EAMON de VALERA

A Biography

BY

M. J. MACMANUS

THE TALBOT PRESS LIMITED
EIGHTY-NINE TALBOT STREET, DUBLIN

First published ... ... May, 1944.
Reprinted ... ... June, 1944.
Printed with additional matter ... Oct., 1945.
Printed with further additional matter Sept., 1947.

AMERICAN EDITION
Ziff-Davis Publishing Company,
Chicago, U.S.A.

DUTCH EDITION
"Scriptura", Troonstaat 57,
Bruxelles, Belgique.

FRENCH EDITION
Les Ecrits de France,
Paris, France.

Printed in Ireland at the Talbot Press, Dublin.

FOR SEAN O'SULLIVAN

Contents

FOREWORD

WHAT I have attempted in this book is the story of a living statesman as seen by a contemporary who has watched its development with interest and sympathy and who has found in many of its phases the stuff of drama.

For the best part of thirty years Eamon de Valera has been the central figure in a series of striking events. He has been a man of action and a maker of history who has lived in a time of revolution. His aims and his methods have been the subject of fierce controversy: his character and personality of diverse interpretations. The winds of controversy blow less violently to-day, but they still blow. At this moment of crisis his capacity for leadership is unquestioned and his policy generally approved, but echoes of the tumultuous years are still to be heard. That, of itself, makes the biographer's task no easy one. A legend has grown up, and legendary mists are notoriously hard to disperse.

Biographies that strive to be wholly objective, that present a cold factual account of a stirring career, and that leave judgment of the events chronicled to the reader or posterity, are seldom successful. They suffer from a worse defect than dullness: they also fail to give any true picture of the man or the measure of his achievements. An honest rather than an impartial account has, therefore, been my aim. In a biography written from the standpoint of an admirer, there is no possibility of doing adequate justice to those who were de Valera's opponents. They, inevitably, must remain more or less in shadow; their share of the high-lights is rigidly restricted by the limitations of space and by the dramatic necessities of the situation; save when their actions impinge on those of the central character they are bound to remain negative figures, whose motives and purposes cannot be fully represented or analysed. In other words, the biographer's task differs fundamentally from that of the historian.

. . . . . .

My acknowledgments are many and deep. The biographies of de Valera that already exist—by Mr. David T. Dwane, Mr. Desmond Ryan, Mr. Sean O'Faolain, Mr. Denis Gwynn and Mr. Mathew Butler—have rendered my task considerably easier than it would otherwise have been. To Miss Dorothy Macardle, whose great work, *The Irish Republic*, is the standard volume on the history of most of the period covered; to Dr. Patrick MacCartan, whose *With de Valera in America* provides a vivid first-hand account of an important episode; to Frank Pakenham, whose *Peace by Ordeal* is a masterly analysis of the dramatic events that led up to the signing of the Anglo-Irish Treaty of 1921; to Mr. Padraig de Burca and Mr. John F. Boyle, joint authors of *Free State or Republic?*—a series of brilliant pen-pictures of the historic Treaty debate in Dail Eireann: to all these my indebtedness is very great indeed. I have also to thank Mr. Aengus O'Daly, Librarian of the *Irish Press,* for help generously given; Mr. Cathal O'Shannon, Mr. Liam Redmond and Mr. Eoin O'Keeffe for some useful suggestions; Mr. Cyril Connolly, for permission to incorporate extracts from an article which I contributed to *Horizon;* Mr. R. H. Lyon, of the Talbot Press, for advice and encouragement; and, in a very special manner, Mr. Sean O'Sullivan and Mr. J. P. Reihill for permission to reproduce the former's portrait of Mr. de Valera.

It only remains to say that I have neither sought nor received any assistance from the subject of this biography. He was not even aware that it was being written.

Note to the Second Edition

In this edition I have taken the opportunity of correcting some minor errors of fact. I have also brought the narrative up to the General Election of May, 1944, as the result of which Mr. de Valera was returned to power for the sixth successive time.

"In the opinion of an English statesman, no man is good for Ireland until he is dead and buried. Perhaps the day may come when I may get a good word from English statesmen as being a moderate man, after I am dead and buried."

—CHARLES STEWART PARNELL.

EAMON de VALERA

CHAPTER ONE
The Beginning

And Spanish ale shall give you hope,
My dark Rosaleen.
—*From the Irish,* by JAMES CLARENCE MANGAN.

(I)

THE year 1882 dawned gloomily over Ireland.

"As Charon ferries the barque of 1881 across the waters of the past," observed a Dublin newspaper on New Year's Day, "no one can fail to see Famine at the prow and Revolution at the helm. We bid adieu to the old year with feelings of sorrow and of shame. Almost without hope, we hail the commencement of the new."

The picture was not overpainted. Three bad harvests in four years had reduced the rack-rented tenant-farmers to a state of misery not equalled since Black Forty-seven. Visiting British and American journalists sent harrowing descriptions of conditions in Ireland to their newspapers. "The calamities and horrors which have given the agrarian history of Ireland a terrible celebrity are now intensified beyond parallel," wrote one. "Unless the present system of landlordism ends, and ends soon, Ireland is doomed," wrote another.

The Duchess of Marlborough's Distress Relief Fund, vigorously organised by her son, Lord Randolph Churchill, and contributed to, according to the London *Times,* by "Canadian legislatures. Hindoo princes, sailors in Chinese waters, citizens of London, Irish Frenchmen in Paris, and Indian squaws in Minnesota wigwams," had proved only a drop in the ocean, although the landlords' organ in Ireland referred to its success as "a victory which transcends Blenheim." Ireland's wrongs were not going to be cured by English charity. But the world, it was evident, was beginning to show awareness of them.

Throughout a large part of the Irish countryside the conditions that existed were—to quote a phrase of William O'Brien's—"those of civil war only tempered by the scarcity of firearms." The tenants were hitting back at the rack-renters with a vengeance. When men working on the bogs heard the sound of a stray shot—it might only be the gun of a fowler in pursuit of snipe—they would lift their heads for a moment and remark with grim humour, "There goes another landlord!"

But random shooting was not likely to solve the problem of landlordism. There were some 20,000 landlords in all, of whom 750 owned half of Ireland. More than 1,500 were permanently domiciled outside the country, and these included many owners of the biggest estates. Others, who had resided at home, were hurriedly packing up and leaving their troubles in the hands of their agents. Some, like Lord Leitrim—who had added to his ejectment activities an occasional exercise of the *droit de seigneur*—were lying peacefully in the green earth which they had ruled with a more than feudal arrogance.

Captain Moonlight, aided by his trusty lieutenant, Captain Boycott, was in command of the ragged troops of the countryside. The people's leader, Charles Stewart Parnell, was in Kilmainham Jail: an uneasy and restive prisoner tortured by claustrophobia, given to long silences during which it was evident that he was thinking not so much of Land Acts as of a comfortable fireside and a pair of comforting arms in a villa in Surrey, angrily refusing to sleep under a richly-embroidered counterpane presented to him by the Ladies' Land League because they had chosen green—his "unlucky" colour—and reluctantly putting his name to a "No Rent" manifesto drawn up by his colleagues. William Ewart Gladstone, Prime Minister of England for the second time, having announced to a wildly-cheering audience that "the resources of civilisation were not exhausted," had put Parnell under lock and key, and all England had applauded as if a major battle had been won. With the Chief in Kilmainham were his colleagues, John Dillon, Thomas Sexton, and William O'Brien, the last-named editing his weekly newspaper, *United Ireland,* as easily as if he were sitting in his office in Middle Abbey Street. Tim Healy had escaped to America, Joe Biggar to Paris. Michael Davitt was back in the stone quarries of Portland Prison. The two Captains, Moonlight and Boycott, had the field to themselves.

As the spring wore on, however, the political horizon began to clear a little. Gladstone was slowly beginning to realise that Parnell jailed was a bigger problem than Parnell free, an opinion shared by his Cabinet colleague, Joseph Chamberlain. Pourparlers began behind the scenes. Mrs. Katharine O'Shea and her husband proved useful intermediaries, and when April came the gates of Kilmainham swung open. An understanding had been reached that the "No Rent" manifesto would be withdrawn and violence discouraged. In return, the English Government promised to amend the Land Act and to abandon coercion. General rejoicings followed, but these did not extend to Dublin Castle or to a certain public-house in Dorset Street where a small group of desperate men were in the habit of meeting. "Buckshot" Forster, British Chief Secretary of Ireland, handed Mr. Gladstone his resignation and the Invincibles went on perfecting their plans.

For a whole week the Irish sky remained more serene than it had been for years. On May 6 Parnell, John Dillon and J. J. O'Kelly travelled down from London to Portland to meet Davitt on his release from prison. The four men journeyed back in high spirits. But while their train was speeding through the peaceful shires of Southern England, a deed was being done at home that was destined to blanch their faces and numb their hearts. Knives had flashed in the green pleasaunce of the Phœnix Park, and there under the trees in the mocking sunshine of a May evening, Lord Frederick

(D1238)

Cavendish, the bearer of Gladstone's olive-branch, the gentle successor of "Buckshot" Forster, nephew by marriage of the G.O.M. himself, lay dead beside Thomas Henry Burke, Dublin Castle's hated instrument of coercion. The Invincibles had struck, suddenly, swiftly, remorselessly.

The Irish sky grew blacker than ever. From one end of Britain to the other the cry for vengeance resounded. Coercion was redoubled, curfew was enforced, the police were empowered to search any house at any hour of the day or night, and the Land Act was forgotten. Evictions increased, and soon there was a trail of roofless cabins and cold hearthstones from Donegal to Kerry.

"To-day," wrote Mr. Bernard H. Becker, of the *Daily News*, "Ireland is not only the most distressful country in Europe, but in the whole wide world."

(II)

But in that same gloomy year of 1882 a faint, far star appeared on the horizon. On October 14th Eamon de Valera was born in New York City.

His father, the son of a Cuban sugar-planter, was a Spaniard, and his mother was a native of Bruree, in the County Limerick. Of Vivion de Valera there is little to be said. He was a musician who died—a young man of about thirty—when his son was only two years old.

Eamon's mother, Catharine Coll, was, when she married Vivion de Valera, a well-built, handsome girl, gifted with intelligence, humour and personality. When, in 1879, she emigrated to the United States, she was accompanied by her brother

Edmond, who became a land steward in Connecticut (he is still alive in the United States). At one of the old "National" schools Catharine had received an education of the solid type dispensed by nineteenth century Irish schoolmasters—the three R's, some geography, some English history—and she supplemented it by constant reading. A somewhat remarkable young woman this, according to the accounts left by those who knew her in her early years in America. A later glimpse is afforded in an article which the pastor of the church she attended in Rochester, N.J.—whither she had removed after her second marriage—published in his parish magazine in 1942.

"The pastor invited all present in the old school hall on Monroe Avenue to participate in a Spelling Bee. About fifty accepted the invitation, including lawyers, teachers and a number of others. Then something unexpected happened. A frail-looking woman came forward. She was plainly dressed, and as she started to mount the steps of the stage some of those present began to laugh at her simplicity, and she was asked by one of the participants if she realised that a spelling match was about to be held. She smiled, and without answering the question took her place with the others.

"After half-an-hour or so only four remained in the contest—a lawyer, a teacher, a business man, and the plainly-dressed and unassuming-looking lady. In five minutes more only two sat upon the stage—the school-teacher and the frail-looking woman.

"The people in the hall were now greatly excited. Surely the school-teacher would win! The last word given out to spell was a most difficult one. It was the teacher's turn to make the first attempt. She became nervous, asked for a glass of water, and failed to spell it. The plainly-dressed lady, without a moment's hesitation, spelt the word as it should be.

"Who was this simple-looking woman sitting alone on the stage? She was no other than the mother of Eamon de Valera, President of the Irish Free State. At that time she was known to the members of the parish as Mrs. Charles Wheelwright, having married again after the death of her first husband."

The death of her husband confronted Mrs. de Valera with a problem that faces many young widows left in straitened circumstances. There was a living to be made and a child to be cared for, and in a city like New York it was extremely difficult to manage both. But almost at once a satisfactory way of solving the problem appeared. Edmond Coll, who had contracted malarial fever, was about to pay a return visit to Ireland in search of health, and it was arranged that the child should accompany him. Another uncle, Patrick Coll, who resided in the old house at Knockmore, Bruree, had agreed to take over the responsibility of his upbringing. Fate was already at work, for the liner had hardly sailed when Vivion de Valera's father arrived in New York from Cuba, with the intention of taking charge of his grandson. He saw his daughter-in-law, but the decision had been made, and he returned home disappointed.

And so it came about that Eamon de Valera's earliest memories are not those of the noisy, forward-thrusting city of New York in the late eighties, with its horse-drawn trams, its eddying cosmopolitan populace, its first sky-scrapers, its garish saloons, its Irish policemen and navvies, its parasols and sombreros, its sirens for ever moaning across the harbour, its icy winters and tropical summers, and its perpetual air of hustle and bustle; instead, it was a quiet-watered pastoral Irish countryside that moulded his first impressions and changed the American accent that was just beginning to sound on his tongue into the flat, slightly harsh County Limerick brogue that has never left him. Bruree and the Maigue river—a stream that once nourished a nest of Gaelic poets on its banks—stand where there was an ancient pass-way from the hills of Clare into the rich lands of Limerick and the Golden Vale that runs past Slieve Phelim to the Rock of Cashel. The ruined castles that stud the valley speak eloquently of ancient wars, and the City of the Sieges and the Broken Treaty is not far away. Always it has been a country of lush grass and fat cattle, of dairy-farmers and butter, and—until recent times—of high-walled demesnes and stately mansions.

But when the three-year-old Eamon de Valera, sturdy and solemn-eyed, first looked upon it, it was not altogether as peaceful as it is to-day. Bruree was not by any means one of the storm-centres of the agrarian revolution, but it did not escape all the winds that were blowing, and Patrick Coll himself was a Land Leaguer. In 1885—the very year that Edmond Coll arrived home with his charge—that observant and cultivated, but cynical Frenchman, the Baron de Mandat-Grancey, was visiting a nearby locality, and he has described how he saw a body of the Royal Irish Constabulary setting out for an eviction. "The men are in marching dress, knapsack on back, rifle on shoulder. The cars waiting for them are painted red and driven by officials belonging to the Government. There is no owner of private cars who dare provide them with one." The same observer noted, too, that even in the Golden Vale there was grinding poverty. Many of the women whom he saw walked barefooted, "scarcely covered with a chemise and a petticoat," although on Sunday, going to Mass, they managed to find "boots, and bonnets with flowers."

In the house of Patrick Coll, however, there was peace and frugal comfort. Patrick's mother—an Irish speaker from whom young Eamon learnt his first Gaelic words—carried on the old Irish countryside tradition of good plain cooking, and there was always a sufficiency of milk and butter, eggs and oatmeal stirabout, potatoes and griddle-cakes. The bacon might be American and disagreeably salty, for it was not until de Valera himself began to revolutionise agricultural economy fifty years later that the small Irish farmer began to kill and consume his own pigs, but, on the whole, the food provided was good and wholesome. The boy thrived on it and became sturdy, if a trifle too tall and lanky for his years.

(III)

When he was five he went to the local school at Bruree, where, as his first biographer has recorded, the schoolmaster, an old man named

John Kelly, put him at the head of the class and told him that, if he persevered, "he would one day have a bicycle and a grand watch and chain." At fourteen he went to the school of the Christian Brothers at Charleville—now Rathluirc—a distance of some six miles, making the journey by train in the morning, returning on foot if the weather was fine.

In Patrick Coll's house of an evening he would hear, when the neighbours dropped in, long and sometimes impassioned arguments. There would be a whirl of words from which the same names, like corks bobbing up and down on a turbulent stream, would emerge again and again. Parnell and Healy, Gladstone and Chamberlain, Davitt and Dillon—a thousand times these names smote his boyish, unresponsive ears. Another name, too, would occasionally be spat out with venom by some frieze-coated old farmer—that of Kitty O'Shea. To the fourteen-year-old boy it meant very little. Some of his school-mates called themselves Parnellites, others were Healyites, but what was it all about? The boys were only pinning labels on their coats and cheering somebody or something about which their parents had grown angry and excited. None of them could be aware of the great tragedy that had descended upon the country, or sense, however dimly, the reason for the bad blood and the dark passions that were setting their elders at one another's throats. But thirty years later Eamon de Valera was to recall that tragic phase in Irish life and to reflect, with however little consolation, that even a civil war did not unloose passions so terrifyingly bitter as those of the Parnellite split.

The Christian Brothers found de Valera a model pupil—serious-minded, industrious, talented. At home of a summer evening he would sometimes, like Abraham Lincoln, be found lying with a book on top of a haystack or working out sums by the light of the kitchen fire when he should have been in bed. He liked his books and his lessons—particularly the sums. For the theoretical side of elementary mathematics he displayed an unusual aptitude. Patrick Coll, a man of good natural sensibilities—unlike Lincoln's father, who vainly tried to stop his son "fooling hisself with eddication"—looked on with an approving eye. Eamon de Valera was lucky in his uncle.

Any books that he could lay hands on he read. There was a Life of Sarsfield lying about—as there would be in many Limerick houses—and a Life of Napoleon. Jane Porter's *Scottish Chiefs*—always a favourite in the countryside in nineteenth century Ireland—was also available, and it was books like these that first fired the boy's imagination and set him dreaming romantic dreams as he lay reading on the grassy banks of the Maigue. From the Christian Brothers he got tales of Spanish ships in Galway Bay, of Spanish soldiers at Kinsale, of a lonely grave at Valladolid, and it strengthened his pride in his Spanish ancestry. A Brother who taught him history told Sean O'Faolain how on one occasion, when Wellington's victories were being discussed, the boy exclaimed, "But, Brother, have we no Generals of our own?" When the old monk went on to speak of Hugh O'Neill, and Red Hugh and Owen Roe and Sarsfield, "Eamon sat there gripping the desk, all on fire."

At sixteen when a scholarship took him from Bruree to Blackrock College, which stands overlooking the Bay in a Dublin suburb, he was tall and thin, but strongly-built and athletic. His stature, his somewhat foreign-looking appearance, and his strange but pleasant-sounding foreign name at once made him an object of interest to his classmates. They twitted him now and then, in schoolboy fashion, about his Spanish origin, but they never carried the joke too far. De Valera was not the sort of boy who provides an easy target for "ragging." His athletic build, his prowess on the playing-fields, the position of pre-eminence which he soon attained in class, and, above all, an easily-apparent strength of character, gave him a dominance at Blackrock that he had no difficulty in maintaining.

Of his school-days there one of his old professors has left a story that is worth recalling. The long-legged youth was the College's champion runner. At the annual sports on one occasion he looked like sweeping all before him. He had won the 100 yards, the 220, and the 440. There only remained the mile, and success in that event meant carrying off the coveted President's Prize. De Valera started an easy favourite. There was only one other boy in the race who was likely to give him any trouble, and after three quarters of a mile or so the two were running neck-and-neck. At that point de Valera noticed that his rival was breathing heavily, as if in distress. He had passed him out when he heard a thud and, looking back, he saw that the boy had fallen. The tape was only a few hundred yards away and the prize was within his grasp. He hesitated a moment and then ran to render first aid. Another boy, who had been out of the running, came up, passed the two of them out, and won the race. "But the laurels were on Eamon's head," said the old professor.

The year of his arrival at Blackrock was 1898—the centenary year of the great Rising and of the most romantic period in Irish history. In Dublin there were meetings, processions, banquets and other celebrations. The Parliamentarians were vocal with sunburst oratory, but it was the young men and women of the recently-founded Gaelic League and the members of the Irish Republican Brotherhood who were making the '98 Commemoration an occasion for national resurgence. Maud Gonne, radiant with beauty and filled with crusading ardour, was in evidence everywhere, and William Butler Yeats, "the poet who looked like a poet," might be seen tossing his raven locks on many a platform.

Even within the cloistered walls of the College of the Holy Ghost Fathers, some rumour of these resurgent stirrings must have found their way. But Eamon de Valera, busy with his books and his games, took little heed of them.

(IV)

At Blackrock the years slipped by quickly. De Valera soon became known as one of the most promising students at the College, with a strong bent towards mathematics, physics and astronomy. At Christmas and midsummer he would return for holidays to Bruree, where he would lend a hand with the work of the farm or go out of an evening walking or shooting with his Uncle Patrick. Nearly fifty years later he recalled those days when replying in the Dail to the charge that he and his Ministers knew nothing about farming, "There is not an operation on the farm, with perhaps one exception," he said, "that I as a youngster had not to perform. I lived in a labourer's cottage, but the tenant, in his way, could be regarded as a small farmer. From my earliest days I participated in every operation that takes place on a farm. One thing I did not learn, how to plough, but until I was sixteen years of age, there was no farm work, from the spancelling of a goat and milking of a cow, that I had not to deal with. I cleaned out the cowhouses. I followed the tumbler rake. I took my place on top of the rick. I took my place on the cart and filled the load of hay. I took milk to the creamery. I harnessed the donkey, the jennet, and the horse."

After reading a brilliant Intermediate and University course he was appointed a junior master in the Intermediate College at Blackrock, the first step on what seemed to be the destined road to a scholastic career. Before he was twenty he was entrusted with the higher classes, and a little later he left Blackrock to take up a Professorship in Mathematics and Physics at Rockwell College, near Cashel. Whilst at Rockwell he graduated in Mathematical Science at the old Royal University. The year was 1904 and he was twenty-two.

The young man had made good. With a degree to his name he came back to Dublin, where there were plenty of openings awaiting him. His industry was amazing. In addition to reading a post-graduate

Photo

De Valera at twenty-two.

course in Higher Mathematics and taking a Diploma in Education, he taught at different periods in University College, in Belvedere, in Clonliffe, in several schools attached to convents, and in the Carysfort Training College for Teachers. His subjects included Latin and French, but Mathematics was his speciality and his chief delight. In educational circles in Dublin his reputation grew steadily. All the gathered records agree that he was a born teacher, painstaking, patient, lucid, master of his subject and, despite a gravity and high-mindedness beyond his years, popular both in the class-room and on the playing-field. His career appeared settled, though there was a short period during which he seriously thought of becoming a priest. But after a week-end spent in retreat with the Jesuits at Milltown he came to the conclusion that his vocation lay elsewhere.

In 1908 he joined the Gaelic League—an event that was destined to have a profound effect not only on his cultural and educational development but on his domestic life and later career. Founded some fifteen years before by a young Trinity College graduate named Douglas Hyde—a Protestant of Ascendancy stock—it had rapidly become the well-spring of the new resurgence. The Parnellites and anti-Parnellites might go on filling the air with their outworn slogans, but the more earnest-minded of the young men and women of the time, wearied by rancorous mouthings that never seemed to lead anywhere, turned more and more to the language classes and the ceilidhes of the League. There, at any rate, something was being achieved.

What Sinn Fein, already started by Arthur Griffith, was doing on the political side, the Gaelic League was doing in the cultural sphere. No longer, for these crusading young people, was Westminster the centre of interest and excitement. If anything worth while came from the British Parliament (the Wyndham Land Act of 1903 which sounded the death-knell of landlordism was the biggest thing for a century) well and good; but it was on their own people and on their own resources that the Sinn Feiners and the Gaelic Leaguers placed final reliance.

De Valera had learnt his first Irish phrases from his grandmother, and there was still an old Gaelic story-teller in Bruree with whom he conversed, for the sake of improving his knowledge of the language, when he visited his home. Now, infected by the spreading enthusiasm for native culture, he enrolled himself as a student at the Leinster College of Irish, and a young teacher there, Miss Janie O'Flanagan (Sinead ni Fhlannagain) was duly impressed when she found that amongst her pupils was a Professor of Mathematics. The Professor was also impressed. Miss O'Flanagan, *petite*, golden-haired and pretty, was a talented amateur actress who was keenly interested in Gaelic drama, at that time in its infancy. She had appeared in one of the first Gaelic plays ever produced—a piece written by Eamon O'Neill about his namesake, the great Hugh O'Neill—in which she took the part of the Spanish Ambassador. Amongst other Irish plays in which she acted was Douglas Hyde's "The Tinker and the Fairy," produced in the open air in the garden of George Moore's house in Ely Place, with Moore looking on approvingly, and Kuno Meyer, the eminent Celtic scholar, acting as prompter. Friendship ripened quickly between pupil and teacher, and in January, 1910, they were married.

The fateful years of the second Home Rule struggle came, bringing excitements that penetrated into even the Gaelic classrooms. Carson was arming his Orangemen; Winston Churchill was mobbed in Belfast; Bonar Law, the leader of the British Tory Party, came to Ireland to review a parade of 80,000 Ulstermen; thousands of Catholics were driven from the Belfast shipyards; when Carson was charged with fomenting treason, he replied acidly that " he did not care twopence whether it was treason or not." The spate of talk that had lasted since Parnell's death was giving way before the onrush of forces that would not be denied.

Eamon de Valera's thoughts began to find a new centre of interest. Soon—who knew?—he might find himself called upon to take a part, in however small a way, in solving problems far more complex than any arising out of Gaelic syntax or the higher mathematics.

CHAPTER TWO

Easter Week

> "But where can we draw water,"
> Said Pearse to Connolly,
> "When all the wells are parched away?
> O plain as plain can be
> There's nothing but our own red blood
> Can make a right Rose Tree."
> —W. B. YEATS.

(I)

IN the year 1913 the march of events began to quicken rapidly. The Ulster Volunteers were training in a blaze of publicity, drilling, parading, forming corps of dispatch riders. Field-Marshal Lord Roberts gave them his blessing and General Sir Henry Wilson, of Currygrane, County Longford, his expert advice.

In Britain the politicians and high military officers were acting with a recklessness that amazed observers in foreign countries, so long accustomed to admiring English statesmen's celebrated "genius for compromise." Intelligent Frenchmen, Germans and Americans rubbed their eyes with wonder as they witnessed the unprecedented spectacle of Britain's Tory Party—the traditional upholders of law and order—setting all law at defiance, striking at the roots of an old, established security, turning their legislative assembly into a nightly bear-garden. They knew, of course, those intelligent foreigners, that there was more behind the Tory support of

Carson than anger at a proposal to grant a strictly-limited measure of self-government to Ireland. They realised that at bottom, the Tory rebellion was a last-ditch fight in defence of privilege. If civil war came in Britain and Ireland that would be the fundamental issue.

The Irish Parliamentary leader, John Redmond, was as worried about it all as was Herbert Henry Asquith, Prime Minister of England. But in public Redmond took care not to betray his anxiety. Bands of men drilling in the fields of Ulster with dummy rifles could not, he declared, hope to thwart the will of the Imperial Parliament. Home Rule was coming "at no far distant date."

But a Dublin schoolmaster named Padraic Pearse did not share Redmond's complacent view. "Personally," he said, "I think the Orangeman with a rifle a much less ridiculous figure than a Nationalist without one," an opinion in which another schoolmaster named Eamon de Valera fully concurred. But when Pearse and his friends urged the immediate formation of a body of Nationalist Volunteers to meet the Tory challenge, Redmond refused. He would not do anything "unconstitutional."

De Valera, still busy with his text-books, found time to turn a steady, appraising gaze on the forces that were gathering. No academic walls were strong enough in the Dublin of 1913 to shut out the winds that had begun to blow so fiercely. For, suddenly, passions were let loose in the streets that had nothing to do with Home Rule and that had everything to do with the right of a man to earn a living wage. At the call of James Larkin—that tall, impressive figure with turbulent black hair, burning eyes and a trumpet voice—the Dublin workers swarmed out of the slums to engage in unequal combat with the all-powerful Federation of Employers—Mr. William Martin Murphy's "Four Hundred." There were strikes, lock-outs, evictions, riots, baton charges and widespread hunger. At Larkin's elbow stood James Connolly, the intellectual leader of the Irish Labour movement, outwardly unemotional, but inwardly exulting in the militant spirit of the workers. In Liberty Hall, Labour's headquarters, the Countess Markievicz was running a soup-kitchen. In August Larkin called upon the workers to arm. "What is legal for Carson and the Orangemen," he told them, "is legal for us." The response was immediate and enthusiastic. The Citizen Army was born.

(II)

De Valera's sympathies—like those of the rest of the men in the forward movement, with the notable exception of Arthur Griffith—were with the workers. An Irish Bishop might refer to Larkin as "anti-Christ," but behind the Labour agitator's activities loomed the stark, ugly fact that Dublin's slums were the worst in the world and Dublin's workers amongst the worst-paid. At home in Bruree, Uncle Patrick Coll was doing in a small way what Larkin was doing in Dublin. He was founder of the local branch of the Trade and Labour Organization, a body formed to further the cause of landless men, agricultural labourers, cottiers and others who had taken part in the Land War, but who had gained little or nothing when victory was achieved. A "small man" himself, he was a champion of the

(D1238)

small men. Many a time uncle and nephew had talked far into the night about the rights of the worker, more particularly of the rural worker—and there was little difference in their outlook.

But in Dublin, for the moment, there was no point of contact between the collar-and-tie class to which de Valera belonged and the men who followed Larkin and Connolly. The soldiers of the Citizen Army were almost a hundred per cent manual workers. Before the year 1913 closed, however, another army sprang into existence. At a meeting held in Dublin in November, to which the name of the chairman, Eoin MacNeill, Professor of Ancient Irish in the National University and Vice-President of the Gaelic League, gave the required prestige, a new body of Volunteers was formed. Its purpose was not, as MacNeill emphasised, to take any hostile action against Carson's Ulster Volunteers, but to meet the challenge thrown out by one of the great English political parties. "We welcome the evident truth," he said, "that they (the Orangemen) have opened the way for a National Volunteer movement." There were now three armies in existence in Ireland, and physical force, for the first time since '67, was in the ascendant.

De Valera was one of the first to join the new body. Here, at last, was something more tangible more purposeful than the wordy conflicts of political warfare. The young men were getting together, the young men of the Gaelic class-rooms and the hurling-fields, earnest, studious young men who had read *Sinn Fein* week by week, who had gathered in Tom Clarke's little shop in Parnell Street to hear the Separatist doctrine expounded, who had cheered

Yeats's *Cathleen ni Houlihan* and Lady Gregory's *Rising of the Moon* at the Abbey Theatre. Soon there were 150,000 of them, and at the top, along with MacNeill, were poets and professors and intellectuals. Behind the whole movement, watching, planning, and secretly directing, were the men of the Irish Republican Brotherhood.

De Valera did not make his decision lightly. As a married man he had to consider his responsibilities. That the physical force movement would end in war and bloodshed he had no doubt whatever. It was only after a long interval of heart-searching that he decided to throw in his lot with the men who believed that a blood-sacrifice was necessary to redeem the nation.

As a Volunteer de Valera soon made his mark, and within a few months he had attained the rank of Captain. He was now in his thirty-first year, "exceptionally tall"—to quote Denis Gwynn, who studied under him about this time—"considerably over six feet in height, a very serious-looking man in his early thirties, with a long nose and spectacles and a strangely foreign complexion." He wore rough, Irish-made homespuns and a deerstalker's cap. A singularly impressive figure he must have been, with his commanding stature, his sombre, burning eyes, his harsh strong voice, his foreign look and his homely garb.

The men he drilled in the fields around Rathfarnham soon learnt to respect him. Here was an officer who gave of his best and expected the best to be given. He brought the same zeal and the same high order of intelligence to field tactics that he had formerly devoted to problems of mathematics. He studied the art of street-fighting as assiduously as Robert Emmet had done more than a century before. What was even more important, he displayed an unusual capacity for leadership. There had never been any symptoms of either boredom or insubordination in the classes over which he had presided in so many colleges; there was none in the ranks of the Volunteers whom he drilled. His serious-mindedness, his capacity for hard work, his slight air of reserve, his physical make-up—all these combined to impose discipline. But he was neither a martinet nor a prig. Prigs are never popular and, according to all accounts that have been handed down, de Valera was as popular as he was efficient.

(III)

In 1914 the cauldron which had been bubbling since Carson had begun to raise an army in the North started to boil over. In March there was mutiny at British Army Headquarters at the Curragh, actively fomented by highly-placed officers like Sir Henry Wilson from within the walls of the British War Office itself. British Army men were enrolling themselves in a conspiracy to defeat the plans of the British Parliament. In April there was gun-running at Larne and 35,000 German rifles were landed without opposition from the authorities and distributed amongst Carson's Volunteers.

The Nationalist Volunteers were still virtually unarmed, but in London a small group, including Mrs. Erskine Childers, Mrs. Stopford Green, widow of the historian, Mary Spring-Rice, daughter of

Lord Monteagle, and Sir Roger Casement, were busy collecting money and making plans. In July King George, in a last effort for peace, called a conference of the Parliamentary Parties at Buckingham Palace. On the day that Austria delivered an ultimatum to Serbia it ended in failure.

Three days later the Irish Volunteers set out on a route march from Dublin to Howth, with Thomas MacDonagh, Bulmer Hobson, and Cathal Brugha in charge of operations. There they met the yacht, the *Asgard,* manned by Erskine Childers, his wife, and Mary Spring-Rice, which had brought a cargo of rifles across the North Sea, and they landed the guns openly. But this time there was no connivance on the part of the British authorities in Ireland. On the way to Dublin the Volunteers were intercepted by a column of British troops and there was a scrimmage during which both sides broke their ranks. Amongst those who kept their heads on that critical occasion was de Valera, who, according to an eye-witness account, remained "cool and resolute." It was his first approach to real war. The Howth gun-running ended with British troops firing on a jeering crowd in the streets of Dublin.

A few days later the first World War broke out, and in the new circumstances that had arisen Irishmen of all shades of political thought began to take their bearings. Asquith's government placed a badly-mutilated Home Rule Bill on the Statute Book, but a Suspensory Act postponing its operation accompanied it. Redmond, however, accepted the position, and called upon the Volunteers not only to stand ready to guard Ireland in case of invasion, but to join the British forces in defence of "right, religion and freedom." A split in the Volunteers followed at once. "Ireland," declared Casement, "has no blood to give any land or any cause but that of Ireland." The majority of the Volunteers followed Redmond, and before the war finished more than fifty thousand Irishmen died fighting under the British flag: a minority numbering some ten or twelve thousand remained with MacNeill and the other leaders who believed in neutrality or who held that if Irishmen were to fight for the liberties of small nations it should be on Irish soil. De Valera was one of the minority.

In 1915 he was appointed Adjutant of the Dublin Brigade, of which Thomas MacDonagh was Commandant. MacDonagh was a gay and exuberant spirit, a poet as well as a professor, a good talker in a city where good talk was commonplace. He would have been at home in the Johnson circle or amongst those mediæval university students who regarded disputation, flavoured with the salt of wit, as a glorious pastime. The figure in history that appealed to him most was the contemplative man turned revolutionist, such a one as the old Roman, Tiberius Gracchus, or Washington. The drama of the righteous man taking arms against overwhelming odds in pursuit of a noble ideal exercised a tremendous fascination over him and he was fated to act it in his own person to the last gallant scene.

Between MacDonagh and his Adjutant there was a strong bond of comradeship. They had met casually at Gaelic League functions, but it was not until the formation of the Volunteers that they became really intimate. MacDonagh lived in the small gate-lodge of a large house in the shadow of the Dublin mountains, where all literary Dublin used to repair to listen to fine talk. But the time came when he put to the company one of his last questions: "When are you lads going to stop writing and do something?"

De Valera had led a much more secluded life. From the time he had left Blackrock until he joined the Volunteers his main interests were his studies, his classes and, later, his home. Attendance at a Gaelic League ceilidhe or concert was almost his sole relaxation. In Dublin's literary world, where men like Yeats, Synge, "A.E.," James Stephens, Padraic Colum, Seamus O'Sullivan, MacDonagh, and the rest met and talked and quarrelled, he was unknown. He rarely went to the Abbey and never to the presentations of the commercial theatres.

In the Volunteers he had made his first wide contacts with men of his own age. Now, owing to his comradeship with MacDonagh, his horizon broadened rapidly. MacDonagh, like de Valera, was an ardent Gaelic Leaguer, but not one of those distressingly narrow ones thrown up later in such numbers by the revival movement. He was as familiar with the Elizabethans and the French romanticists as he was with the traditional Irish poets. The two men often walked home together after parades or route marches and, with the robe of scholarship cast aside, found that they had much in common to discuss. Always, however, the dominant topic was—what was going to happen in Ireland?

One night MacDonagh asked his friend to join the Irish Republican Brotherhood. De Valera hesitated. He had scruples on religious grounds (for the I.R.B.

was under the ban of the Church), and he also had the cautious man's natural fear that a secret society might provide an easy doorway for spies to enter the highest councils of the movement. Finally, he consented, stipulating, however, that he would be asked to do no more than take orders when the time came.

(IV)

All through the year 1915 the I.R.B. went steadily ahead perfecting their plans. From the moment that the European War had broken out they were resolved that a Rising would take place. The only question was, when? Connolly, impetuous and daring, was all for immediate action. He was with difficulty restrained from marching the Citizen Army to the Mansion House and seizing it when Asquith addressed a recruiting meeting there. Casement was in Germany looking for arms and attempting to form an Irish Brigade. There was constant communication with John Devoy and other friends of the movement in America. But the I.R.B. did not take into its confidence men like MacNeill, the Volunteer Chief of Staff, or Arthur Griffith, or any of those, in fact, who held that a Fabian policy was wisest and that the Volunteers should only strike if an attempt was made to enforce conscription or if they themselves were attacked.

Easter Sunday, 1916—which fell on April 23rd—was finally selected as the date of the Rising. Pearse, who had been appointed Commander-in-Chief by the Revolutionary Council, gave public orders for a route march and field operations to be held on that day. A rumour of what was intended reached

MacNeill and at once he sought out Pearse and insisted on being told the truth. Pearse was frank. He told MacNeill that a Rising had been decided upon and begged of him not to interfere. MacNeill refused. Short of giving information to the British, he would, he declared, use every means in his power to prevent the outbreak.

Meanwhile Casement, disappointed and embittered, was returning from Germany to Ireland by submarine. His project of forming an Irish Brigade amongst the prisoners of war had failed and, instead of the large German expedition that he had hoped for, only a single cargo of twenty thousand rifles was being sent. He landed on the Kerry coast on Good Friday morning and was captured within a few hours, tormented in mind because he had not been able to get in touch with the leaders and stop the Rising. On the same day the German arms ship, which had waited in vain throughout the previous night in Tralee Bay for a signal from the Irish shore, was captured by a British fleet and scuttled by its crew. A party of Volunteers had been dispatched from Dublin by motor to "contact" it, but the driver, mistaking the sea for a moonlit road, drove over the pier at Ballykissane. The driver escaped, but the passengers were drowned.

Once again, on the eve of an Irish insurrection, everything had gone wrong. What John Mitchel termed the "British Providence" had intervened to set carefully-laid plans awry. Red Hugh's impetuosity at Kinsale, the contrary winds that baffled Wolfe Tone at Bantry Bay, the great snowstorm in '67—these had their parallel in the chapter of disasters that occurred in Holy Week, 1916. But things had gone too far now for the I.R.B. to draw back. Connolly, in fact, would have led a Rising single-handed if there was any further attempt at postponement.

On Easter Sunday morning an order from MacNeill cancelling the parades and manœuvres was published in the *Sunday Independent,* and later on the same day de Valera, Adjutant of the Dublin Brigade, received from MacNeill the following message:

> COMMT. EAMON DE VALERA,
> As Commt. MacDonagh is not accessible, I have to give you this order direct. Commt. MacDonagh left me last night with the understanding that he would return or send me a message. He has done neither.
> As Chief of Staff I have ordered, and hereby order, that no movement whatsoever of Irish Volunteers is to be made to-day. You will carry out this order in your own command and make it known to other commands.
> EOIN MACNEILL.

De Valera received the message with a troubled mind. For MacNeill he had not only the highest personal regard but all the respect due to Ireland's greatest living scholar. Not only that, but he held the view that, in the circumstances, it would be wiser to postpone the Rising. As a result of the announcement in the *Sunday Independent* there was a good deal of confusion. Many of the Dublin Volunteers, in view of the cancellation of manœuvres, had gone away for the day and the Volunteers in the provinces were out of reach. Yet he knew that a Rising was now inevitable. On Easter Sunday morning, before he received

MacNeill's message, the Revolutionary Council had met and decided to strike at noon on the following day, and in the afternoon the final plans for mobilisation were made. For de Valera, that was sufficient. Pearse was his Commander-in-Chief and he would obey Pearse's orders. There would be a Rising on Easter Monday and he would take part in it, however slender the chances of success.

(v)

The livelier our interest in any historical period the more we are apt to falsify our recollections. The sentiment it evokes is in itself a disadvantage. While less entertaining periods remain prosaic, there gathers around a familiar and exciting chapter of the past a nebulous star-cluster of names and romantic happenings.

Easter Week, for all that it is only a little more than a quarter-of-a-century distant, has become one with Ninety-Eight and Sixty-Seven. It is encrusted in legend, blurred with sentiment. The highlights continue to dazzle: seven resolute men seated around a table in Liberty Hall as the hands of the clock of the Custom House opposite point to nine on Easter Monday morning; golden sunlight flooding the streets of a city in holiday mood; the officers of the British Garrison speeding along the Navan road to the Fairyhouse Races; a column of grim-faced men swinging in at noon through the doorway of the G.P.O.; the crashing of glass, the hoisting of the Tricolour; the reading of the Proclamation of the Republic. Then the calm starlit nights with an uncanny silence between the bursts of gunfire; the boom of exploding shells on Liberty Hall and the Post Office; the fires that lighted up the midnight sky as the heart of Dublin burnt itself out; the final conference beside the wounded Connolly's bed; the surrender; the volleys of the execution squads in the dawn of a May morning. They have been told and retold, these happenings that were the stirring to life of a nation that had seemed dead upon its bier. They have been the theme of song and ballad. They will continue to provide rich material for novelist and playwright. But not all the weaving around them of romantic imaginings can destroy the reality of their historical significance. For Ireland, Easter Week was an end and a beginning.

(VI)

For de Valera, too, it was an end and a beginning. A few days before he had walked out of his classroom at the Carysfort Park College for the last time. Now he was taking a road of which he could not foresee even the nearest turning.

On Holy Thursday night he slept at home without taking off his uniform and with his revolver lying close to his bedside. He did not sleep there again. Good Friday and Easter Saturday were filled with feverish activities, receiving and sending messages, giving orders, perfecting the final plans. On Easter Sunday night he returned home for a few hours and left late, after having gone upstairs for a few moments to have a look at his four sleeping children. To his wife he gave no inkling of what was to happen next day.

Early on Easter Monday morning the Volunteers

and the men of the Citizen Army were astir. Now, to be sure, there was no longer a Volunteer Army or a Citizen Army: fused into one, they had become the Army of the Irish Republic. A pitifully small army it was, as it was mobilised in the streets of Dublin that morning; perhaps a thousand in all; and of that number something less than a hundred were assigned to Commandant de Valera.

At Liberty Hall the last salutes were given and the last instructions taken and de Valera's little column wheeled southwards through the city. For the moment all thought of the high adventure on which he and his comrades were setting out was obscured by the instant need of getting certain things done. The task assigned to him was one of tremendous difficulty, and was evidence in itself of the complete confidence reposed in his practical ability by the men at the top. Reinforcements for the Garrison in Dublin would, inevitably, be dispatched from Britain as soon as news of the Rising reached the authorities, and it was the business of de Valera and his men of the Third Battalion to hold them up as long as possible when they landed at Kingstown and marched on the city.

Leaving a dozen men in occupation of Westland Row Station, the terminus of the Kingstown-Dublin railway, which was seized without difficulty, he halted at Mount Street Bridge, which crosses the canal where it bisects the coastal road. Here, with careful and unavoidable economy, he selected other handfuls and placed them, four in one house, three in another, two in a third. The remainder, some seventy or eighty, he marched to the building which was to be his headquarters,

Boland's Flour Mills, a grey, many-windowed limestone edifice standing on the banks of the canal overlooking the slums of Ringsend. There, and on an old nearby distillery—this was a blind, for during the week it was virtually unoccupied—he hoisted the Tricolour.

Curious crowds, who as yet had hardly come to realise the significance of what was happening, began to gather. These had to be dispersed and sentries posted, for there was grim work ahead. All through Easter Monday and late into the night the job of fortifying the place went on, and only when every window had been barricaded with flour sacks and every possible avenue of approach covered did the work cease. At last, having satisfied himself that he had done everything possible, de Valera told his men to get what sleep they could. Other nights were coming, he knew, when sleep would be out of the question. He himself went from floor to floor, out into the cobbled yards, along the railway line, inspecting the sentry posts, giving an order here and there.

At one point he found the posts deserted, and when he looked for the sentries he found them on their knees in a hut saying the Rosary, their rifles stacked in a corner! He reprimanded them sternly, telling them that there was a time for prayer and a time for duty. It is an incident that could hardly have happened in any other country in the world. It illustrates the religious fervour which went hand in hand with the intense nationalism of the time and which was in evidence throughout the whole period of the Rising. Later in the week, when the British troops were closing in late in the night around the Countess Markievicz's men in the College of Surgeons, a Cockney soldier was heard to remark: "A rum lot of coves, these Shinners! I thought they were singing, but, blimey, it's chanting 'ymns they were!" He had been listening to them intoning the responses of the Rosary.

When everything was strangely silent and dawn not far away, de Valera stood for a while, before stretching himself on the sack-strewn floor, looking out on the star-filled waters of the canal, on the little slated houses of Ringsend's poor, on the roofs of the neat and prosperous suburban villas a little farther away. What were his thoughts at that moment? One can guess more nearly at the mind of his friend MacDonagh, across the city in Jacob's Factory, or at that of Clarke or Pearse or Connolly in the Post Office, for these men have left documents for illumination. Did he find a moment to spare from immediate anxieties in which his thoughts might rest on wider values and more ultimate purposes? Did he ask himself, surveying this event which he was helping to shape, *quid hoc ad aeternitatem?* Or did he, in that terrifying moment of loneliness, find a mood of exultation as one who shared the secret of a people "who believed so much in the soul and so little in anything else that they were never entirely certain that the earth was solid under the footsole"? There is no answer to these questions. About his personal share in the drama of Easter Week, about his emotions and aspirations, de Valera has maintained an unbroken silence; almost his only references have been the tributes he has paid at the gravesides of his comrades. But there can be no doubt that it was a high purpose that lured the mathematician from his books, the astronomer from his contemplation of the stellar spaces. And one may be sure that there was a softening of the tense look in his sombre eyes as he gazed across the roof-tops of the silent city towards a little house where a young wife was sleeping—or praying.

(VII)

Tuesday brought little change in the situation. There were barricades to be looked to and weak spots to be strengthened, but it was mostly a day of waiting. The men posted at Westland Row were recalled and they joined their comrades in the Mill. Rumours were carefully disseminated that reinforcements of Volunteers had arrived during the night and that the old distillery was strongly garrisoned.

On Wednesday the insurrection began to blaze up fiercely in other parts of the city. Troops were converging from the Curragh, from the North, and from other places. Heavy guns were operating from Trinity College and machine-guns barked from the roofs of the Custom House and the Tivoli music-hall. The gunboat *Helga* steamed up the river to batter the walls of Liberty Hall, but the Hall had already been evacuated. The upper storey of the Post Office was wrecked and many buildings in O'Connell Street were set on fire by shells.

Troops had now been landed at Kingstown and they were marching along the route held by de Valera's men. Many of them, it would seem, were not tested veterans from France or Flanders, but "rookies" without any war experience. At any rate, they walked straight into a death-trap. As they approached Haddington Road nests of snipers opened fire from adjoining houses and the men of the Sherwood Foresters retired in confusion. Again and again they advanced, but each time with the same result. From Clanwilliam House, commanding Mount Street Bridge, occupied by Captain Malone, de Valera's aide-de-camp, and six Volunteers, volley after volley was poured into the ranks of the Foresters with deadly effect, and it was not until the house, attacked by a Gatling gun and hand-grenades, had gone up in flames, burying Malone and two of his comrades under its debris, that the bridge was captured. In his Report to the Government afterwards, General Sir John Maxwell described how "after careful arrangements the whole column, accompanied by bombing parties, attacked the schools and the houses where the chief opposition lay, and the battalions charging in successive waves carried all before them." When he wrote that Sir John was hardly aware that the opposition came from no more than some fourteen men. The British losses were two hundred and thirty-four killed and wounded, or about half of the total incurred in the Rising. The Volunteers lost six. The battle had lasted for five hours.

Out at Ringsend the fighting grew more intense as the week wore on. British snipers took up positions in the tall Mount Street houses and the Mill was continually under fire. A field gun was mounted in Percy Place and a shell crashed through the outer wall of the Bakery. De Valera dispatched an officer to send out semaphore messages from the roof of the nearby distillery. The messages meant

 (D1238)

nothing at all, but they succeeded in their purpose of drawing away the fire from the Mill. The British, believing that the distillery was the area headquarters, began to pound that building with artillery. Some of the shells went wide and fell into the sea near the *Helga,* which had steamed down the river to take part in the bombardment. The *Helga's* captain mistook the shells for Republican artillery fire and trained his guns on the empty distillery, which was thus bombarded from land and sea. The Mill remained intact and the barricades unbreached. Along with the Four Courts, held by Commandant Daly, Boland's Mill remained to the end the most strongly-defended post in the city.

The fires of Thursday night told de Valera that all was not well with his comrades in the central positions. Communications with the Post Office had been severed, but the murky orange-red sky above the heart of Dublin told its own tale. No thought of surrender, however, had as yet occurred to him and he moved about giving orders quietly and methodically. His grey-green uniform was white with flour-dust; his unshaven face was worn and haggard; his eyes were weary from lack of sleep; but he still contrived to maintain his cheerfulness and to encourage his men. When they upbraided him for exposing himself recklessly to the flying bullets, he said, "Better men have been killed." All through Friday and Saturday, when the drama of the burning Post Office was over and Pearse had surrendered his sword, when the Tricolour had been hauled down from Jacob's Factory, when Cathal Brugha, bearing on him the marks of seventeen bullet wounds, had been carried

D

out from the South Dublin Union, when the Countess Markievicz had marched out of the College of Surgeons, the Mill was still offering defiance and the men of the Third Battalion were still fighting fiercely on roofs, at barricades and at street corners. But as the week drew to its close the end was in sight. Then, for the first time, de Valera betrayed some emotion. To a bakery employee who was permitted to tend the horses, he said, "Ah, if the people had only come out with knives and forks!"

(VIII)

The Rising was over. Dublin was encircled by a cordon of steel and Sir John Maxwell had declared that he would not hesitate to raze the city to dust if he encountered further opposition. So, "to prevent further slaughter and in the hope of saving the lives of our followers now surrounded and hopelessly outnumbered," Pearse gave the order to surrender. But not before the men of the Rising "had redeemed Dublin from many shames."

It was not until Sunday that the order to lay down arms reached de Valera. He marshalled his men, spoke to them quietly for a few moments, saw to it that the doors of the Mill were made safe against possible looting, and then marched them to the nearest military post. To the British officer with whom he parleyed, he said: "You may shoot me, but my men must not be molested when surrendering." The date was April 30, a date that he was to recall seven years later when it brought an even fuller measure of bitterness.

He was put on trial eleven days later and

De Valera a prisoner after the surrender in Easter Week.

sentenced to death. Twelve executions had already taken place and protests were beginning to be raised in the House of Commons and in the British and American press. "These executions are becoming an atrocity," said the *Manchester Guardian.* "The men who were shot in cold blood after capture or surrender," wrote Bernard Shaw, "were prisoners of war, and it was therefore entirely incorrect to slaughter them. I cannot regard as a traitor any Irishman taken in a fight for Irish Independence against the British Government, which was a fair fight in everything except the enormous odds my countrymen had to face." At Westminster John Dillon appealed to Asquith. "It is not murderers who are being executed," he declared, "but men who fought a clean fight, a brave fight." Asquith admitted that the insurgents "had conducted themselves with great humanity" and Maxwell's hand was stayed. The pit he had dug to hold a hundred was, after all, going to prove too large. When, on May 12, the wounded Connolly was shot as he lay propped up in a chair, and Sean MacDermott after he had limped from his cell to the prison yard, the tale of death was complete. De Valera's sentence was commuted to penal servitude for life.

Sir John Maxwell's biographer has said of him that "his readiness to take action on his own responsibility never forsook him in any emergency." But he had never heard of Mazzini's dictum: "Ideas ripen quickly when watered by the blood of martyrs."

CHAPTER THREE

The Banner County

With gladness now we re-begin the quest
That destiny commands. Though where we go
Or guided by what star, no man doth know.
Uncharted is our course! Our hearts untried!
And we may weary ere we take the tide,
Or make fair haven from the moaning sea.
Be ye propitious, winds of destiny!
On us at first blow not too boisterous bold!
All Ireland hath is packed into this hold!

—JAMES STEPHENS.

(I)

WHEN de Valera and his comrades were marched along the quays of Dublin, silent, dispirited, but with defiant eyes, there were some who hooted and none who cheered. To cheer, indeed, would have been highly dangerous in a city under the Terror. Of those who called down curses on the insurgents many were "Separation Women," as the wives of the soldiers in the British Army who were fighting in Flanders and Salonika were called. They, poor things, had been told that the Rising was "a stab in the back" for the nation which was fighting on the Continent for the cause of small nations. And, unbelievably, they believed it.

But the thoughtful men and women were thinking harder than ever. With Walt Whitman they began to say to themselves, "How beggarly are all arguments before a valiant deed!" James

Stephens, writing whilst the ruins of the Post Office were still smoking, said of the leaders that "they were good men—men, that is, who willed no evil, and whose movements of body or brain were unselfish and healthy." W. B. Yeats, away in London, realised, after one wavering, emotional moment, that he was wrong when he declared that romantic Ireland was dead and gone, and he wrote an unforgettable poem with the refrain:

A terrible beauty is born.

All over Ireland, where troops and police were roping in Sinn Feiners (and catching in their indiscriminate net many a loud-mouthed "pathriot" whose claim to the heroic virtues was very slight indeed) for transportation to English jails, there was, once the first shock was over, an almost instant revulsion of feeling. People who had been reared in the Nationalist tradition began to sense, however incompletely, that there was a fitness and a sort of inevitability in what had happened; that the Insurrection was an event compounded of many forces in Ireland's national life; that it sprang from the centuries of oppression; from the blood-bath of '98; from the resurgent gospel of the Young Irelanders; from the horrors of the Famine and the long-sustained memories of the exiles; from the oath of the Fenians; from the unroofed cabins of the Land War; from Arthur Griffith's doctrine of Sinn Fein and self-reliance; from the failure of the Parliamentarians; from the slums of Dublin and the ruthlessly-suppressed Great Strike of 1913; from the very boards of the Abbey Theatre.

John Redmond had become Britain's "recruiting

agent" in the Great War and he had been repudiated by men who knew that their manner of repudiation would cost them their lives. He had offered to Britain something that it was beyond his power to give—the lives and fortunes of a people who could not be disloyal to Britain because they had never been loyal. He had spoken as if he had had Ireland in his pocket, and the first shot fired from the windows of the G.P.O. had blown the whole fallacy that lay behind his words to fragments. From that moment Parliamentarianism was dead: as dead as Parnell, who would never have given a pledge unless he had received a cast-iron, unbreakable pledge in return.

(II)

De Valera was in Dartmoor. His chronicle of jails had begun. On the long journey from North Wales he had caught his first glimpse of the country whose pride and caution and stubbornness were to shape the biggest problems of his future career. He had seen the towering chimney stacks of cities that had made Britain industrially great; he had seen the green and pleasant land that had bred Shakespeare and Blake. In his own island, he knew, there were few factory chimneys and little or none of the green prosperity. What he saw from a railway carriage-window was the rich, thickly-populated, arrogant and unfriendly nation that, for all the hymns to liberty her poets had written, had kept his own little nation impoverished, depopulated, and unfree. Nevertheless, looking at it, he did not, even though his hands were manacled, feel any bitterness welling up within him. His mood was rather one of despondency and puzzlement. How could such things happen after more than nineteen centuries of Christian civilisation? Was justice and fair dealing between nations, after all, a fantastic and impossible dream?

Brooding in his cell at Dartmoor, he found no answer to these questions. There, possessed of mental reserves which helped him to bear it better than most, he did not suffer from the appalling isolation which had so often driven Irishmen mad in English convict prisons. Tom Clarke, during his fifteen years in Portland and Millbank, had set himself incredible tasks to occupy his mind and preserve his sanity. He had counted every brick in the walls and every nail in the iron-studded door a thousand times; he had taught himself shorthand and had transcribed the whole of the Bible, from Genesis to Revelation, twice over; he had even contrived to keep his sense of humour, and in the printer's shop of one convict establishment had printed surreptitiously a "newspaper" entitled *The Irish Felon*, "published at Her Majesty's Convict Prison, Chatham"!

De Valera was determined that, like Clarke, he would pit his resolution against that of his jailers; that no solitude would break his spirit or make him morose or bitter. There might be long years of penal servitude ahead; well, he would face them as unflinchingly as might be. Some day release would come and he would be met again with the task of supporting his wife and children. Blackrock or Carysfort might take him back when the jail gates opened. He asked for some books from the prison library; it would not do to let his mathematics grow rusty.

Day succeeded day, week succeeded week, month succeeded month. The black-and-white walls, the damp, barely-lighted cells, the drab figures of the convicts, the blue-coated warders, the meagre prison dietary, the single-file "ring" of morning exercise taken with measured paces and in dead silence,

. . . the little tent of blue
That prisoners call the sky,

de Valera and his sixty-four Irish comrades came to know it all in the full horror of Wilde's ballad. Deadly, demoralising, unbroken monotony.

Once only in those early months at Dartmoor had there been a thrill and a break in the gloom. Eoin MacNeill had come to serve his sentence, and one morning when the Irish prisoners were lined up in the central hall for inspection, his spare figure was seen descending the iron stairs to take his place in their ranks.

> "We were all conscious," says Robert Brennan, who has told the story, "that the prisoners had mixed feelings about him, as he had stopped the Rising. To our amazement Eamon de Valera stepped out from our ranks and faced us. His voice rang out with the command: 'Irish Volunteers! Attention! Eyes left!' The command—a salute for MacNeill—was obeyed with military precision, and de Valera stepped back into the ranks, leaving us a bit dazed by his chivalry and courage."

It was an illuminating incident. It indicated a mind swift to grasp the necessities of an unexpected occasion and it showed a ready capacity for leadership. The Senior Officer of the Volunteer prisoners was honouring his former Chief of Staff. Not only that, but he was making it plain that he agreed with Pearse when the latter said—in a manifesto issued from the Post Office: "Both Eoin MacNeill and we have acted in the best interests of Ireland."

Six dreary months went by. The summer with its grateful warmth passed into autumn, and autumn into the frosts and fogs of a Dartmoor winter. Then, after a short hunger-and-thirst strike carried out as a protest against what he considered the unfair punishment of a comrade for a minor act of insubordination, de Valera was removed to Maidstone. Before the year was out he was lodged in Lewes Jail, where all the convicted insurgents were now concentrated.

(III)

At home, events were moving rapidly. All through the summer and autumn the country lay under martial law and Sir John Maxwell held absolute power. But in spite of daily arrests and deportations Ireland was awakening. An Irish National Aid Association and an Irish Volunteers' Dependents' Fund were formed, and these organisations, in addition to carrying out relief work, became the spearhead of a new advance. When, in August, Roger Casement was hanged, the process of re-awakening was quickened. Even the most obtuse Irishman was quick to grasp the irony of a situation in which a man who three years before had declared that he "would refuse to recognise any law" if Ireland were granted Home Rule, was acting as

Prosecuting Counsel in a trial for treason. "The difference between us," Casement had said in the dock, with his eyes fixed on F. E. Smith, "is that the Unionist champions chose a path that they felt would lead to the Woolsack, while I went a road that I knew must lead to the dock." Casement's words were noted by his own people. Speeches from the dock have always been part of Ireland's revolutionary literature.

In certain political quarters in England some anxiety began to manifest itself with regard to the Irish situation. It was not easy, it was felt, in the prevailing circumstances, to convince America, still hesitating about entering the war on the side of the Allies, that "government by consent of the governed"—one of President Wilson's famous Points—existed in Ireland. The British Ambassador in Washington did not conceal his opinion that the executions after Easter Week were a blunder and he pressed strongly for a policy of moderation.

The nimble brain of Lloyd George—who became Prime Minister in November—got busy. Already a Home Rule Bill, from the operation of which six out of Ulster's nine counties were provisionally excluded, had been introduced in the British House of Commons (but not before Lloyd George had given Carson a private written pledge in which he stated that "we must make it clear that at the end of the provisional period Ulster does not, *whether she wills it or not,* merge in the rest of Ireland.") Partition was under way. The Bill, in spite of the fact that Redmond favoured its acceptance, was greeted in Ireland with a storm of protest and derision.

Lloyd George played his next card. At Christmas the prisoners in the internment camps—but not the leaders in Lewes—were released. They received a tumultuous welcome. Torchlight processions filled the city streets and bonfires blazed on the hillsides.

(IV)

Amongst the released prisoners were Arthur Griffith, the "Father of Sinn Fein," and a young Corkman named Michael Collins.

Griffith, stockily-built, heavy-moustached, keen-eyed, had been, since his return from South Africa eighteen years before, the implacable foe of Parliamentarianism. "Get away from Westminster and its corrupting influences," he had cried week after week in the organ of Sinn Fein; "be Irish; wear Irish; buy Irish; rely on yourselves." He wielded a wizard pen that was forever being dipped in acid and one that he could have sold profitably at any moment. But nobody could wean him from his crusade, even though his shoes often leaked and there were times when he could not pay his compositors. The young men read him week by week and the intellectuals contributed to the columns of his paper. Political though his primary intent was, his cultural influence was almost as great as that of Dr. Hyde. The Sinn Fein Clubs and the Gaelic League classes were, in fact, ofttimes hardly distinguishable in either purpose or personnel. But although he was in his writings as fiercely anti-English as John Mitchel—the only Irish journalist of the same stature in more than half a century—he was not, like the Easter Week men, a

Separatist. He had, indeed, after the Rising had broken out, gone to the Post Office and asked to be permitted to take his share in the fighting, only to be told by Sean MacDermott that his work lay elsewhere; but not once had he breathed the word "Republic," and he had made it sufficiently clear that his ideal Irish State was a return to Grattan's Parliament of 1782—Dual Monarchy, Irish Lords and Commons. He was, too, almost alone among the leaders of the time, curiously antipathetic towards Labour; for Connolly he had a warm personal regard, but from the movement that culminated in the Great Strike of 1913 he had remained coldly aloof. A grim, granitic man, who in any other country except Ireland would have been a solid Conservative, his doctrine of Sinn Fein, by a curious irony, and through a confusion of names and ideas, provided the label by which the Rising and the Republican movement which followed it came to be known.

Michael Collins was a young man of twenty-seven, tall, handsome, with dark, rebellious hair and a rich Cork brogue. At fifteen he had entered the British postal service in London and later on had become a bank clerk. More " typically Irish " than de Valera or Griffith, he was possessed of a fund of boisterous humour, the gift of easy comradeship, and a capacity for strong language.

Mick was a youth with a manly air
Whose golden laugh was a cure for care,

one of the makers of ballads wrote about him. After fighting in the Rising he had been interned in Frongoch, where he had acquired a good deal of influence, and where he had organised a secret oath-bound society intended to become a branch of the I.R.B., of which he was already a member. Ardent, generous-minded, impulsive, he had as yet worked out no political philosophy, and was indistinguishable from thousands of other young Irishmen in the movement save by his strong personality and undoubted ability.

Men like Griffith and Collins had hardly set foot in Ireland after their release before an opportunity presented itself for taking up the work which the holocaust of the Rising had so tragically interrupted and to which, at the same time, it had given such a tremendous stimulus. There was a bye-election in Roscommon and it was decided to contest it. The Redmondites threw all their weight into the struggle, but the young men came from all airts and parts, dragging their bicycles across the February snow-drifts of 1917, cheering the torrential eloquence of Father Michael O'Flanagan, and sweeping the Sinn Fein candidate, Count Plunkett, to easy victory. In May there was another bye-election, this time in Longford, and the candidate chosen to carry the Tricolour was Joseph McGuinness, one of de Valera's fellow-convicts in Lewes Jail. The Parliamentarians asked the staid, slow-thinking farmers of the Irish midlands not to sacrifice "the certain boon of Home Rule" for the illusory promise of an Irish Republic. Once again they suffered defeat. The old Parliamentary Party—whose leader had boasted that he could smash Sinn Fein "like that" (crashing one fist into the other)—was being swept away at a pace unparalleled in Irish political history.

(v)

Within the jail walls at Lewes there was excitement of another kind. Under de Valera's leadership the prisoners were in revolt. Rebelling against their "convict" status they had demanded the rights and treatment of prisoners of war and, when these were refused, they proceeded to disobey all regulations, to smash up furniture, and generally to make life inside the prison a prolonged riot. The authorities retaliated by dividing them up into dozens and half-dozens and scattering them through other English jails.

Release, however, was not far away. Mr. Lloyd George was once again calling upon the inexhaustible resources of his ingenuity. America had by this time entered the war, and it was considered desirable to placate the powerful Irish-American element. The British Ambassador at Washington reported that the effect of the Easter Week executions on opinion in America had been "disastrous." "The Irish here have blood in their eyes when they look our way," he said. He strongly favoured a conciliatory policy. It was impossible, of course, for the British Prime Minister to invite men who were wearing convict dress in British prisons to one of his celebrated Downing Street breakfasts and to talk to them in a spirit of sweet reasonableness, but another way out occurred to his quick intelligence. Why not, as a magnanimous gesture, release all the Irish prisoners, call a round table conference of all shades of Irish opinion, keep them talking as long as possible, and then when they had disagreed (as by the terms of reference he could ensure they would) turn to America and the world and say: "Look at that, now! England wants to do the right thing by Ireland, but the Irish themselves won't agree as to what should be done."

The Convention was duly decided upon, and the remaining prisoners were released. It was a memorable home-coming. All night long, crowds waited on the quays of Dublin, singing rebel songs, straining their eyes as the dawn came for the sight of an incoming ship. Someone brought word eventually that the prisoners were being landed at Kingstown, whereupon the crowds got into military formation and marched to meet them at the Westland Row terminus. As they stepped from the train a roar of cheering broke out, followed by the Soldier's Song, and through the densely-packed streets of Dublin, where a little more than a year before they had gone out to challenge the might of an Empire, they were escorted with bands and banners.

One tall, spare figure, with closely-cropped hair and eyes that were smiling now, seemed to attract universal attention. "There he is!" people exclaimed; "there's de Valera!" The fame of Boland's Mill had spread abroad.

(VI)

As he had stepped out of the gates of Pentonville—where he spent the last weeks of his imprisonment—de Valera was handed a telegram. It informed him that he had been selected to contest a forthcoming bye-election in East Clare as Sinn Fein candidate.

The turning-point in his career had arrived. The decision he had to make was a fateful one, though he could not, at that moment, have been aware of the extent to which it would shape his life. Up to now he had thought of release in terms of taking up the old existence which had been interrupted; in terms of home and family, of studies to be resumed, of teaching posts to be looked for. Now, suddenly and unexpectedly, there loomed up before him a new road, a road where there would be few signposts and many pitfalls, a road that might lead anywhere. It was a prospect both exciting and disturbing.

What qualifications had he to bring with him into the political arena? Of helpful experience he had had none. Until he had joined the Volunteers four years before, he had been something of a recluse, known to few outside a limited academic circle. Spare-time soldiering in the evenings and at week-ends, culminating in one short week of bloody warfare, had, no doubt, sharpened his outlook on men and things tremendously, but it was not necessarily a good preparation for a political career. "Career," in fact, was a word that never entered into his head as the Irish Mail thundered through the shires of England on the night of his home-coming. No man was ever less of a careerist. If he made his mind up to accept the invitation offered to him (as he actually did before he sighted Kingstown Harbour), personal ambition was not the dominating factor.

What he was about to embark upon, of course, was not politics in the ordinary restricted sense of the word. Easter Week had blown all hitherto accepted political values to atoms. The uprising of

(D1238)

the nation had begun and a revolutionary crusade rather than a new political movement had been launched—a crusade which might necessitate other methods than those which were termed "constitutional." British rule in Ireland would not fall easily and—whatever Arthur Griffith might think or desire—the guns might very well go off again.

If de Valera had any hesitation in coming to a decision, one may be sure that it was not due to any want of self-confidence. To a sturdy belief in his own abilities was added a standard of values acquired in the testing-time of the Rising and its prison aftermath, and to that standard could be attributed a serenity and a self-assurance which would serve him well in a time of crisis. His leadership had already been proved and accepted to a certain extent; now that it was about to be tried in a wider and somewhat different sphere, he did not fear the result.

He had heard, of course, of Roscommon and Longford, of the amazing changes that a single year had brought, of the new and rapid stirring of the nation's pulse; and it all helped to make his mind up. Easter Week was not an end but a beginning, and Clare had called on him to lift the standard. Well, to Clare he would go.

(VII)

Willie Redmond, best-loved of the Parliamentarians, brother of their leader, had fallen fighting at Messines. Patrick Lynch, a King's Counsel, well-known and popular—a "decent" man, in the phrase of the countryside—had been chosen to take his place. He was a strong candidate.

But the young men who had carried the Tricolour to triumph in Roscommon and Longford were in no doubt about the result. Was not Clare the "Banner" County—the constituency forever associated with the great days of O'Connell and Emancipation? Clare would not let them down. Once more they oiled their bicycles and took the long road to Ennis, carrying with them an exultant air of enthusiasm. Every young man was an idealist and a crusader. In the ranks of the re-organised Volunteers discipline was at its highest; nobody drank, and even the use of strong language was frowned upon. There were no doubts or heart-searchings; in their youthful minds all was simplified. The cause was everything; labour and hardships counted for nothing.

What made Clare different from Roscommon and Longford was the appearance of a leader. No longer was the work of electioneering being carried out by a band of inexperienced amateurs, but by soldiers who took orders and obeyed them unquestioningly. When de Valera, donning his Volunteer uniform, rang out his commands from a platform that overlooked the market square at Ennis, there was not only a soldierly clicking of heels, but also a quick beating of boyish hearts.

Bliss was it in that dawn to be alive,
But to be young was very heaven.

From Ennis the Volunteers cycled out across the heathery hills, through the fields of stones, along the rim of Clare's hungry sea, to Burren and

Bodyke, canvassing, cajoling, speech-making, doing as unsoldierly a job as soldiers were ever called on to do. They found many a tough nut to crack. The farmers of Clare were not easily weaned from their old allegiance. To many of them Easter Week was still a mad escapade that had brought trouble on the country and that might well bring more; and as for Eamon de Valera, that unknown young man with a foreign name, who was he that they should be expected to follow him in pursuit of the mirage of a visionary Republic? John Redmond they knew, and Patrick Lynch they knew; and they knew what men like these stood for. Was it any wonder that they hesitated?

In some instances the young men took drastic and, no doubt, highly immoral steps to prevent votes being cast against their hero, and there was the case of the Redmondite veteran who, when his sons had hidden his boots to prevent him voting against de Valera, walked the four miles from his home to the polling-booth in his bare feet. Even the ranks of Tuscany had to applaud that. In contrast, there was the case of another ancient farmer, who, when a group of Republican canvassers had addressed him for five minutes as if he were a public meeting, took the pipe out of his mouth, looked at them quizzically, and said: "Boys, I was out in '67; isn't that enough for ye?"

Clare was a good fight and a clean fight. If there was an ugly tradition in Irish elections, this one showed a break. It was fair enough to ask the voters to "choose between the Crown Prosecutor (Patrick Lynch held a Government post) and the Crown Prosecuted," but when a poster insultingly depicting John Redmond and John Dillon was produced de Valera ordered it to be destroyed. He would fight on principles, not personalities.

What of the central figure in the contest? One thing was certain: he was no mere symbol or standard-bearer as Joseph McGuinness had been in Longford. He was there for all to see, and even the most indifferent or most hostile of observers could not fail to be aware that a new and striking personality had come amongst them. His oratory, it is true, was not impressive; in a country renowned for orators it fell far short of what was demanded by a great tradition. John Redmond, a speaker in the grand Gladstonian manner, or Joseph Devlin, the battling "duodecimo Demosthenes," could sway an Irish crowd much more readily.

The fact was, of course, that until he went to Clare de Valera had never made a platform speech in his life. The roar of cheering that greeted him when he made his first appearance in the market square at Ennis was not a welcome to an orator from whom golden eloquence was expected; it was a tribute to the soldier who had fought a gallant fight in Easter Week. Yet unknown as he was, inexperienced as he was, devoid as he was of the natural gift of oratory, he nevertheless impressed when he spoke. He was lucid, vigorous and direct, hammering home his points with force and sincerity. There were no flourishes, no conventional embellishments, but there was a grave dignity, which has ever since remained the most striking feature of his manner of speaking in public.

The electors of Clare were left in no doubt as to what de Valera stood for, though they might have no very clear idea as to how it was to be achieved. He issued no election address, but he made it plain that, if returned, he would never set foot in Westminster. With Griffith he held that Parliamentarianism was "useless, degrading, and demoralising," and he sought election to the British Parliament solely that he might be the better able to protest against that Parliament's claim to legislate for Ireland. For the rest, his policy was the policy of Easter Week—"in the name of God and of the dead generations from which she receives her old tradition of nationhood . . . we declare the right of the people of Ireland to the ownership of Ireland, and to the unfettered control of Irish destinies, to be sovereign and indefeasible." That, at any rate, was clear and unmistakable. It was the Separatism that Wolfe Tone formulated when he called upon the people "to break the connection with England": it was the Separatism of the Fenians; it was the Separatism of the Republican Brotherhood.

Was Ireland ready for it, with British rule as firmly rooted in Irish soil as at any time during six centuries, with two hundred thousand of her sons fighting at that moment under the British flag? Was Clare ready for it?

On June 23 Clare gave the answer. De Valera received 5,010 votes; Lynch, 2,035.

Once again the tar-barrels blazed and the beacon fires leapt in the night from hill to hill.

CHAPTER FOUR

President de Valera

> " It is easy to describe second-rate talents, because they fall into a class, and enlist under a standard; but first-rate powers defy calculation or comparison, and can be defined only by themselves."
>
> —WILLIAM HAZLITT.

(I)

FROM the excitements of Clare de Valera returned to his quiet little home in Dublin, tired but happy. He had won a resounding victory and the Republican movement was sweeping Ireland like a prairie fire. That what had happened was due chiefly to the reflected glory of Easter Week and to the essential rightness of the cause, he knew perfectly well, but at the same time he was quite aware of his own personal contribution to the triumph. He had come out of the ordeal well; congratulations had been showered on him by friends, and even the special correspondents of English newspapers had revealed in their dispatches how much they had been impressed. " The young men appear ready to follow de Valera anywhere," said one. " This tall, stern man, in his early thirties, with angular features and burning eyes, seems destined to be the leader of Sinn Fein," said another. The name de Valera was already flaming across the Irish skies. The ballad-makers were busy, as always, and the boys and girls of the countryside were singing:

Up de Valera! he's the champion of the right,
We'll follow him to battle 'neath the Orange, Green and White,
And when next we challenge England we'll beat her in the fight
And we'll crown de Valera king of Ireland.

He might smile at that, but he did not underestimate its significance. In what was taking place there was more than the emotionalism of the time or the insuppressible extravagance of youth. Through all the trumpetings and flag-wavings, through all the turmoil and the shouting, the call for a leader was coming, clear as a bell.

Of the men who were lying in quick-lime graves in Arbour Hill, how many could, had they lived, have answered that call? How many of them possessed the rare combination of qualities requisite for popular leadership? Pearse, perhaps; MacDonagh, less certainly; Connolly, for all his dynamic character, not at all. But these men were dead, and all that was speculative. Was the mantle about to fall on de Valera's shoulders? He was not left in doubt very long.

(II)

There were many eyes on the victor of Clare. There were, of course, the hostile eyes of the Parliamentarians and the worshipping uncritical eyes of the young people. But there were others whose glance was more penetrating and purposeful. Arthur Griffith was surveying him keenly through his steel-rimmed spectacles and the members of the Irish Republican Brotherhood were cautiously turning his name over in their minds. Between  Sinn Fein—the original Sinn Fein, that is, with its limitation of the national objective—and the Brotherhood, there was a very wide gap indeed, though for the moment their conflicting ideals appeared to be harmonised. They might be regarded as the Right and Left wings of the forward movement, and it would require a leader possessed of unusual strength of character and with a flair for political finesse to fuse them into a weapon that would not break when the final crisis came.

Already de Valera had displayed some of the essential qualities. His transparent sincerity, his maturity, his dignity, his air of reserve, his unemotionalism—all these counted in his favour. So far, he had shown no desire to grasp authority, but he had let nobody encroach upon the powers vested in him. There were prominent Republicans who would have banished Eoin MacNeill from the platform of Clare on account of his action in calling off the Rising, but de Valera made it clear that MacNeill would go there, and MacNeill went. The grumblers were silenced and unity was preserved.

A month after the Clare election Lloyd George's Convention began its sittings in Dublin. Boycotted by the Republicans, by organised Labour, and by William O'Brien's "All-for-Ireland League," it was representative of only minority sections of Irish opinion—the Redmondites, the Carsonites, the dwindling remnants of landlordism.

A few able and sincere Independents like Erskine Childers, who was its secretary, and George Russell ("A. E."), the poet and economist, took part in its deliberations, but they soon became convinced that the end would be disillusionment. Apart entirely from the unrepresentative character of the Convention, things were happening in the country every day that rendered its sessions, held in the cloistered peace of Trinity College, as remote from actuality as if they had been held on Mars. Coercion was in full swing; raids, arrests and clashes with the police were of daily occurrence; the jails were filling up again. Men were being imprisoned for whistling the "Soldier's Song," as they had been imprisoned in the Land League days for whistling "The Peeler and the Goat." The wearing of the Volunteer uniform and the hoisting of the Tricolour were forbidden. Hunger-strikes and the technique of furniture-smashing, learnt in English prisons, were now being adopted at home. The revolution was sweeping ahead, leaving the men who were talking in Trinity College like sea-wrack abandoned by the tide. In July another bye-election took place, this time in Kilkenny City. The candidate chosen by Sinn Fein—on de Valera's suggestion—was William Cosgrave, an Alderman of the Dublin Corporation, who had been sentenced to death for his part in the Rising, a sentence afterwards commuted to penal servitude for life. He had the easiest of victories.

(III)

In October both the national programme and the question of leadership were settled. De Valera, who had been co-opted on the National Council of Sinn Fein after his release, worked untiringly behind the scenes to bring Right and Left together, and when the Ard-fheis met on the 25th to decide upon a new Constitution and to elect a new President, the last obstacles to unity had been removed. It had been no easy task. Griffith and his followers were reluctant to subscribe to the full Republican programme, whilst men like Cathal Brugha would have the Republic or nothing. It was a formula devised by de Valera that bridged the gulf. "Sinn Fein," it ran, "aims at securing international recognition of Ireland as an independent, Irish Republic. Having achieved that status the Irish people may by referendum choose their own form of government." Both sections were satisfied, and the seventeen hundred delegates, representing twelve hundred Sinn Fein Clubs, gave the new Constitution enthusiastic approval.

Then came the business of electing a leader. There were three candidates—Arthur Griffith, the founder of Sinn Fein; Count Plunkett, the victor of Roscommon and father of the poet executed in Easter Week; and de Valera. Count Plunkett was an elderly man, Griffith was forty-seven, de Valera was thirty-five. If long years of service and achievement counted, Griffith's claim was very strong; he had been President of Sinn Fein for six years and the driving intelligence behind it from the beginning. But his chances of election were slight, for he lacked the support of the militant sections. To avoid a division, both Griffith and Plunkett stepped down and Griffith proposed de Valera, "a man," he declared, "in whom you have a statesman as well as a leader." Once again, there was unanimity and enthusiasm. The great hall of the Mansion

House was filled with cheering as de Valera rose to return thanks.

"I stand for what I stood in East Clare," he said—"international recognition of an Irish Republic; and it is because I stand for that that I was elected here."

Two days later, at another Convention, he was elected President of the Volunteers, who remained independent of Sinn Fein.

It was an extraordinary tribute to a man whose name was virtually unknown in Ireland eighteen months before, who had had no political training, and who was endowed with none of the more obvious political gifts. Now he had been invested with powers such as even Parnell, at the height of his fame, had not possessed. Yet nobody seemed to doubt the wisdom of the choice. Griffith was not covering any secret disappointment when he gave de Valera his warm support. Leaving the Mansion House he said to a friend, "Thank God for de Valera; heaven must have sent him." The Volunteers, naturally, were jubilant, and even the Republican Brotherhood—from which he had resigned before the election—were satisfied. In Britain Lloyd George began to sit up and take notice. "I have read the speeches of the Honourable Member for East Clare," he said. "They are not excited, and so far as the language is concerned they are not violent. They are plain, deliberate and, I might almost say, cold-blooded incitements to rebellion." And he went on to add that de Valera, in his opinion, was "a man of great ability and considerable influence."

Clearly, Britain was awaking to the fact that the

"Irish problem," as she had known it for fifty years, no longer existed, that a problem infinitely greater now lay at her doors, and that a new Irish leader, very different in character and pledged to use very different methods, had suddenly sprung up from nowhere.

When, less than six months later, the Trinity College Convention broke up (in spite of F. E. Smith's "Why not let them keep on talking?") without having achieved anything, and John Redmond, disillusioned and broken-hearted, died, an epoch in Irish history came to a very definite end.

(IV)

Did the new leader look on the burden he had taken on his shoulders with some misgiving? Did he pause to glance back with any regret at the quiet academic life that he had left behind forever? He would have been less than human if he did not. Only a year-and-a-half before he had gone day by day with punctual and rigid routine, to his lectures at Carysfort Park and, apart from his evenings with the Volunteers, he had had few interests save his home life, his studies and the classes of the Gaelic League. Now he had achieved leadership or, it may be, leadership had been thrust upon him. From now onwards, in the stormy and dangerous times that he knew lay ahead, there would be for him very few of the familiar delights of home and fireside, none of the quiet joys that attend upon the studious mind. Henceforth he would have to ride the whirlwind; to endure the tyranny of fame and the spotlight of publicity; to be something of a prophet and something of an actor; to retain poise and dignity and calm in the midst of tumultuous clamour; to lead a nation, not a party, along a tortuous road where danger lurked at every turning.

But whatever his private anxieties may have been, he gave no hint of them in public. He had taken on a job and he would carry it out, as he had carried out every other task that he had undertaken, with all the thoroughness of which he was capable. Come what might, he had faith in the cause, and faith in the people. Statesmanship might be a complex affair, but in his political philosophy it was greatly simplified. Make sure of the goal, use every means consonant with morality and ethics to attain it, and drive ahead whatever winds might blow or storms rage. It was naïve, no doubt, but it was to prove remarkably effective.

The great advantage that he started with—and almost the only one—was that his leadership rested solidly and fundamentally on certain rock-like qualities that he possessed. There was his integrity, which even his enemies have never questioned, and which was rare and refreshing in a country where servitude had too often been the foster-mother of political corruption; there was his gift of patience, which would be increasingly needed to preserve a *via media* between the two wings of the movement; there was, above all, that indefinable something called personality of which nobody with whom he came in contact could fail to be aware.

(v)

A big accession to the ranks of Sinn Fein came with the Conscription crisis which loomed up in the spring of 1918. The British army was fighting with its back to the wall in France, the cry had gone up for more recruits, and Lloyd George, badgered by Generals like Sir Henry Wilson, came to the decision to conscript Irishmen, in spite of the fact that, according to the warning given him by his own officials in Dublin Castle, "it would require three Army Corps to get one out of Ireland." The Conscription Bill was passed in the British House of Commons in April.

Its immediate effect was to unify all sections of Nationalist opinion in Ireland. John Dillon, who had succeeded Redmond as leader of the Parliamentary Party, adopted Sinn Fein tactics and withdrew the Irish Members from Westminster. In Dublin a "National Cabinet," composed of representatives of Sinn Fein, the Parliamentarians, Labour, and the veteran Independents, William O'Brien and Tim Healy, met to organise resistance.

De Valera's special gifts were never seen to better advantage than at that Conference where Old Ireland and Young Ireland met for the first time around a common table. John Dillon, who sat opposite to him, had been in Kilmainham Jail with Parnell in the year the Republican leader was born. Now the old Parliamentarian was looking appraisingly through his pince-nez at the man who was destined to supplant him, and de Valera was returning the glance with interest. Tim Healy noted in his diary that de Valera was "as chatterful as Griffith was reserved," but added that he seemed "a resolute fellow." William O'Brien was struck by his "transparent sincerity," his "gentleness and equability," and "the obstinacy with which he would defend a thesis, as though it were a point in pure mathematics." "My husband brought away," says Mrs. William O'Brien, in an unpublished book of memoirs, "a pleasant impression of Mr. de Valera, as of a man ready to own he was in the wrong. Once, it was essential to act quickly. Mr. de Valera's speech was long, time was passing. Recalled to the necessity to act he excused himself on the plea that he was an old schoolmaster. In a modest fashion that took my husband's fancy."

A declaration passed by the Conference and drawn up by de Valera declared that "the passing of the Conscription Bill by the British House of Commons must be regarded as a declaration of war on the Irish nation," and called upon the people "to resist it by the most effective means at their disposal." The support of the Catholic Hierarchy was secured, a twenty-four hour general strike took place by way of protest from organised Labour, and an anti-Conscription pledge was signed at the church doors by the whole of Nationalist Ireland. It was a demonstration of unity and solidarity such as had seldom been witnessed in Irish history.

Lloyd George's answer was soon forthcoming. Ireland was placed under military law with Field-Marshal Lord French in supreme command. Then a mythical "German Plot" was discovered and an immediate swoop made on the leading Sinn Feiners. De Valera was arrested as he alighted for his home at Greystones. The net had been thrown very wide and nearly every notable figure in the movement was captured, including most of the senior officers of the Volunteers. Michael Collins and Cathal Brugha, however, succeeded in escaping. Seventy-three of the prisoners were deported to England. As de Valera walked down the gangway at Kingstown between two files of soldiers someone in the crowd of onlookers asked for a message. He waved back and said: "Be calm and confident." He was lodged in Lincoln Jail.

(VI)

1882 was repeating itself. The man who had best claim to the title of national leader was in jail and the nation was responding, as it had always responded in similar circumstances. There was plenty of law, but little order. Meetings were banned; newspapers were suppressed; courts-martial were set up; raids and arrests mounted rapidly. "Chaos is come again," wrote the special correspondent of the *Daily News*.

The Great War, in which fifty thousand Irishmen had fallen, came to an end, and with it the Conscription menace disappeared. A month later there was a General Election which, so far as Ireland was concerned, was regarded as a plebiscite. Sinn Fein was faced with appalling difficulties: its leaders and election organisers were in jail, its newspapers were suppressed, and the country was under military rule. But the result was never in doubt. A Republican candidate was put forward for every constituency in Ireland except Trinity College, and out of 105 seats 73 were captured. Only six Parliamentarians had been returned; the remaining 26 seats were held by the Unionists of North-East Ulster. De Valera, whose election address had been stopped by the prison authorities, was returned both for East Clare and East Mayo. In the latter constituency he received twice the number of votes cast for his opponent, John Dillon.

Sinn Fein, as the London *Times* admitted after the result, had "swept the country," and it had done so on the full Republican programme. Nobody pretended to misunderstand what had happened. The fiction, so sedulously propagated by British Ministers and the British Press, that Sinn Fein was a movement supported only by cranks and fanatics, was blown sky-high. Home Rule was dead and the stage was now set for the inevitable struggle between Imperial Britain and Republican Ireland.

In Ireland there was a tremendous outburst of jubilation. There was jubilation, too, within the walls of Lincoln Jail.

(VII)

Lincoln was as grim and forbidding as any other English jail, though mercifully free from the fogs of Dartmoor; and out of its high, iron-barred windows the prisoners could catch a glimpse of a pleasant green countryside. De Valera passed the long days studying books that dealt with the mysteries of logarithms and quaternions (but now, from pure love of the subject rather than with any utilitarian purpose), reading Wolfe Tone's *Autobiography* (a book the prison authorities had never heard of and did not therefore suspect of being treasonable), running races in the exercise yards with his comrades, (and, to their astonishment, beating the youngest of them by virtue of his long legs), wondering what was happening in Ireland, and attempting, with the aid of such data as he possessed, to make plans for the future.

He knew that the war was over and that the movement of which he was leader had won a memorable victory. News of big happenings manage to penetrate through even the thickest prison walls. It was good news, but at the same time it left him more than a little anxious. What would Sinn Fein do with its victory, now that nearly all the leaders were behind prison bars? A blunder at this moment might easily prove disastrous.

In the solitude of his cell at Lincoln he began to turn his eyes to wider horizons. The end of the war had brought new opportunities and new problems. Britain, no doubt, would veto any attempt to present Ireland's case at the Peace Conference, but what about America? Surely there was no small nation in the world to which President Wilson's famous principle of self-determination and "government with the consent of the governed" could be applied with greater force than to Ireland? Already he had begun to think in terms of world politics, and it is not surprising if he chafed at his enforced idleness in Lincoln Jail.

The Christmas of 1918 came. De Valera, who was in the habit of serving Mass for the Catholic chaplain of the prison, suddenly got an idea. Why not make an effort to escape? The chaplain usually left his keys on a table in the sacristy and it would be no very difficult matter to obtain an impression; an altar candle would provide the wax. Besides the main entrance to the jail there was a door in one of the walls which appeared to give access to the outside world, and if a key could be procured for this it might be possible to plan a jail-break.

The rest of the story is familiar. A humorous post-card on which there was a drawing of a key was sent out of the jail and its significance was grasped by de Valera's friends in Dublin. A cake, containing a key cut to the size indicated on the post-card, was baked (Michael Collins superintended the icing!) and sent to the jail as a gift to the prisoners. The key proved to be too small. Another one was sent, but this was also a failure. Finally, a third cake, containing not only a key but files as well, reached the prison, and out of these materials one of the prisoners manufactured a master key. Meanwhile Collins and Harry Boland had crossed over from Ireland to superintend the rescue from outside.

The date fixed for the escape was February 3rd, and on that night Collins and Boland, accompanied by Frank Kelly, were waiting in a field at the back of the jail, having left a taxi in readiness nearby. At a pre-arranged hour they flashed a light, which was immediately answered by a similar signal from one of the prison windows. When Collins reached the door he discovered that it was guarded on the outside by an iron gate. He had, however, brought a duplicate key with him which fitted, but when he started to turn it, it broke in the lock. Almost at the same moment the inside door swung open and through it emerged the shadowy figures of de Valera and two of his fellow-prisoners, Sean Milroy and Sean MacGarry. Collins was in despair. It looked as if the careful planning of months was about to be wrecked at the last moment. "I've broken the key in the lock, Dev!" he said in a tragic whisper. De Valera paused a moment and then inserted his own key from the other side. Luck was with him; the broken piece fell out, his key turned smoothly, the iron gate opened, and he stepped out a free man.

The escape created a tremendous sensation on both sides of the Irish Channel. There were angry questions in the British House of Commons and wild speculation in the British Press. Was there no prison in the country strong enough to hold an Irishman (only ten days previously four other Irish prisoners had escaped from the jail at Usk)? Where was de Valera?

"This Irish Scarlet Pimpernel," said one English newspaper, "has disappeared as completely as if the ground had swallowed him up." Within a week of the escape the Press of two countries and the Continent had discovered that he had been seen in London, in Glasgow, in Paris, in Dublin, in a fishing-smack, in a small boat, in Skibbereen, in one of the Hebridean islands. Other accounts stated that he had escaped by balloon to France, where he was waiting to encounter President Wilson. An Exchange message starred the rumour that he was dead. The *Daily Express* had a theory all of its own. "Ireland," it said, "is full of stories of banshees and leprechauns and quaint spirits, and de Valera is just a distillation of these mystic things."

Actually, he had reached Manchester on the night of the rescue in relays of cars arranged for by Collins and he was resting there in the house of an Irish friend.

CHAPTER FIVE

Across the Atlantic

"A mind not to be changed by place or time."
—MILTON. *Paradise Lost.*

(1)

A GOOD deal had happened at home during the nine months of de Valera's imprisonment.

In January, following the victory at the December elections, the first Dail Eireann met and, in a historic session, reaffirmed Ireland's claim to independence. Cathal Brugha, who presided in the absence of the imprisoned leaders, declared: "We are now done with England; let the world know it and those who are concerned bear it in mind." An Address to the Free Nations of the World was issued and three delegates—de Valera, Griffith and Count Plunkett—were appointed to represent Ireland at the Peace Conference. Cathal Brugha was elected Acting-President, and he nominated as Ministers, Michael Collins for Home Affairs, Eoin MacNeill for Finance, Count Plunkett for Foreign Affairs, and Richard Mulcahy for Defence.

Home affairs, in a somewhat different sense of the term, had already passed very much into the hands of Collins. His escape when most of the other leaders were rounded up at the time of the "German Plot" in the previous May had given him a position of power and importance. He was high in the councils of the I.R.B. and his influence in the Volunteers was enormous. For all Brugha's role as Acting-President he was, although he only gradually came to realise it, playing second fiddle to the young Corkman. Collins's energy was boundless. He was re-organising the Volunteers, perfecting an intelligence system, honeycombing British Government departments with secret agents, making contacts with friendly detectives, importing arms and manufacturing explosives. Britain's espionage system in Ireland had never been effectively countered until Collins set to work.

A month after de Valera's escape the rest of the Irish prisoners in English jails were released. It was a sensible step, said a London morning paper: "the more freedom you give Sinn Fein orators in Ireland the sooner they will tire their countrymen with talking and exhaust themselves." But a distinguished French observer, Monsieur Y. M. Goblet, knew that more than oratory was in question, and he wrote: "A new epoch is beginning and one that will be terrible." With the constituent assembly throwing out a challenge to Britain, with the youth of Ireland arming, and with Britain answering Ireland's demand with a chilly, contemptuous "No!" the clash could not be far away.

(II)

The people of Dublin wanted to give de Valera, who was now free to return to Ireland, a civic welcome of royal proportions, and the Lord Mayor arranged a ceremony in which the leader would be paid an honour never previously accorded to anyone except British Sovereigns—the presentation of keys at the City Boundary. Dublin Castle at once banned the ceremony and rushed troops to the city from the Curragh. De Valera felt that to permit the reception would, in the circumstances, be playing into the hands of the British authorities, who were, according to a writer in the *English Review,* "hoping against hope for a bit of a scrap." Besides, he had other plans which made it desirable that there should be no disturbance at that particular moment. So he called off the reception and returned quietly to Dublin.

When the second session of Dail Eireann met in private on April 1st, de Valera was elected *Priomh-Aire,* which was translated "President" in the official report, the title by which he was to be known for the next three years. He at once formed a new Ministry, which included Griffith, Collins, Brugha, MacNeill, Count Plunkett, the Countess Markievicz, Cosgrave, Robert Barton and Laurence Ginnell. Collins became Minister for Finance and Brugha for Defence. Richard Mulcahy was appointed Chief of Staff of the Irish Republican Army, as the Volunteers were now officially styled.

It was during these April sessions of the newly-established Dail that de Valera first gave proof that he was no mere traditional agitator or verbose orator, but a leader of commanding stature. In Clare he had borne himself with dignity and restraint and had displayed a refreshing dislike for scoring petty points of political controversy. But in Clare his audience had been limited, and he was, besides, speaking there more as a soldier than as a politician. Now, in Dail Eireann, he was speaking, not only to the whole Irish Nation, but to Britain and to the world as well. Maybe the world, with its eyes fixed on the Peace Conference, was not listening very intently at that moment, but Britain was listening carefully, and of the Irish people's profound interest there could be no doubt. Here was a leader who, not satisfied with drawing away the eyes of the nation from Westminster, showed, even in those early days, a determination to make the world hear that Ireland was something more than a lonely, forgotten, spiritless island set in the Western mists.

"Our first duty," he declared in the Dail, "is to make clear to the world the position in which Ireland now stands. There is in Ireland at this moment only one lawful authority, and that authority is the elected Government of the Irish Republic. Of the other power claiming authority we can only say, adapting the words of Cardinal Mercier: 'The authority of that power is no lawful authority.'"

More than once he quoted Cardinal Mercier, a name respected in Britain as the outspoken champion of the Belgian people during the German occupation, and one that, naturally, carried weight with the Hierarchy at home. The great majority of the Irish Bishops were still hostile to Sinn Fein, but de Valera made at least one convert. "The fight for Irish freedom," said Dr. Fogarty, Bishop of Killaloe, "has passed into the hands of the young men of Ireland, and when the young men of Ireland hit back at their oppressors it is not for an old man like me to cry 'Foul.'"

With regard to the League of Nations, de Valera said that Ireland was willing to take part in world affairs and to become a constituent unit in a League "based on the only principle on which it could stand—the equality of rights among nations, great and small."

When, in the same month of April, the Ard Feis of Sinn Fein met and de Valera was unanimously re-elected President of the organisation, Arthur Griffith took occasion to pay him a striking tribute:

> "In President de Valera," he said, "we have a man whose judgment and rectitude we can absolutely trust. I know that there is no man who feels more embarrassed at hearing himself praised, but I want you to realise that in de Valera Ireland has a great leader—a man who lives in thousands and millions of hearts, a man with a wonderful judgment, such as I have never met in a young man, save Parnell. Since Parnell there has been no man to equal de Valera, and I am sure that in following and standing by him loyally he will bring the Irish cause to that goal for which many Irishmen in hopeless generations suffered."

Praise from Sir Bedivere was praise indeed! Griffith was twelve years older than de Valera; he had been twenty years in the political movement: de Valera, with whom on the fundamental question he did not see eye to eye, had supplanted him in the leadership of the organisation which he had founded; yet this stolid, hard-headed man, who had found no leader in a quarter of a century worthy of support, acclaimed de Valera in language of emotion.

(III)

From the moment of his escape from Lincoln de Valera had been turning over in his mind the possibilities of a propaganda mission to America.

There was no doubt at all that Britain would veto Ireland's claim to be heard at the Peace Conference, but if the sympathy of the great Republic could be enlisted on behalf of the little Republic something might be done. Congress had already passed a resolution in which it expressed the hope that the Peace Conference would "favourably consider the claims of Ireland to self-determination," and it was obvious that the principles President Wilson had so often and so emphatically enunciated bore a very special application to Ireland. A visit by an Irish leader might, therefore, have important results. Wilson was already under fire, not only from the strong Irish-American element, but from quarters where the traditional "isolationist" opposition to European entanglements was as powerful as ever. Besides, in America there would be a platform from which the carrying-power of an Irish leader's voice would be infinitely greater than at home. Finally, there were precedents in plenty for the step which he proposed to take. Parnell had gone to America, had been enthusiastically welcomed by the exiles there, and had been accorded the signal privilege, previously granted to only two foreigners, Kossuth and Lafayette, of addressing Congress. In later years, visits by other notable Irish politicians had been frequent.

Not all of de Valera's colleagues agreed with the President that the proposed visit was, in the circumstances, wise. One or two urged that his absence at that critical juncture might adversely affect the fortunes of the movement. But the majority felt that he was doing the right thing and wished him God-speed.

(IV)

Once again, after an interval of thirty-four years, de Valera was crossing the Atlantic. He had outwitted the vigilance of the British authorities, and was a stowaway in the hold of a liner, where such comfort and attention as were possible was given him by two faithful Irish sailors. Harry Boland had already preceded him to make preparations for his reception, and the indefatigable Irish Republican Envoy to the States, Dr. Patrick McCartan, had been on the spot for two years.

De Valera had plenty to occupy his mind on the voyage. No doubt the movement was in safe hands at home, with men like Griffith, Brugha and Collins at the head. But the crisis was reaching boiling-point and much might happen before he reached the shores of Ireland again. To all intents and purposes war had been declared on Britain, and so far Britain had not yielded an inch. On the contrary, coercion grew with every day that passed. The Volunteers were becoming restive, shootings had taken place, and it would need a firm hand to impose the necessary discipline. Collins and Brugha did not always see eye to eye, and if there were divided counsels at the top, the military organisation was bound to suffer in morale and efficiency. Collins had been one of those who thought the American mission was unwise, but he had accepted the final decision with a shrug and the remark: "You know what it is to try and argue with Dev. He says he made his mind up in prison and that he can be more useful at the moment in America than at home."

In America, too, there were people who were soon to discover what it was like "to argue with Dev." On June 11th he passed the Statue of Liberty and during the night he was smuggled ashore. Rats had eaten through the clothes that he had brought in a sailor's bundle and ready-made garments had to be procured for him.

"We kept secret the manner of his coming," records Dr. McCartan. "His arrival when announced created a great sensation, and the mysterious ease with which he had eluded the British added to the popular interest in him. Nothing was lacking to make him a popular hero."

His first care was to visit his mother, and then he went to stay at the home of Joseph McGarrity, in Philadelphia, where he began to take his bearings. He was in no danger of underestimating the difficulties that lay ahead. That he would receive a cordial welcome from the vast bulk of his countrymen he had no reason to doubt, but the enduring of tumultuous receptions and handshakes by the thousand was the least part of his job. It was necessary to tread warily, to look from the immediate platform to the wider audience, to speak with one eye on Washington, another on Paris, and a third, if he had it to spare, on Dublin. There was a strong anti-Irish element in America which had to be taken into account, and even amongst those who were not definitely hostile there were many who, alienated by the blustering of some of the traditional Irish—or half-Irish—professional agitators, had come to regard the 'Irish question' as a joke—or a nuisance. Many Americans, who knew no other Ireland than that represented by generations of ragged and often unlettered immigrants and who regarded Tammany Hall as the perfect synonym for graft, would be slow to change their views. In some respects, in fact, there was not much to choose between the attitude of New England and old England.

Of all that de Valera was aware. What he was not aware of, however, was the size of the problem that he was to encounter in dealing with those of his own countrymen on whom it was natural to count for ready and generous support. The object of his mission was three-fold: to secure recognition of the Irish Republic from the Government of the United States, to float the Dail Eireann External Loan, and to give Ireland's national claim the widest possible publicity. It was already clear that, unless extraordinary pressure was brought to bear on President Wilson by his own people, nothing was to be hoped for from the Peace Conference. On the very day de Valera arrived in New York, Wilson had granted an interview to three delegates who had been dispatched to Paris by the "Friends of Irish Freedom" in America, and had informed them that no small nation would be allowed to present its case before the "Big Four" unless the Four unanimously agreed to receive it; in other words, he was permitting Lloyd George to keep Ireland out. When reminded of his own words about self-determination and the hopes they had aroused in the hearts of millions of people, he ran his fingers through his hair wearily and said, "You have touched on the great metaphysical tragedy of to-day."

(v)

To unravel the complex fabric of Irish-American politics and to try and disentangle them from the local and nation-wide American politics with which they were inextricably bound up, was a task as dismaying as it was, to a certain extent, unprofitable. Yet something like this de Valera was called upon to do—and almost at a moment's notice. Beyond the reports which McCartan and Boland had in readiness when he arrived he had little to guide him. Of the bewildering political complexities he was about to encounter he had neither suspicion nor foreboding.

These were centred chiefly around the personalities of two men—John Devoy, the old Fenian, and Daniel F. Cohalan, Judge of the Supreme Court of the State of New York.

Devoy was an old man of seventy-seven, deaf, irritable and obstinate. More than fifty years before he had shouted a contemptuous " Guilty, my Lord! " at Judge Keogh in the dock at Green Street, Dublin, and had gone to pick oakum for five years in an English convict prison. After that he had lived all his life in America, where he was the driving force behind the Clan na Gael—the American counterpart of the I.R.B.—and editor of the Clan's organ, the *Gaelic American.* In journalism, it was his boast that " he always gave better than he got "; in other words, when the editor of the *Gaelic American* set out to trounce a man or a movement, the adjectival resources of even the largest dictionary were discovered to be hopelessly inadequate. He suffered from the loneliness that is common to deaf people and he was given to sudden outbursts of rage. But no man ever doubted his sincerity.

His close friend and associate, Judge Cohalan, was of a very different stamp. Described as " the peerless leader of twenty millions of the Irish Race in America," he was able, arrogant, and overbearing; meticulous in his Americanism; ruthless where his own personal interests were concerned; and as accomplished a master of intrigue as ever American politics had produced. He had quarrelled violently with President Wilson and was determined to use every means in his power to bring about the President's downfall. His enemies, in fact, declared that the industry and enthusiasm which he had brought to the building up of the great organisation known as the " Friends of Irish Freedom " were inspired as much by the hope of smashing Wilson and his League of Nations as by any ardour he might have for the cause of Irish independence. The " Nine Old Men " of the Bench of the Supreme Court of the United States never gave Franklin Delano Roosevelt more trouble in the days of the New Deal than Judge Cohalan gave Woodrow Wilson in the year 1919. Over Devoy his ascendancy was complete, and it was widely believed that many of the editorials in the *Gaelic American* were directly inspired, if not actually written, by the eminent Judge. Devoy in his old age had become a Shagpat almost completely innocent of the fact that his power lay in a hair of Cohalan's head.

Dr. McCartan, the accredited envoy from the Government of the Irish Republic, had already had trouble with Devoy and Cohalan long before de Valera arrived. " There is no Irish Republic," the

Judge had declared again and again, and therefore there could be no question of seeking official American recognition for it; "self-determination," not Republicanism, was the issue. Devoy, who agreed with Cohalan in everything, appeared to take the same view. McCartan, however, refused to be discouraged and went on steadily with his lobbying and his publicity campaigns.

(VI)

No foreign visitor to the United States ever received a more enthusiastic welcome than President de Valera. So far as public appearances went, it was roses, roses all the way. He toured the Continent from coast to coast, visiting all the principal cities and receiving tremendous ovations all along the route. New York and Chicago made him a freeman of their cities; in San Francisco he was officially welcomed by the Governor and the Mayor; he was invited to address both Houses of the Massachusetts Legislature; at Cleveland, Ohio, he was met at the city boundary by an escort of planes and automobiles, and on entering the city was honoured with a salute of twenty-one guns; he was gang-interviewed, photographed, fêted, and banqueted, and his name was front-page news from Manhattan to the Golden Gate. When he visited Chicago during the Republican Convention a cartoon appeared in one of the leading dailies with the wisecrack: "De Valera assures us that he is not a candidate for the Presidency of the United States."

A contemporary report of one of his meetings may

be quoted as an indication of the enthusiasm that awaited him wherever he went:

> "Chicago last night gave vigorous and vociferous evidence of its desire for recognition of the Irish Republic. Eamon de Valera, President of Ireland, when introduced to an audience of one hundred thousand that jammed the auditorium and packed the streets for blocks around, commanded one of the greatest ovations ever accorded an American or foreign statesman. For twenty-six minutes the President stood unable to speak, while the huge crowd cheered in a frenzy of enthusiasm. The President was lifted to the shoulders of his uniformed bodyguard, composed of American veterans of the World War. Flags, American and Irish, rippled over the sea of faces; and all the while the crowd yelled, screamed, and in many cases broke into tears in the intensity of enthusiasm."

"Smashing British propaganda as he goes," said another newspaper, "Eamon de Valera continues his tour. . . . What Sherman's march to the sea was to the Union, de Valera's tour from ocean to ocean is likely to be to the cause of Irish and world freedom."

It was all very exhilarating, but it was also very exhausting; and it was a relief when he could take an occasional hour or two off to play a game of handball in a secluded New York ball-alley with Harry Boland or spend a quiet evening in his mother's home.

But there was one man who was not impressed. Almost from the first moment that the cold, searching eyes of Judge Cohalan rested upon the calm, carven face of de Valera there was a clashing of temperaments, soon to be followed by a conflict of

G

wills. The Judge, much to his surprise, found the newcomer to American politics a singularly intractable piece of material. He discovered what it was like " to try and argue with Dev." The Irish leader listened courteously and attentively to the eminent American jurist as he explained what should and what should not be done, and then committed the unpardonable offence of talking back forcibly and pointedly. If Judge Cohalan had had a personal quarrel with President Wilson, he—de Valera—had none, (" I well recognise President Wilson's difficulties in Paris," he had said), however much he might deplore the President's policy, or absence of policy, with regard to Ireland. If the Judge was the sworn foe of the proposed League of Nations, he—de Valera—was a believer in a League of Nations founded on the principle of self-determination: a League of which the United States would be a member and in which Ireland would take its place as an independent constituent unit. Besides, de Valera made it clear by his attitude that he was not interested in any purely anti-Wilsonian intrigue and that he would resent the Irish movement in America being used as a weapon for any other purpose than that of furthering Ireland's national claim. Judge Cohalan was considerably annoyed. This obstinate Irishman, with no experience of American politics, with only two years' experience of politics all told, seemed to be bent on following a line of his own; a line, moreover, that did not fit in at all with the Judge's plans.

The first open clash occurred over the question of floating an Irish loan in America—one of the principal objects of de Valera's mission. Cohalan contended that the project was both impolitic and illegal; that it contravened the "Blue-Sky" Laws (designed to protect investors from bucket-shop financiers); and that, if tried out, it would prove a disastrous failure. Had not his own organisation, the Friends of Irish Freedom, established an Irish Victory Fund which had already raised over a million dollars? Why not leave well alone?

Cohalan was supported by many prominent leaders of Irish-American opinion, and de Valera, according to McCartan, was "coaxed, bullied, and finally informed that if he did not do as the people in that room advised, he could do nothing in the United States."

It was evident that the Friends of Irish Freedom had not even begun to know their man. Instead of crumpling up under the barrage, de Valera dealt point by point with the objections raised, said that he had come there to carry out the instructions given him by the Dail, and announced that, come what might, he intended launching a Bond Drive for five million dollars without further delay. He spoke so firmly, so earnestly, so courteously, that by the time he had finished he had demolished most of the opposition.

Cohalan took his defeat badly. From that time onwards the feud grew in intensity and was liable to break out in small matters as well as large. When de Valera wrote a circular advertising the Loan Bonds he used in it the words "peasants" and "steers." Cohalan objected. He contended, says McCartan, "that the term 'peasant' was associated in the American mind with 'peon' and conveyed the idea of an inferior type of humanity; and that the word 'steer' was also objectionable to Americans. President de Valera maintained that 'peasant' had a poetic flavour and that 'steer' was expressive; and, as he met me, he voiced his satisfaction that he had not given in to Judge Cohalan."

It is an illuminating, if somewhat comic, incident. De Valera's feeling for the use of words is one of his most pronounced traits: a legacy, no doubt, from his schoolmaster days. It is noticeable in his broadcasts, in his prepared speeches, and in all his public pronouncements. He makes a virtue of verbal precision, so much so that he has sometimes exasperated colleagues and officials who have not the same interest in delicate niceties of expression.

Judge Cohalan's irritation continued to grow.

(VII)

The Bond Drive was a sensational success. Irish-American business men dipped their hands deeply into their pockets, Irish servant-girls contributed their dollars, and, with the Loan speedily out-topping the five million mark, Cohalan's gloomy prophecies were blown to the winds.

De Valera's stock was rising rapidly. Even the anti-Irish elements in America became aware that the man who had come amongst them was something more than a mere "Irish agitator." "He had conducted himself in public," says McCartan, "with so much circumspection and dignity as to bring to him universal respect." But the Cohalan-Devoy group refused to be won over. De Valera firmly occupied the centre of the stage, and their own power was on the wane. Cohalan, with the Irish

Victory Fund at his back, was carrying out an intensive campaign against President Wilson and the League of Nations. In every State and every city he pursued him with defamatory and highly expensive newspaper advertisements. He was determined to make the League of Nations the outstanding issue in American politics.

It was an issue that de Valera could not evade, even if he had wanted to. It cropped up at nearly all the public meetings he addressed; meetings which were representative of every shade of American politics. Democrats, as a whole, favoured the League, whilst Republicans opposed it, and there were both Democrats and Republicans on all de Valera's platforms and on all his reception committees. "To speak under the auspices of such committees without giving offence to some of their members seemed almost impossible, yet"—McCartan bears witness—"President de Valera gave offence to none."

During his stay in America, de Valera kept in constant touch with his colleagues at home. The "Sinn Fein Mail" operated secretly and smoothly and couriers were constantly crossing and recrossing the Atlantic. Griffith, who told the Dail that "it is in the United States the centre of gravity of the political situation is for the present fixed," regularly sent across messages of encouragement, and Michael Collins wrote letters in which he told of visits to Mrs. de Valera and the children at Greystones. But the general news from Ireland, which spoke of mounting terrorism, was calculated to cause him the deepest anxiety, even if its immediate effect was to win sympathy for his mission.

In February, 1920, the long-smouldering Cohalan-de Valera feud burst into flame. On the 6th of the month de Valera gave an interview to the *Westminster Gazette,* in which he replied to the argument that an independent Ireland might be used as a base from which an enemy of Britain might attack her at any time. Having quoted the Monroe Doctrine, he went on to declare that a free Ireland would be willing to offer Britain all the legitimate international guarantees necessary for her security, and instanced the article in the Cuban Settlement under which Cuba engaged to preserve its independence against any foreign power. " Why," de Valera asked, " doesn't Britain make a stipulation like this to safeguard herself against foreign attack as the United States did with Cuba? "

The parallel was, in all the circumstances, somewhat unfortunate. The Cuban Settlement had been a matter of fierce controversy in American politics, and it was evident that de Valera, when he gave the interview, did not realise the full implications of his words. In quoting the relevant paragraph of the Platt Amendment relating to Cuba, he had intended nothing more than a declaration of Ireland's willingness to discuss safeguards for English security compatible with Ireland's independence (just as, in May, 1935, he made it clear that in no circumstances would Irish territory be allowed to be used as a base for an attack on Britain.)

That it was open to other interpretations, however, was soon made clear. Honest Pat McCartan was horrified and jumped to the entirely mistaken conclusion that the Republic was being let down. The interview was featured by several American newspapers, one of which printed it with the heading: "De Valera Opens the Door."

To Cohalan and Devoy de Valera's slip came as a heaven-sent opportunity. Without waiting for or asking for an explanation they swooped down on the interview. Devoy launched a frontal attack on it in the *Gaelic American,* using all his noted powers of invective. As for Cohalan, "the Cuban interview seemed to offer a chance to rid himself of de Valera's presence; that chance was at once seized." (*McCartan*).

De Valera felt that the time had arrived for a show-down. Already he had written to Griffith stating his opinion that "big as this country is, it is not big enough to hold the Judge and myself." Now, in a letter to Cohalan, in which by describing himself as "the responsible head of the Republic sent here to seek recognition," he contemptuously brushed aside the charge of "letting down the Republic," he demanded an explanation of the Judge's attitude—and that of the *Gaelic American*—towards his mission. It was a fair demand. Cohalan had never shown any enthusiasm for the Republic; on the contrary, he had time and again denied its existence. He had refused, until strong pressure had been brought to bear upon him, to send a single dollar of the Victory Fund to Ireland, even though there were Deputies there who had so little money that they could not afford to pay their railway fares to Dublin to attend the Dail. He had spent thousands of dollars of the Fund campaigning against Wilson and had left nobody in doubt—except, possibly, Devoy—that the Irish cause was only a secondary interest with him.

His reply to de Valera was not lacking in arrogance or acidity. " What I have done for the cause of the independence of the Irish people recently, and for many years past, I have done as an American, whose only allegiance is to America, and as one to whom the interest and security of my country are ever to be preferred to those of any and all other lands." The eminent American jurist, the old and experienced politician, the Judge of the Supreme Court of the State of New York, was telling the Irish interloper " where he got off." He spoke—to the man who had fought in Easter Week—of " a British Monroe Doctrine that would make Ireland the ally of England and thus buttress the falling British Empire," and finally he thundered (with total irrelevance): " Do you think for a moment that American public opinion will permit any citizen of another country to interfere as you suggest in American affairs? "

To this letter de Valera did not reply.

(VIII)

Cohalan now felt his position so strong that he decided, as McCartan phrased it, " to put de Valera on trial," with a view to forcing him to leave the country. The place selected was the Park Avenue Hotel, New York City, and the date was March 19. Seventy-five of Cohalan's associates, and others on whom he believed pressure could be brought to bear, were secretly invited to the meeting. The defendant's presence was not desired, and so it was arranged that an invitation to attend a " phoney " banquet in Chicago on the same night should be sent to him.

But the plans miscarried. On the day before the meeting the American Senate ratified the Peace Treaty with a remarkable reservation in which it declared that "the United States adheres to the principle of self-determination and the resolution of sympathy with the expectations of the Irish people for a government of their own choice adopted by the Senate, June 6th, 1919, and declares that when such government is attained by Ireland—a consummation which it is hoped is at hand—it should promptly be admitted as a member of the League of Nations."

It was a notable triumph for de Valera—on the eve of his "trial." The arduous and patient work of nine months, work that some of those on whom it would have been natural to count for assistance had made doubly difficult, had at last borne tangible fruit. De Valera was able to cable to Griffith: "Our mission has been successful. The principle of self-determination has been formally adopted in an international instrument. Ireland has been given her place among the nations by the greatest nation of them all."

Cohalan had experienced a set-back, but, nevertheless, he decided to proceed with his arraignment. It was a big company that assembled in the spacious room at the Park Avenue Hotel, and it included business men, clergymen, and professional men of all sorts. Judge Goff was there, and so was Bishop Turner, of Buffalo. When the doors were closed the chairman asked for credentials. Joe McGarrity, whose presence was unwelcome, ignoring the chairman's demand, strode up to the table, and signed the book with the rest. Then the chairman called upon Judge Cohalan.

Cohalan rose and delivered his judgment against de Valera. The President, he declared, was utterly ignorant of America and American politics; he had refused to take advice from those best fitted to give it to him; he had, by his arrogance, disrupted the unity of the cause in America and he had alienated those willing to help him; by his British Monroe Doctrine proposal he was making Ireland an ally of Britain. The Judge even went farther. He charged de Valera (whose frugality even in those days was a byword) with living in palatial hotel suites and thus wasting the money that had been raised to help the gallant people fighting at home.

It was too much. McGarrity, ignoring cries of protest, jumped up and demanded that de Valera be given a hearing. There was consternation among the Cohalanites. "But he is in Chicago!" someone shouted. "No, he isn't," retorted McGarrity, "he is at the Waldorf." Harry Boland, it seemed, had got wind of the secret inquisition and of the trick to spirit de Valera away to Chicago and had kept his Chief at home. McGarrity then insisted that de Valera be telephoned for, a proposal that was supported by Bishop Turner and Judge Goff, and finally agreed to. After an interval of uneasy silence, the doors opened and de Valera entered, accompanied by Harry Boland. They walked quietly up to the platform and de Valera began to address the meeting.

He explained the purpose of his mission and his

responsibility to the Government of the Republic and to the people of Ireland. He said that he had made it his chief care at all times never to interfere in American affairs, and described how from the very beginning he had been hampered in his work by the hostility of Cohalan and Devoy, who had attempted "to treat him like a schoolboy." He was aware, he added, that this meeting had been called for the purpose of driving him back to Ireland, and—when cries of dissent were raised—he asked would the company believe him if he produced a letter showing that the conspiracy was at least six months old. There were cries of "Who wrote the letter?" and Boland replied "John Devoy." The old man, listening with his hand to his ear, cried out, "What's that, what's that?" When told of the accusation, he jumped up and shouted furiously, "It's a lie!" "Produce the letter, Joe," said de Valera quietly to McGarrity.

Immediately there was uproar, some calling for the letter, others declaring that it should not be produced. In the midst of the clamour Judge Goff stood up and called upon Cohalan to apologise. Bishop Turner added a plea for peace. Cohalan rose, retracted his charges, and offered de Valera his hand. De Valera, who, McCartan noted, had maintained his dignity throughout the whole astonishing scene, did not refuse it. Then the Bishop called upon everyone present to kneel down and pray.

There was peace, but it was the peace of Munich.

(IX)

In spite of the difficulties that he had to contend with, de Valera's work in America continued to prosper. There, respect for and understanding of Ireland's national claim grew steadily, so much so that the British Government sent out a small army of writers and publicists as a countermove. But one of them cabled home sadly: "De Valera has left us no standing-room in America." From home there came praise and encouragement when, in June, on the motion of Griffith, the following message was sent to the President: "Dail Eireann assembled in full session to-day unanimously re-affirms the allegiance of the citizens of Ireland to your policy, expresses complete satisfaction with the work you have performed, and relies with confidence upon the great American nation to accord recognition to the Republic of Ireland now in fact and in law established." It was not merely a notable tribute to the work of the President; it was also—in view of later events—remarkable for its complete acceptance by Griffith of the Republican position.

Despite Bishop Turner's prayers, the peace of the Park Avenue Hotel was of short duration. Dissension broke out again over the "Irish Victory Fund" of which less than one-fifth had been expended up to date for demonstrably Irish purposes, and it grew into open hostility when Cohalan, at the Convention held in Chicago to select a Republican candidate for the Presidency of America, wrecked de Valera's efforts to have recognition of Ireland's Government made a plank in the platform.

The breach was now complete and de Valera, whom Cohalan had refused to meet in Chicago, decided to take action. Establishing headquarters at Washington he launched a new organisation bearing the significant title of the "American Association for the Recognition of the Irish Republic." Within a matter of weeks it brought to an end the power of the Cohalan-Devoy combination. "The Association," writes McCartan, "soon contained most of the Friends of Irish Freedom, the best friends Ireland had in America. When they thought Cohalan was leading for Ireland they flocked into his organisation, which numbered at its peak in 1919 about 250,000 members. In the reception to de Valera, in the Bond Drive, and in all the other work for Ireland they were asked to do, they responded nobly. From February, 1920, when Devoy began to attack Ireland in the person of de Valera, the membership began to wane. The attempts to expel de Valera and the refusal to send more money to Ireland caused the membership to dwindle fast. . . . To the new Association these American friends of Ireland passed over and laboured unselfishly." A further blow for unity was struck when Boland, who had been sent to Ireland to report, and who was a member of the Supreme Council of the I.R.B., returned with orders that the group opposing the President be no longer considered as affiliated with that body. Ireland had finished—for the time being—with Cohalan and Devoy.

The history of the Irish in America has produced few episodes more curious than this bitter vendetta in which de Valera, through no apparent fault of his own, was made the central figure. Cohalan's attitude one can understand. The Irish blood that ran through his veins was, at best, no more than a sluggish stream, and he never troubled to conceal the fact that the only country to which he owed allegiance was America. He was, in fact, an American politician first and last, and it was that, rather than any mere temperamental antipathies, that lay at the root of his quarrel with de Valera, who had insisted all along on maintaining a scrupulously correct attitude where American affairs were concerned.

But Devoy? There the problem is not so easy. He was, it is true, a deaf, difficult old man of nearly eighty who had been a dictator in Irish-American revolutionary circles for so long that he had grown intolerant of all criticism and suspicious of any power near the throne. Besides, he was susceptible to Cohalan's influence at every turn of the political wheel. Yet one would have imagined that the old Fenian, who had come to terms thirty-five years before with Parnell and Parliamentarianism, would have cordially welcomed the Republican envoy, the sole survivor of the men who had led the Rising which he—Devoy—had actively helped to bring about. But it just did not happen. The two men were incompatibles. Harry Boland, who was present when they met for the first time—a night or two after de Valera's landing—once described to a friend that remarkable encounter. De Valera was conducted to Devoy's apartment, greeted him gravely with a Gaelic salutation, and was rewarded with a formal, silent handshake. Then the old Fenian and the new leader sat down, each staring at the other, neither speaking. Minutes passed and the silence remained unbroken, until finally somebody in the room eased the tension with a word. "I could have screamed," said Boland.

It is unlikely that de Valera could have achieved much more than he did even if there had been no dissension. He had succeeded in stirring the imagination and winning the sympathy, not only of the Irish exiles with long and bitter memories, but of the bulk of the American people. To have won the full recognition he sought would, in the circumstances of the time have been a miracle. President Wilson was a dying man, his term of office was about to expire, and Warren Harding, who succeeded him, was hardly the type of President to take a step which, had it been pressed, would have strained the relations between the United States and Britain—her recent ally—to breaking-point. De Valera himself said to his colleagues after his return: "If I were President of the United States I would not and could not recognise the Irish Republic." But at the same time he—de Valera—would not and could not reduce his full claim, and the American platform gave him the opportunity he needed of urging it on the attention of the world.

In any event, the American mission was at an end. From Ireland came news that Arthur Griffith had been arrested, and at once de Valera started for home.

He had been eighteen months in America and he had progressed along the razor-edge of American politics with singular skill and singular courage. Of the many tributes to his work that are on record, two may be quoted. "In America," said Griffith in the Dail, " the work accomplished by the President has been extraordinary; he has welded the Irish Race into a united force and has raised the Irish question there into the position of an international issue." Liam Mellowes, who had been associated with him in his mission, wrote afterwards: " He [de Valera] made the name of Ireland respected where it was despised and the Irish cause an ideal where it had been regarded as political humbug."

CHAPTER SIX

War and Peace

"England and Ireland may flourish together: the world is large enough for us both."
—EDMUND BURKE.

(1)

DE VALERA arrived home secretly on Christmas Eve, 1920. The liner *Celtic* on which he had sailed was searched for him when it arrived at an English port, but once again he outwitted the British authorities and succeeded in reaching Dublin safely.

Much had happened during his absence. The War of Independence had begun and a reign of terror such as Ireland had not known for a hundred-and-twenty-two years had the country in its grip. The methods that Mountjoy had used in 1600, that Cromwell had used in 1649, that Castlereagh had used in 1798, were being adopted again—with modern improvements—in the twentieth century. Lloyd George, boasting that he would soon "have murder by the throat," had let loose the Black-and-Tans on the Irish populace. Assassination, arson and looting were the order of the day. Towns were being sacked and pillaged. Martial law and curfew were in operation. The people's assembly had been suppressed and its leaders thrown into prison. The Lord Mayor of Cork had been murdered, and his successor, Terence MacSwiney, after focusing the eyes of the world on his cell in Brixton Jail, had died on the 74th day of a hunger-strike. In an attempt to strangle the country's economic life creameries had been burnt down and fairs and markets disrupted. The heart of Cork city had been burnt out. Executions of captured prisoners were beginning. "Frightfulness," in short, had become the keynote of British policy towards a small nation in which, to borrow a phrase of John Mitchel, "even the old men, the women and the children were engaged in a criminal conspiracy to set their country free."

The Volunteers on their part were hitting back with a vengeance. Brugha, as Minister for Defence, and Collins, as Director of Organisation, had welded them into a strong, well-disciplined, though ill-equipped body. The flying columns were out on the hills and units of the Dublin Brigade were carrying out ambushes in the streets of the city. Men of the Republican Intelligence Service were to be found everywhere, and there was not a department of British officialdom in Ireland in which Collins had not succeeded in placing his men. The secret service of Dublin Castle had been regarded as one of the most efficient in the world. Working through the Royal Irish Constabulary, it had its agents, not only in every town and village in Ireland, but on the docks of New York and San Francisco, and in the slums of London and Glasgow. Now, for the first time, it was being challenged and beaten.

Side by side with the war-effort a resolute attempt was being made to give the Republic the requisite machinery of government. Departments of Finance, Trade, Local Government, Labour and Propaganda were functioning in spite of almost insuperable difficulties. A Land Bank was brought into being and a Land Commission was set up. Another Commission was established to investigate Ireland's natural resources. Most successful of all were the Republican Civil and Criminal Courts, which, backed by a new force of Republican Police, were the sole guardians of justice in many areas. As Mr. Bonar Law admitted in the British House of Commons, Sinn Fein possessed "all the symbols and all the realities of a Government." Government was passing from British control into the hands of the elected representatives of the people; and the people, or at any rate, a big majority of them, were wholeheartedly behind the struggle for independence, even though, guerilla warfare being what it is, the civilians suffered most. Lloyd George looked for a break, but none came. British terrorism, in fact, was bringing new recruits to the Republican banner every day. When young Kevin Barry was hanged scores of his fellow-students at the National University joined the Volunteers. Lloyd George was beginning to realise—though not very clearly as yet—that he was dealing, not with a "murder gang," but with a nation.

(II)

In an old Georgian house not far from the centre of Dublin city a hiding-place was found for de Valera in the New Year of 1921. There, as head of the Government, he had his headquarters; there he worked day after day, reading reports, giving instructions, receiving messages, conferring, advising, planning. Always a robust man, he was able to work with insatiable energy—often eighteen hours a day—for weeks on end without showing much outward sign of the terrific mental and physical struggle he was enduring. America, to be sure, had left its mark on him. "You're looking older, Dev.," was a colleague's greeting after he arrived back from America. "Am I?" he said with a smile; "what matter; I'm feeling all right."

It was a respectable house in a respectable street where not all the residents were in sympathy with the movement or admirers of the President. Great care had to be taken with regard to visitors and messages, and there were times when de Valera was as much a prisoner as if he were back in Lincoln. At night when the curfew order came into operation there was a sinister silence outside in the pitch-dark streets, broken every now and then when a lorry of Black-and-Tans came tearing by, its occupants often roaring drunk. Sometimes one of these lorries or an armoured car would stop nearby to raid some house in the locality, and there would be a thunder of knocks on a door and maybe the crash of revolver shots. Once the very house in which he himself was staying was raided and ransacked, but Collins had provided a secret cubicle and the raiders went away empty-handed.

No wonder he was looking older. Nearly five years had passed since the studious schoolmaster had given up his quiet tutorial routine to take part in the great adventure that was to change the whole course of his life. They had been hectic, hurrying, bewildering years, bereft of all the normal domestic joys, filled to overflowing with the excitements of war, electioneering, prison experiences, jail breaks, dangerous journeys, strange vicissitudes, and frenzied popular acclaim. To stand up against such a concentrated experience without breaking required unusual strength of character and a definite philosophy of life. De Valera had both. His calm demeanour was the result of a stern self-discipline and of the fixed determination of an indomitable will.

But if his temper seldom cracked, and if outward serenity was his most pronounced characteristic, he was far from being unmoved by the agonies of the time. The horrors which he now saw at first-hand lacerated his soul. A friend who was admitted to see him late one night at Mount Street found him leaning over a table with his head between his hands. "Have you a headache, Dev.?" he said. "No, a heartache," was the reply. Six Republican prisoners had been hanged in Mountjoy Jail that morning. One has the image of a pair of sombre brown eyes looking out suddenly beyond those imprisoning walls and seeing another world—a world of the future—in which there would be none of these calamities, no midnight terrors, no hangings at dawn, but, instead, the peace of the council chamber, opportunities for scholarship, and the ordered progress of a civilised community. And yet, such is the potency of malice and propaganda, at that moment three out of every four citizens of Britain regarded de Valera as a cross between the stage Irishman and an American film gangster. The official organ of Dublin Castle, *The Weekly Summary*, established by the British Chief Secretary for Ireland, Sir Hamar Greenwood, for the purpose, as he stated, of "reviving the morale" of the Police Forces, made him a special target. He was described as having sprung from "a race of treacherous murderers" and as "a man with a fancy for ditch murders"; "if the fellow," it went on, "had a thousand lives they would be less than dung."

(III)

Michael Collins, on whose head the Castle was said to have put £10,000, was doing mighty work. He was Minister for Finance; he was Director of Organisation of the I.R.A.; he was the head of Intelligence; he was the driving force behind the I.R.B. His daring, his resource, his tireless energy, and his hair-breadth escapes had made his name known throughout Ireland. Already he was a legendary figure. Few saw him, but everybody had heard of him. His lines of communication stretched everywhere and his contacts were innumerable.

Those who worked under him worshipped him; to them he was the "Big Fellow." They liked his rough-and-ready manner, his scorn of formality, his boisterous humour, his easy sociability. They did not even mind the rasp of his tongue. But it was otherwise with some of his colleagues. Brugha and Stack were often at loggerheads with him. Brugha, dogged, determined, uncompromising, entirely without fear, a man who believed in shooting British Ministers as a fair reprisal for terrorism, was Minister for Defence, and Collins, in theory, was bound to accept his orders in everything relating to the Army and the conduct of the war. But in practice it did not work out like that. Collins, who had more organising executive ability and who was more directly in touch with the fighting men, was impatient of any kind of official routine and took things pretty well into his own hands. Brugha resented that, as he resented Collins's use of the I.R.B. in Army affairs.

The relations between Collins and Austin Stack, Minister for Justice, were much the same. Stack, a brave but gentle idealist nursed in the Fenian tradition, found Collins arrogant, overbearing and, at times, even insulting. "Mick" would burst into Stack's office, looking black as thunder, and demand imperiously why this or that was not being done. "Your office is a bloody joke, Austin," he barked out on one occasion. Stack, naturally enough, was often stung to anger. The "Big Fellow" was no big fellow to him. The result was that during the spring and early summer of 1921 friction in the Cabinet was a frequent occurrence. They were all hunted and sorely-tried men, usually working long hours into the night, and often in a state of nervous tension; it was no wonder if tempers sometimes got frayed.

It was de Valera's job during this period to smooth over differences. The war was reaching its highest peak of intensity and any breach in the ranks would have been disastrous. Already peace feelers were being thrown out and it was essential to present an absolutely united front to the British. To a large extent he was successful. Both sides respected him, both brought their troubles to him, and both found him persuasive and tactful. That neither the Irish nor the British public had the slightest inkling of any differences within the Republican Cabinet in the pre-Treaty period was due in the main to his patient diplomacy.

He could, no doubt, take a clearer view of the fight than the men whose whole time was given up to the conduct of it. He knew that the Declaration of Independence made by Dail Eireann in 1919 was, in effect, a declaration of war on the British. He stood over that. But he had also to consider to what extent the war was achieving its object, how long the resources of the country were likely to last, and how long the people's morale would hold against the ever-increasing onslaught of terrorism. Whilst the British Government, he observed, were piling threat upon threat and whilst tales of fresh horrors flowed in every day, at the same time the volume of protests from humane and enlightened opinion in Britain and elsewhere was rapidly growing. To meet such opinion some easing of the position might be called for, and it was a matter of choosing the best moment.

One thing, he realised, had to be done without delay. The position of the I.R.A. had to be made clear both in Ireland and Britain. British Ministers and propagandists still persisted in representing it as composed of small bands of blood-thirsty irresponsibles (Lloyd George's "murder gangs") and the time for an official declaration of its status was overdue. In a public statement made after he had raised the question in the Dail, de Valera put the matter beyond ambiguity.

"One of our first governmental acts," he said, "was to take over the control of the voluntary armed forces of the nation. From the Irish Volunteers we fashioned the Irish Republican Army to be the military arm of the Government. This Army is, therefore, a regular State force, under the civil control of the elected representatives, and under organisation and a discipline imposed by those representatives, and under officers who hold their commissions under warrant from those representatives. The Government is, therefore, responsible for the actions of this Army."

On the question of the morality of the tactics used by the I.R.A. he was equally clear and explicit. In Britain ambushing was being held up in speeches and in the Press as a cowardly and indefensible method of warfare; as something tantamount to assassination. It was a charge that he had no difficulty in rebutting. " If they " (the British forces), he told an interviewer, " may use their tanks and steel-armoured cars, why should we hesitate to use the cover of stone walls and ditches? Why should the element of surprise be denied to us? . . . If German forces had landed in England during the recent war, would it have been held wrong for Englishmen to surprise them? "

That statement alone is sufficient to dispose of the fantastic story—revived by Frank O'Connor in his biography of Michael Collins—that de Valera, on his return from America, horrified Collins and Mulcahy by a suggestion that guerilla methods should be exchanged for " pitched battles." De Valera's whole training in his Volunteer days had been for warfare of a guerilla nature and the fighting carried out by the men under his command in Easter Week had been of the same type. Now, more than ever, it was the only possible choice. Besides, he knew that the I.R.A. contained, at peak point, no more than three thousand fighting effectives, indifferently armed and equipped. To suggest that he wanted these to indulge in an act of self-immolation by joining open battle with sixty thousand well-armed troops, aided by artillery, armoured cars and Lewis guns, is, on the face of it, nonsensical.

(IV)

As early as December, 1920, whilst de Valera was still in America, moves for peace had been set on foot. Archbishop Clune, of Australia, had interviewed Lloyd George, had found him in a conciliatory mood, and had proceeded hopefully to Dublin, where he sought the views of the Republican leaders. Still more hopeful, he returned to London, but found to his dismay that the British Prime Minister's attitude had changed. If there was to be a truce, Lloyd George declared, it would have to be preceded by a surrender of arms. In the meantime the war on the "murder gang" would be intensified by every means in his power. The Archbishop, after remarking that the British decision "had scarcely been inspired by the Holy Ghost," returned to Australia.

But before the year 1921 was far advanced Lloyd George began to change his mind again. An impressive chorus of protests against his policy was ringing throughout Britain. The *Times,* the *Daily Mail,* the *Manchester Guardian,* and other influential organs denounced it week after week. The Archbishop of Canterbury spoke against it in the House of Lords. Lord Robert Cecil, as a gesture of protest, crossed the floor of the House of Commons. Mr. Asquith described the methods that were being adopted as "hellish." Lord Henry Cavendish-Bentinck established a "Peace with Ireland Council." Notable dignitaries of the Protestant Church in England addressed a letter to the Prime Minister in which they declared that the Government's Irish policy was exposing Britain to "the hostile criticism of the most friendly of the nations of the world."

Lloyd George began to doubt whether, after all, Sir Henry Wilson and Sir Hamar Greenwood were giving him the best advice possible. Soundings were made in Dublin by unofficial intermediaries and reports were brought to Downing Street. Prominent Republicans were constantly being interviewed. One newspaper man who succeeded in making a personal contact with Michael Collins asked him to define his terms of settlement. "Lloyd George has a chance of showing himself a great statesman by recognising the Irish Republic," Collins replied. "Do you mean a Republic within the British Commonwealth?" asked the interviewer. "No, I mean an Irish Republic," said Collins.

De Valera had no great belief in the usefulness of those unofficial peace moves. Lloyd George, he suspected, was looking for a chink in the Republican armour. Of the dozens of unofficial intermediaries who visited Ireland in the first three months of 1921 he saw none, though he gave occasional interviews to pressmen.

In April, however, he met Lord Derby, who arrived in Dublin inadequately disguised by a pair of horn-rimmed spectacles. Nothing came of the conversation, save a reply by de Valera to the question whether, as a preliminary to negotiations, the Republican leaders insisted on the principle of complete independence being first conceded. His answer took the form of another question: Would Lloyd George not consent to meet a representative of the Government of Ireland unless the principle of complete independence were first surrendered? To that question no reply was forthcoming.

A fortnight later de Valera found himself face to face with a more interesting visitor—none other than Sir James Craig, Prime Minister of the Six-County area. The two Irish leaders came together, in conditions of the strictest secrecy, at the house of a well-known solicitor in Clontarf. Each, apparently, had been led to believe that there was some common ground which might serve as the basis of an agreement. De Valera welcomed the opportunity for an exchange of views, but found that he had to do most of the talking. The dour Northerner was a man of few words. He lit his pipe and smoked and listened. De Valera gave him some geography, a certain amount of economics, and quite a lot of history. Sir James smoked and smoked, a perfect picture of the strong, silent man. De Valera, too, was strong, but not at all silent. (He is, in fact, one of the best talkers in Ireland, and he is never more in his element than when expounding a thesis). A couple of hours passed and then Sir James suddenly stretched out his hand, tore a piece of paper from the blank margin of a sheet of music that was lying on a piano-stool, and began to scribble rapidly. Having finished his writing he handed the slip of paper to de Valera. "That," said he, "will do, I think, as an agreed statement for the Press." De Valera stopped talking. He looked at what Sir James had written and smiled. "Yes," he said, "that will do." Then the two rugged-faced men stood up—each of them six-feet-two—looked one another straight in the eye, shook hands, and parted. When Sir James returned to his hotel Lady Craig noticed that his tobacco-pouch, which he had filled when he was starting out, was empty.

(v)

In May, Lloyd George's Better Government of Ireland Act—known in Ireland as the "Partition Act"—came into force, and on the "appointed day" under the Act, Lord Fitzalan, the new Viceroy, came into office. He was a Catholic—the first Catholic Viceroy for centuries—and the British Government hoped that his appointment would be regarded as a gesture of goodwill. "We would as soon have a Catholic hangman," growled old Cardinal Logue.

At the General Election which followed later in the month the Republican Government decided to make use of the British electoral machinery to demonstrate the solidarity of the national movement. The result was never in doubt. In the Twenty-six Counties no contests were necessary; outside Trinity College, which returned four members, Republican candidates were elected unopposed in every constituency. In the Six Counties, where the election was marked by scenes of violence and intimidation, forty Unionists were returned, as against twelve Republicans and Nationalists.

That it was a sweeping victory for the Republican party, even Lloyd George admitted. "Two-thirds of the population of Ireland," he said, "demand the setting up of an independent Republic in that island. At the recent election they have re-affirmed their demand." This was a far cry from his earlier pretence that what the British Government was dealing with in Ireland was a "small band of assassins."

De Valera, who was elected to a seat within the Partitioned area (South Down) as well as for Clare had defined the issue in the election as "nothing less than the legitimacy of the Republic." Those who voted for Sinn Fein, he declared, were voting "for Ireland against England, for freedom against slavery, for right and justice against force and wrong." He warned the people not to allow "the manœuvring of the enemy" to sow disunion in their ranks. "We are advancing steadily to the final settlement. The blossoms are not the fruit, but the precursors of the fruit—beware how you pluck them."

But for the moment it looked as if the victory of Sinn Fein was to be followed by an intensification of the methods the British had been employing. Winston Churchill, who was Chairman of the British Cabinet Committee on Irish Affairs, was in favour of "a tremendous onslaught—the most unlimited exercise of rough-handed force," though he agreed that, as a preliminary, the Irish should be given the refusal of a more generous measure of government than that contained in the Partition Act. The scheme of "rough-handed justice" was to be enforced by an additional army of a hundred thousand specially-trained troops, whose work was to be rendered easier by a blockhouse system covering the entire country. Austen Chamberlain and

Lord Birkenhead gave the plan their full approval, and it was adopted by the Cabinet.

The Republican Army, however, gave no sign that it was in danger of crumpling up in the face of threats. Throughout the countryside the war raged with greater intensity than ever, and in Dublin, on May 25, one of the biggest coups of the struggle was carried out when the Custom House, the headquarters of the most important branches of the British civil government in Ireland, was destroyed. Nevertheless, de Valera had plenty of cause for anxiety. The Republican forces had been seriously depleted (there were some five thousand men in internment camps and about a third of that number in gaol); reports of a growing shortage of rifles and ammunition were coming in from the country every week; the long evenings which would inevitably render the work of the flying columns more difficult and hazardous were at hand. Could another summer campaign be sustained effectively? And if the military arm broke, how was the political position—his own special concern—to be maintained? These were problems which admitted of no easy solution.

At the same time de Valera had no intention of allowing himself to be used as a party to any efforts to bring about a premature truce. Mr. Alfred Cope, the Assistant Under-Secretary in Ireland, was busy exploring possible avenues and had interviewed leading Republicans, including Michael Collins. His reports to Whitehall were becoming more and more optimistic. General Smuts, who was in London, was also taking a hand in the game. But de Valera, who was kept informed of the various moves that were on foot, preferred to watch and wait. Until the British Government showed some realisation of the fact that "Home Rule" was not only dead but damned, negotiations would be worse than useless. To Art O'Brien, President of the Irish Self-Determination League of Great Britain, he wrote in June: "The best line to pursue is to indicate that they [the British] are on the wrong track and that the right way is to propose a treaty with Ireland regarded as a separate State. Irish representatives would then be willing to consider making certain concessions to England's fear and England's interests; there is no other way."

Such was the position when, on June 22, King George the Fifth travelled to Belfast to open the new Six-County Parliament. Peace seemed as far away as ever. The British War Office, where Sir Henry Wilson, Craig's Military Adviser, was Chief of the Imperial Staff, was perfecting its plans to launch in July the "tremendous onslaught" which Churchill had foreshadowed. The Republican Army was fighting hard, sadly hampered by lack of munitions. Mr. Cope was still exploring avenues.

Suddenly, the whole position changed. King George, a man of humane instincts, had long held the opinion that Britain's credit was suffering as a result of the Irish war and was dissatisfied with the speech his Ministers had prepared for him to deliver in Belfast. After taking counsel with Smuts, he submitted a new version to the Cabinet, which accepted it, though with some reluctance. In his speech the King made an earnest appeal to all Irishmen "to pause, to stretch out the hand of forbearance and conciliation, to forgive and forget, and to join in making for the land they loved a new era of peace, contentment and goodwill."

Next day the British Cabinet met hurriedly. Lord Stamfordham, the King's private secretary, saw Lloyd George. "If something is not done at once," he said, "the effect of the King's speech will die away; there is not a moment to be lost." That was more than a hint. Unless the Cabinet were to let the King down, an official peace proposal would have to be made and all the talk about "shaking hands with murder" abandoned.

That was what de Valera had been waiting for. He distrusted intermediaries. Unless and until something concrete and authoritative was offered, there would be no response from the Irish side.

But at the very moment when King George was delivering his address to the Six-County Parliament, British troops were raiding a house in Blackrock. They arrested a man of whose identity they were not aware and brought him for interrogation to Dublin Castle. He proved to be President de Valera. Next day, to his astonishment and theirs, the President was released. Mr. Cope, who was in touch with London, had been busy. The mystery was soon cleared up. Two days after the release a letter reached the President from Lloyd George inviting him and "any colleagues he might select" to a conference in London, "to explore to the utmost the possibility of a settlement." A similar invitation was issued to Sir James Craig. "No British Government in modern times," Winston Churchill has admitted, "ever appeared to make so sudden and complete reversal of policy."

De Valera welcomed the invitation. Here, at last,

was solid ground on which he could put his foot. He replied in a letter that was firm, but friendly, taking care at the outset to emphasise that negotiations were unlikely to be fruitful unless the British agreed to recognise Ireland's "essential unity and the principle of self-determination."

On July 4, America's Independence Day, the Stars and Stripes were flying from the Mansion House in Dublin and the streets were thronged with wildly-excited crowds. The President was conferring with his Republican colleagues and with representatives of the Unionist minority in Ireland. Griffith had been released from Mountjoy and Barton from Portsmouth. MacNeill and Duggan were also free men. The Black-and-Tans were confined to barracks and, for the first time in years, Dubliners breathed a little freely. The crowds around the Mansion House, which de Valera had made his headquarters, laughed and joked hysterically, and as each leader appeared there was a wild outburst of cheering.

A few days later the Truce was signed and it came into force at noon on July 11th. As the Angelus bells rang men took off their hats and prayed that out of the Truce would come a lasting peace. The boys of the Flying Columns came down from the hills into the little towns and villages, where they were welcomed with bands and banners. They, the fighters, were glad of the respite—many of them looked on the Truce as no more than that—and they danced and sang the "Soldier's Song" at the cross-roads in the sunny evenings of that marvellous summer of 1921. But they did not forget the fallen, and there were long processions.

led by the wailing of pipes, when they brought home from the bogs and the mountains the bodies of their comrades who had been hurriedly buried during the dark nights of the Terror.

(VI)

The day following the Truce, de Valera, accompanied by Griffith, Barton, Stack, Count Plunkett, and Erskine Childers, crossed over to London. Ireland gave him a tremendous send-off and cables of encouragement poured across the Atlantic. The Orangemen, characteristically, celebrated the occasion by an anti-Nationalist pogrom in which fifteen Catholics were killed and a hundred and fifty houses belonging to Catholics were burnt to the ground.

Before leaving Ireland the President addressed a proclamation to the people in which he called for discipline and fortitude during the period of the Truce. "Should force be resumed against our nation," he said, "you must be ready once more to resist. Thus alone will you secure the final abandonment of force and the acceptance of justice and reason as the arbiter."

The warning was needed; a truce was not a settlement. But it was impossible to check the people's elation. For the first time in five years they were able to walk about without restraint, to sing the "rebel" songs, to fly the nation's flag, to set their minds on the business of their shops and their farms. Many began to talk glibly about "victory." Had not the peace moves come from the other side? There was a deceptive blue in the sky. It was easy to hope too much, to dream too much, to catch too eagerly at the balloon-strings of illusion. The fighting-men, it is true, were aware that at any moment they might have to take to arms again and resume the fight for the Republic. The average citizen, however, was weary of the struggle; he longed for the time when peace would be permanent, when there would be no curfew, no raids, no ambushes; when a man could go about his daily business without danger to life or limb. In short, he wanted peace and wanted it badly, and that passionate desire of his was to have a profound effect on national events six months later.

De Valera came face to face with the British Prime Minister for the first time on July 14. The advantages, one would have said, were entirely on the side of Lloyd George. He had been in politics for thirty years and a Cabinet Minister for fifteen; he had behind him the prestige and all the resources of a great Empire; he was the Man Who Had Won the Great War; he had traversed the whole maze of diplomacy at Versailles; his personal charm, his nimble wit and his persuasive powers had already become a legend; a formidable opponent, beyond all question. What equipment did de Valera bring with him to arm him for such an encounter? Nothing, seemingly, except a very clear knowledge of what he wanted, a remarkable tenacity in pursuing it, and a certain rock-like quality against which all the wiles of the Welsh Wizard were likely to beat in vain.

Lloyd George—" never," according to Winston Churchill, " a greater artist than in the first moments of a fateful interview "—began by exercising all his hypnotic powers. He was delighted to see the Irish leader. He, too, was a Celt, and, therefore, had an instinctive sympathy with Irish aspirations. There was a close affinity between the Irish language and the Welsh, was there not? But there appeared to be no equivalent for the word "republic" in Welsh. What was the Irish word?

It was a clever opening, perhaps a little too clever. De Valera's devotion to the Irish language was second only to his devotion to the Republic, but—first things first. It was the Republic that mattered now, not Celtic affinities. The Irish leader was wary and watchful. He was courteous in his replies, a model of correctness in his manner. But all the time, through his horn-rimmed spectacles, he was sizing up the voluble and vivacious little Welshman.

Suddenly, the Prime Minister switched on to another topic. Did Mr. de Valera recall the many Irish associations of that Cabinet room in No. 10 Downing Street, in which they were sitting? There, on that very table, Balfour had laid his Coercion Acts; there Gladstone had outlined his scheme of Home Rule; and now, around that table, an Imperial Conference was sitting daily. He pointed dramatically to the various chairs. "This is where the representative of South Africa sits; here is Canada; here is Australia . . . there is one empty chair waiting." Mr. de Valera was apparently expected to, but did not, supply the name of a possible occupant.

The President had four long interviews with Lloyd George within a week, and after each meeting consulted with his colleagues. Little or no progress was made. "Negotiating with de Valera," said Lloyd George afterwards, "is like trying to pick up mercury with a fork." "Why," commented de Valera when the remark was reported to him, "doesn't he use a spoon?"

Still another man had found out "what it was like to argue with Dev." Where fundamental principles were involved neither wiles, nor flattery nor threats had any effect. Lloyd George used all three. When, during the third interview, the British document containing a strictly limited scheme of Dominion Home Rule was produced and rejected, he exclaimed: "You know that this means war? And you realise that the responsibility will rest on your shoulders?" De Valera shrugged the shoulders referred to and replied: "If you attack us the responsibility will be yours, not mine."

Eventually, after making it clear that he could never personally accept the terms offered, de Valera agreed to submit a considered written reply after consultation with his colleagues. Thereupon the delegation returned to Dublin.

(VII)

For an understanding of the events of the next few months, and more particularly of de Valera's part in them, it is necessary to clarify the issues which divided the two leaders. Simple and clear-cut though they were, they were surrounded by a web of circumstances, historic, racial, economic, geographic, and psychological, so complex that their simplicity was greatly obscured at the time. Later, when the big crisis came, and for many a year afterwards, de Valera, because he never lost sight of the main issue, was described on both sides of the Irish Channel as a "visionary," a "fanatic," a "dreamer," a "man with a single-track mind." That all his political conduct was governed by an unswerving allegiance to certain clear and well-defined principles was either not recognised by his critics or deliberately overlooked.

The plain fact is that, in his whole attitude to the problem of Anglo-Irish relations, de Valera, from Easter Week up to the present time, has been a Separatist. At no time, as he himself declared during the Treaty debates, has he been a "doctrinaire Republican." If the people of Ireland wanted a Republic, well and good; he would fight for it. But he was committed to no particular form of government; he saw no special virtue in Republicanism. What he did believe in was Separatism; he was determined—with Tone and the Fenians—"to break the connection with England." His reading of history had convinced him that the connection was not only disastrous for Ireland, but morally bad for England; that there would be no lasting peace or friendship between the two countries save on the basis of equal rights and equal nationhood; that—to use what the English call an Irish bull—Britain and Ireland would never come together until they were separated.

He and Lloyd George looked at the map of the "British Isles" through very different spectacles. De Valera saw his own country as an island nation with frontiers as sharply-defined as any on earth and inhabited by a people who differed in race, religion, tradition and their way of living from the people in the sister island. He looked back across six centuries during which Ireland had been invaded, ravaged, planted and seemingly conquered, and he saw that its people had never once renounced their nationhood and that the conquest, through some miracle, had never become final. Almost every generation had seen its wave of resurgence and his own had seen the greatest of all. Could he, after all the sacrifices that had been made throughout the centuries and in his own lifetime, accept anything less than the full freedom in the long struggle for which so many of his countrymen had been slain, tortured, imprisoned or exiled?

At the same time he was quite aware that a British Prime Minister could never look at the map in the same way as himself. To Lloyd George, now as complete an Imperialist as ever Joseph Chamberlain was, the two islands were a geographical unit which, for political and strategic reasons, must remain indissolubly linked together by the Imperial bond. To him, as to the majority of the British people, the idea that the world's greatest empire, embracing one-fifth of the earth's surface, could ever permit the people of the small neighbouring island to set up an independent State at its very gateway was altogether unthinkable. The British War Office would not give such a proposal a moment's consideration, and as for the House of Commons, flushed with victory and the spoils of Versailles and filled with " hard-faced men who looked as if they had done well out of the war," what earthly chance would there be of getting such a House to give it legislative sanction? Besides even if—unlikely happening!—Lloyd George were to become a convert to the creed of Irish Republicanism, he was no more than the spokesman of a Government whose leading members were Tory Die-hards; in the background there were the menacing figures of Austen Chamberlain, Winston Churchill, and Lord Birkenhead.

How were irreconcilables to be reconciled? On what basis could negotiations even begin? That was the immediate problem with which de Valera had to deal after his return to Dublin. "If peace is to come," he had told a representative of *Le Matin* during the period of his conversations with Lloyd George, "the negotiations must be conducted between nation and nation." That much granted, Ireland would, as he had declared a short time before, be willing "to make concessions to England's fears and England's interests." What shape would those concessions take? How far could they be permitted to go? Those were questions that had to be answered without delay.

(VIII)

The measure of self-government offered by Lloyd George would, if it had not been marred by the Partition clause, have seemed generous to Parnell or Redmond. Pearse and Connolly would not have rejected it in 1912, though neither would for a moment have conceded its finality. Now it had no chance whatsoever of acceptance, and the Republican Cabinet rejected it unanimously, although, according to Austin Stack's unpublished memoirs, Griffith, Collins, and Mulcahy were not as wholeheartedly in favour of rejection as the President, Brugha and himself. That Ireland was to be allowed to raise an army of her own was, apparently, regarded by them as an unexpectedly generous gesture on the part of Britain. But so long as the two vital claims, independence and unity, were denied, there could be no acceptance. What was offered was not, as de Valera pointed out in a letter to Lloyd George, even "Dominion" status. "The freedom which the British Dominions enjoy," he said, "is not so much the result of legal enactments or of treaties as of the immense distances which separate them from Britain. . . . The most explicit guarantees, including the Dominions' acknowledged right to secede, would be necessary to secure for Ireland an equal degree of freedom. There is no suggestion, however, in the proposals of any such guarantees. Instead, the natural position is reversed; our geographical situation with respect to Britain is made the basis of denials and restrictions unheard of in the case of the Dominions. The smaller island must give military safeguards and guarantees to the larger and suffer itself to be reduced to the position of a helpless dependency." Furthermore, he pointed out, no proposal which recognised and perpetuated Partition could be accepted. "We cannot admit the right of the British Government to mutilate our country."

When the second Dail met on August 16 (its members who were still in prison having been released for the purpose) de Valera put the position before them in one of the most lucid and challenging speeches of his career. The British Press was broadcasting threats day after day of the terrible things that would happen if war was renewed. Lord Birkenhead was declaring that if negotiations broke down Great Britain would recommence hostilities "on a scale never hitherto undertaken by this country against Ireland." Other conservative politicians in England were sneering at the negotiations as a waste of time. De Valera met the challenge fully and firmly. Speaking as the leader of "a separate nation—a nation which is defending itself against the encroachment of a foreign nation," he called for rejection of the British offer. "I have made my attitude and the attitude of the Ministry clear to you. It is on that attitude that we are here before you for judgment. I state it here in public session, so that the Irish people may judge, and I feel that, as in the past they have not flinched when force was brought against them, they will not flinch now because more arms are being sent for."

Griffith supported him, stressing the harmony and identity of viewpoints that existed between the Ministry and the Dail, and declared that all were united in their efforts to secure a sovereign Republic.

The Dail met in private session on the 23rd and rejected the British proposals without a single dissentient vote. Three days later de Valera was elected President of the Republic. He was proposed by Commandant Sean MacKeon, the far-famed Blacksmith of Ballinalee, whose exploits in the war were already legendary and whose chivalry had made his name a toast among even the Black-and-Tans. "In no generation for more than a century," declared the Commandant "has any Irish leader equalled his [the President's] achievements . . . The honour and the interests of our nation are alike safe in his hands." General Mulcahy, who seconded, paid him an equally glowing tribute. "President" had been de Valera's title since 1919, but now for the first time the status of his office and its association with the Republic were given formal recognition.

CHAPTER SEVEN

"Mr. Shakespeare is Waiting!"

"Beware of the hoof of the horse, the horn of the bull and the smile of the Saxon."

—*Old Irish proverb.*

"An offence against the light of nations."

—FRANK PAKENHAM.

(I)

NOTHING cataclysmic followed the rejection of the July proposals. The sky did not fall. Winston Churchill's "tremendous onslaught" did not materialise. The British Government, it was evident, had not yet said its last word.

Lloyd George replied to de Valera's letter announcing the Dail's decision with a lengthy document which suggested that he had been indulging in a rapid but intensive study of Irish history. He quoted Grattan, O'Connell and Davis to show that Irish leaders of the past were willing to accept less by way of settlement than Britain was offering to-day. People in Ireland found the spectacle of Lloyd George quoting Davis "at" de Valera not a little entertaining, and the question was asked, "Who's been coaching him?"

But neither leader, it was obvious, wanted a rupture, though in the long correspondence which followed there was little given away by either side. From the Irish point of view it was essential that the Irish delegation should not enter the

Conference with Irish independence in any way compromised. At the same time de Valera knew that the British would not, on their part, accept the independence of Ireland as a preliminary. Lloyd George naturally sought to secure recognition of Imperial supremacy from the Irish leader, and the Irish leader was as naturally determined not to give it; for once given it would preclude the raising of the question of independence at the Conference at all.

To General Smuts, who wrote to de Valera urging acceptance of the July proposals, the latter replied: "An Ireland in fragments nobody cares about, a unified Ireland can be happy and prosperous. To the British Commonwealth group and to Britain itself Ireland would readily become friendly, but it is only in freedom that friendship could come."

As between Lloyd George and de Valera it was a case of two men in search of a formula. On September 8 an acceptable one appeared in a letter from the British Premier proposing that a conference be held "with a view to ascertaining how the association of Ireland with the community of nations known as the British Empire may best be reconciled with Irish national aspirations."

That gave de Valera what he wanted. The operative word was "association," a word which he himself had used in the course of the correspondence, when he had proposed "a treaty of free association with the British Commonwealth group." As de Valera saw it, there was nothing that compromised Irish independence in associating the Republic with Britain and the British Dominions for purposes of common concern, so long as that association was voluntary. It was his solution for meeting a position that he had long foreseen and that he had known would have to be faced sooner or later. It had been present in his mind when, during his American tour, he had made his "Cuban" proposals. It was a practical recognition of the hard facts of geography, of the demands of trade and defence, of the whole question of common interest. Even more compelling was the hope that by accepting the principle of association the minority in the North-east might be reconciled to the separatist idea.

Uncompromising Republicans like Brugha and Stack were not greatly enamoured of this "External Association" scheme, but they were eventually won over by de Valera's arguments. Even the Left wing was forced to realise that some concession to British fears and British sentiment would have to be made.

In his letter accepting the conference proposal, de Valera said:

> "In this final note we deem it our duty to affirm that our position is and can only be as we have defined it throughout this correspondence. Our nation has formally declared its independence and recognises itself as a Sovereign State. It is only as the representative of that State and its chosen guardians that we have any authority or power to act on behalf of our people."

When the letter was delivered at Gairloch, in Scotland, where the British Premier and several members of the British Cabinet were staying, it produced a typical Lloyd George manœuvre. The Premier privately asked Harry Boland, the Irish envoy who had brought the letter, to take it back and have this paragraph deleted; meanwhile "he would regard the letter as undelivered." The request was refused. Lloyd George called off the conference and resumed his efforts to get the Irish leader to pledge himself to remain inside the Empire. He failed, and, realising that further efforts were useless, announced that the previous correspondence was cancelled and sent a fresh invitation to a conference to be held on October 11th. De Valera had won his point. The conference was to sit without any preliminary conditions. In the final exchange of telegrams he told Lloyd George that the Irish delegates could only recognise themselves for what they were, though they could not force recognition of that status from the British. Lest any doubt should remain, however, as to what capacity they went in, de Valera's final acceptance of the conference referred back to the correspondence Lloyd George was anxious to ignore. "Our respective positions," he wrote, "have been stated and are understood."

The correspondence had lasted a month and the Irish leader had given nothing away. Before September was out a Draft Treaty, in the drawing up of which Erskine Childers and Gavan Duffy played principal parts, was laid before the Cabinet, discussed and approved. Five delegates to the conference were appointed. Most people, including the majority of his Cabinet colleagues, expected that de Valera would head the delegation. But the President, for many reasons, preferred to stay at home, and Griffith, Collins, Barton, Gavan Duffy and Duggan were appointed, with Childers as secretary. Brugha and Stack had refused to go to

London at any price, and Collins gave his consent with obvious reluctance.

No step of de Valera's has been more adversely criticised than his decision not to go to London, and there were few of his countrymen who, in the light of after events, did not regret it. But at the time there were excellent reasons for it. As the President pointed out to his colleagues, "he was in the position of head of the State as well as head of the Government and his absence would always be a good reason for the delegates making no hasty agreements in London." Besides, he had already had prolonged conversations with Lloyd George and had broken with him on the two outstanding issues of independence and unity; it might be better for others to take up the discussions where he had left off. At the back of his mind, too, was the case of President Wilson, whose failure at the Peace Conference had been ascribed by many Americans to the fact that he had crossed the Atlantic instead of exercising his enormous power and prestige from Washington.

With de Valera remaining behind, Collins was an obvious choice. At home legend had made him the "strong man" of the war, and the fighting men, at any rate, would feel that the negotiations were safe in his hands. The most "wanted" man in Ireland, one of the spearheads of the fight, the man who had declared publicly a few weeks before that the goal of the struggle was not "a Republic within the British Commonwealth of Nations" but "an Irish Republic," was not likely to accept anything that would compromise the national claim. Even as a stern gesture, sending Collins was good business. It was the final answer to men like Lloyd George and Churchill, one of whom had described him as "Chief of the Murder Gang," and the other who saw in him "a man whose hands had touched the springs of terrible deeds." The Irish people regarded Collins as a gallant soldier, and by sending him as a delegate to the Conference they were showing Britain and the world the contempt in which they held the British pretence that men who had waged a heroic fight for freedom were murderers.

(II)

The long, tangled and highly dramatic story of the negotiations which ended in the Treaty of December 6th has been told with brilliance, impartiality and a wealth of documentation in Frank Pakenham's *Peace by Ordeal.* It need not be told again. But its main features, at least, must be examined here.

Three things have to be borne in mind at the outset (1) Although the delegates were styled "Plenipotentiaries," it was laid down by the Cabinet and instructions given to each of them in writing before their departure that nothing final or binding was to be signed without being referred back to Dublin; (2) the delegation was united in purpose when it left for London; and (3) it carried with it a Draft Treaty which, if not the Republican blue-print that Brugha and Stack (and for that matter everybody else) wanted, nevertheless contained in its main provisions the irreducible minimum never to be lost sight of in the course of the negotiations.

If the position of unity, strength and clarity thus indicated had been maintained there was every reason to hope that ultimate victory would have been achieved and that the tragedy by which a nation, growing in united purpose for five years, was eventually split from end to end would have been avoided. How was that position undermined? How was it brought about that a Treaty, which had not been referred back to Dublin and which represented a disastrous compromise on the two vital issues involved, came to be signed? To answer that question it is necessary to glance at the composition of the two delegations and to make a brief comparative estimate of character, aims and strength.

Britain could hardly, at any period in her history, have fielded a stronger team. Lloyd George, the dictator of the Great War, the victor of Versailles, wiliest and most experienced of negotiators; Austen Chamberlain, cradled in statecraft, a politician almost from boyhood; Lord Birkenhead, the Unionist party's doughtiest fighter, a brilliant lawyer and advocate, a debater whose capacity for the lightning sword-thrust dated back to the days of the Oxford Union; Winston Churchill, the " bulldog aristocrat," an orator and a historian, a dyed-in-the-wool Imperialist, a man possessed of formidable talents and mighty ambitions; against a team that included such men as these, welded together as it had been in the winning of a world war, united as one man on the Imperial issue, backed by a skilled secretariat carefully chosen and having ready access to illimitable resources, sitting proud, arrogant and self-confident in the very hub of Empire, what had Ireland to put in the field?

It would be easy to underestimate the Irish team.

Griffith might be regarded as no more than a brilliant political journalist, and Collins as no more than a daring guerilla chieftain with a genius for intelligence work; Barton as no more than a cultured landowner who had had little experience of politics; Gavan Duffy and Duggan as no more than legal experts. Nevertheless, potentially it was a strong combination. Griffith, silent, tenacious, unemotional, at his best when in-fighting was called for, was an impressive figure at any council table; Collins, big, virile, fearless, seemed of all men least likely to be browbeaten; Barton had walked straight into the Conference room from a British gaol, with all his enthusiasm for the Republican ideal strengthened rather than diminished; Gavan Duffy, a lawyer of great talents and cosmopolitan experience, would be a match for the most acute legal mind pitted against him.

Such was the line-up as it appeared to the outsider. But, unfortunately, the Irish delegation bore within itself the germs of disunity, born partly of differences in political ideology, partly of personal antipathies. Griffith, from the beginning, would have accepted less in full settlement of the national claim than any Republican leader of the time. His watch, so to speak, had stopped in 1782. Collins, who had never looked on himself as a politician, had, owing to his quarrels with Brugha and Stack, fallen more and more under Griffith's influence, and the same influence was powerfully exercised over Duggan, the weakest member of the team. Barton, Gavan Duffy, and Childers, on the other hand, were strong in their determination to resist anything in the nature of a compromise on the main issues.

Between Griffith and Childers there was no love lost—Griffith, in fact, had strongly objected to the appointment of an 'Englishman' (Childers's mother, in fact, was Irish) as secretary to the delegation—and the relations between Griffith and Duffy were not cordial. Therein lay the weakness of the Irish team.

(III)

When the British and Irish Delegations came face to face for the first time on October 11, each had certain fundamentals in mind with regard to which compromise would be resisted to the end. The British were determined that Ireland should remain within the Empire and that the six Partitioned counties of Ulster should be free to choose whether they would enter an all-Ireland Parliament or not. The Irish were equally determined not to accept any settlement under which Ireland would become a Dominion of the British Empire and they were uncompromising on the question of Irish unity.

Many sessions were held, however, before a clash on any major issue occurred. Such things as trade, defence and finance—none of which was likely to bring about a breakdown of negotiations—were under discussion. Griffith was in constant communication with de Valera, from whom he was receiving advice and encouragement, tempered by an occasional warning. "Lloyd George," the President wrote at an early stage in the proceedings, "seems to be covering again the ground that he covered with me; you will have to pick him up soon on this 'further than this we can't go' stunt."

After some three weeks of parleying the main problem was reached and Griffith propounded the plan—the Cabinet's plan, not his—of External Association. It was not turned down at once. The British were curious to know what precisely it meant. "Does it mean," asked Lloyd George, "that if all other conditions are satisfied, you are prepared to come inside the Empire as New Zealand, Canada?" "That," replied Griffith, "is not quite our idea of association." But what about the Crown? Where did the Irish Delegation stand in regard to that? Lloyd George pressed the point home. "We are willing," said Griffith, "to accept the Crown as head of the Association."

In that interchange the gulf that had to be bridged, if the negotiations were to be successful, and the extent of the concession that Ireland was willing to make, were made sufficiently clear. External Association would preserve the ideal of Irish independence. It would associate Ireland with the Dominions of the British Empire from the *outside.* Under it Ireland would not become a member of the British Commonwealth of Nations, but would recognise the Crown as the head of the free association which the plan envisaged. The distinction was a big one and a vital one. It was not—as was suggested later—a question of hair-splitting or vague symbolism. It was a question of whether Ireland would achieve independence—whether she would go into the Empire or preserve her national integrity. The qualified acceptance of the Crown as an associating link was Ireland's concession to British sentiment.

Had the North-east corner of Ireland never been

"planted" and had no "Ulster" question existed, the issue would have been free from further complexities. But, behind all the negotiations, standing somewhere in the shadows but at the same time a very solid and menacing presence, was the grim figure of Sir James Craig. His contribution to the task of settlement could be summed up in the only three words of his which are remembered to-day: "Not an inch!" The Orangemen had been given their six counties—two of which contained Catholic and Nationalist majorities—by Lloyd George's Partition Act of 1920, and those six counties they were determined to keep. Let the British and the Sinn Feiners make what arrangements they liked, so long as they did not interfere with "Ulster." Craig knew his strength. His life-long friends and associates were members of the all-powerful Conservative Party, upon whom Lloyd George was now dependent for his political existence. They had given him their pledges and they would not let him down.

In the intransigeance of the Orange leader Griffith recognised that he had a strong card to play. If it could be shown to the world that the only obstacle to an honourable and permanent settlement of the centuries-old feud between England and Ireland was the bigotry and stubbornness of the politicians in a piece of Irish territory smaller in area than Yorkshire, there was no doubt where the sympathies of the world would rest. If a break had to come, thought Griffith, better let it come on the question of "Ulster" than on that of the Crown. But that was exactly what Lloyd George wanted to avoid.

He saw the strength of the Irish position in regard to unity, but he had committed himself to Partition. When he discussed the matter at the Conference, however, he was sweet reasonableness itself. If the majority and minority sections of Irish opinion—or, as Lloyd George preferred to phrase it, "South" and "North"—would only come to an agreement, Britain would not stand in the way. The obvious answer to that was, let Britain stand aside. But that was something that Britain had no intention of doing, as the Irish delegates soon discovered; and so long as Craig had the backing of Britain—or, at any rate, of what in the circumstances amounted to the same thing, of Britain's Conservative Party—there would be little progress so far as the question of unity was concerned.

That much is clear now; it was not quite so clear at the time. The British, it is evident, were not only determined that Ireland would remain within the Empire, but that it would be a Partitioned and, therefore, a weakened Ireland ("We must make it clear," Lloyd George had written to Carson in 1916, "that Ulster does not, whether she wills it or not, merge into the rest of Ireland.") Craig was being assured that no coercion would be employed against him, whatever happened, but to Griffith and his colleagues the impression was being conveyed that if the Orangemen proved to be the final stumbling-block in the way of peace they would be disowned by the British. In fact, if an understanding on the Crown could be reached, Lloyd George intimated, he would present an ultimatum to Craig and, if it were rejected, he would go down to the

House of Commons, announce his resignation, and retire from public life.

It was the sharpest of sharp practices.

(IV)

At home de Valera was reading Griffith's bulletins with both hopefulness and anxiety. He, too, wanted the break, if it came, to come on "Ulster," and he was happy to see Griffith's strategy directed towards that end. He wrote congratulating the delegation on the admirable way in which they were handling this particular issue. But once again he sent a warning. The Conference had lasted a month and the biggest issue—*i.e.* national status—would soon have to be settled once and for all. "The danger now," he wrote, "is that we shall be tempted, in order to put them (Craig and Co.) more hopelessly in the wrong, to make further advances on our side. I think, as far as the Crown-Empire connection is concerned, we should not budge an inch from the point to which the negotiations have now led us."

The warning was needed. Griffith, for all the magnificent work he had been doing, was showing signs of "slipping." He and Collins had fallen into the bad habit of accepting invitations to private meetings with British Ministers. On October 30th Griffith had seen Lloyd George alone at Winston Churchill's house. Three days later he and Collins met Birkenhead. Barton and Duffy did not like those private interviews, which were obviously part of the British strategy. Still less did they like Griffith's proposal that he (Griffith) should write a personal letter to Lloyd George—at the latter's suggestion—containing some documentary evidence which the Prime Minister said he wanted to use in his dealings with the Unionists. They objected both to the terms of the letter—which left Ireland's very qualified acceptance of the Crown open to serious misinterpretation—and to the fact that it was being sent by a single member of the delegation instead of coming from the delegation as a whole. Griffith gave way, but only after an unpleasant scene. The British were succeeding in their purpose of disrupting the unity of the Irish team.

On November 12th Griffith made his crowning blunder. He met Lloyd George at the house of Sir Philip Sassoon, in Park Lane, and walked—unwittingly—into a trap. The Prime Minister told him that he was sending an ultimatum to Craig; that he was giving "Ulster" the right of voting itself out of an All-Ireland Parliament within twelve months, but if it did, that a Boundary Commission would be set up, by which the Ulster Boundary would be adjusted as nearly as possible in accordance with the wishes of the inhabitants. He was, in fact, he declared, putting the screw on "Ulster," and he wanted Griffith's help. Would Mr. Griffith give him an assurance that in this difficult matter—in which the British Conservative Party as well as the Orange leaders would have to be bludgeoned—the Irish Delegation would not let him down? Griffith agreed. Unsuspectingly, he gave the assurance asked for in writing. Not only that, but, for some reason that has never been fully explained, he refrained from mentioning what had happened either to de Valera or to any of his colleagues. Griffith, indeed, thought that he had done well, and when he wrote to de Valera he declared that "Ulster had fallen into the pit they had digged for us."

After another week had dragged on we find de Valera issuing a further warning. "There has been so much beating about the bush that I think we should now get down to definite business and send them as far as possible our final word." As the parleying had lasted for more than five weeks nobody could accuse de Valera of becoming unduly impatient.

Griffith was on a slope more slippery than anybody in Dublin could guess, but Barton, Duffy and Childers were not altogether unaware of the danger, and more than one heated scene occurred at Hans Place. Griffith was becoming increasingly conscious of Childers's watchful eye and, in a moment of temper, accused him of working against a settlement, an accusation he soon withdrew. Barton and Duffy became more and more resentful of sub-conferences and private meetings and seriously thought of resigning. The delegation was not a happy family. But neither Barton nor Duffy—nor, of course, de Valera—had up to that time any idea that Griffith or Collins even contemplated accepting Empire status.

In point of fact, there had so far been no real surrender. Griffith had given a pledge which would be used against him with deadly effect in the final stage of the proceedings, and the proposal of a Boundary Commission was being discussed as a possibility instead of the "essential unity" which was one of the two rocks on which the delegation had been instructed to stand. But as late as

November 22nd, when a new Irish Memorandum was presented to the British, it did not appear that anything vital was being given away. The Memorandum insisted upon the sovereignty of Ireland, upon the preservation of independence, upon equality with Britain in the League of Nations, and of the maintenance by Ireland of her own defence forces. If these were conceded, and if unity was maintained, Ireland offered in return acceptance of the Crown as the symbol and accepted Head of the Association, consultation with the States of the British Commonwealth on matters of common concern, an undertaking to refuse to any foreign nation control over Irish territory which might be inimical to Britain, consideration of claims by Britain for naval facilities for not more than five years, and a recommendation that the Irish Government should conclude trade conventions with the States of the British Commonwealth.

Griffith, it is plain, was not only fighting valiantly, but fighting for something which he had come to regard as a forlorn hope. That the British would give way on the question of allegiance he did not believe, and as for himself, he was prepared to accept that position. It was Griffith's personal tragedy that Ireland was being offered at that moment all that he had dreamt of ever since he had started his Sinn Fein campaign twenty years before—a Parliament and a Dual Monarchy—and now he found himself so placed that he could not accept it. Did he, one wonders, in those critical last days of November, 1921, ever pause to consider that, next to the Rising of Easter Week, it was his own passionate and fiercely anti-British writings over two decades which had inspired the War of Independence and rendered his "1782" solution as out of date as the Home Rule Bill of 1912?

The Irish proposals envisaged an honourable and lasting settlement, they afforded Britain all the guarantees that one nation could legitimately ask from another, but once again they proved unacceptable. They filled Lloyd George, his private secretary told the delegation, "with despair." The negotiations looked like breaking down. Only one man was happy. Sir James Craig was able to tell a Belfast audience on November 29th that he had received a promise from Lloyd George that "the rights of Ulster would be in no way sacrificed or compromised."

At home preparations were being made to face a renewal of the war. De Valera was busy reviewing Republican troops in the South and West. On the last day of November, addressing the Mid-Clare Brigade, he made it clear that peace might vanish at any moment, and he warned the people that they might have to endure a period of renewed and intensified terrorism. "We know," he declared, "what can be done by this powerful nation; we know the terrorism and we know the savagery that can be used against us, and we defy it."

Everywhere he was received with enthusiasm. The feeling of the people at that critical moment was demonstrated by an address which the Clare County Council presented to him: "We would prefer to consummate our independence without further bloodshed, but if it should be, as recent events entitle us to suspect, that British Statesmen are planning another betrayal, then, on behalf of the people of Clare, we tell you we are ready. We have unqualified confidence in you and in our Government and in the cause of Irish independence. We will follow you if needs be to the death."

(v)

Events now moved swiftly to their tragic conclusion. On December 3rd the delegation was back in Dublin for a final consultation with the Cabinet, bringing with it a draft of the latest British proposals.

These proved to be almost identical in substance with the July proposals which had been unanimously rejected by the Cabinet and Dail. The British proposed to set up an "Irish Free State" within the Empire; in time of war the British Government was to receive any defence facilities it required; the Partitioned Ulster Counties were to be permitted to "opt out" of an All-Ireland Parliament, but, if they did, a Boundary Commission was to be established; and the following Oath was proposed: "I . . . do solemnly swear to bear true faith and allegiance to the Constitution of the Irish Free State; to the Community of Nations known as the British Empire; and to the King as Head of the State and Empire."

It was obvious that there was no real advance here, and that, without an almost complete surrender, such terms could not be accepted. When the Cabinet met at the Mansion House in Dublin on December 3rd the President said so at once. He was supported by Brugha, Stack, Barton, and Duffy. Barton pointed out that what was offered was not even Dominion status and that there was no guarantee against Partition. Duffy held that by maintaining a strong united front the Irish scheme, or at any rate all that was vital in it, could be secured. Childers, when consulted, declared that the proposals took away Ireland's national status and would inevitably involve Ireland in all England's wars.

Griffith, however, was strongly in favour of acceptance; it was England's last word, he was convinced, and the alternative was war. So was Duggan; and so, in a general way (he disliked the Oath) was Collins. But the President declared that he personally could not subscribe to the Oath of Allegiance nor could he sign any document which would give North-East Ulster the right to vote itself out. De Valera then, as always, was adamant on the two main questions of independence and unity. Whatever concessions might have to be made, there could be no surrender on these.

That fateful Cabinet meeting lasted for seven hours. Griffith continued to plead for a settlement and peace. Collins was unusually silent. Griffith's refusal "to break on the Crown" was the centre of a large portion of the discussion, and Brugha was particularly acid in his criticism. He wanted to know how it had come about that the delegation had been split, so that two of its members—Griffith and Collins—were frequently seeing the British alone. "It looks," said the Minister of Defence, "as if the British had selected their men." Later on Brugha suddenly turned on Griffith again and said, prophetically, "Don't you realise that if you sign this thing you will split Ireland from top to bottom?" "I suppose that's so," said Griffith slowly. "But I'll tell you what I'll do. I'll go back to London. I'll not sign that document, but I'll bring it back and submit it to the Dail and, if necessary, to the people."

That satisfied everybody. De Valera, whom Barton had begged to go over to London and take charge of the negotiations himself, decided that there was now no need for him to go. With a pledge given that nothing would be signed without reference back to the Cabinet in Dublin, the immediate position seemed to be safeguarded.

The final stages of the meeting were devoted to the question of the Oath, which Brugha objected to in its entirety, but which Collins described as "sugar coating" which might help the British to swallow a settlement. De Valera was unwilling to let the Oath stand in the way of settlement, so long as it was an Oath that did not imply a surrender of national independence. He proposed a form that would be innocuous: "I do solemnly swear true faith and allegiance to the Constitution of the Irish Free State, to the Treaty of Association, and to recognise the King of Great Britain as Head of the Association." Not, be it observed, to the King as "Head of the Associated States." There was a world of difference between a free and independent Ireland allied for purposes of common concern with the States of the British Commonwealth and an Ireland possessed of no more than the subordinate status of one of those States. Again, everybody seemed satisfied.

De Valera returned to the West to continue reviewing the Volunteers and the delegation hurried back to London. It was noticed that, whilst Barton, Duffy and Childers took the boat at North Wall, Griffith, Collins and Duggan chose the alternative Kingstown-Mail route.

(VI)

Six tired, overwrought, and dispirited men were up early at Hans Place on the following morning—Sunday, December 4th. Three of them, Barton, Duffy and Childers, were hard at work drafting amendments to the proposed Treaty in accordance with the conclusions arrived at in Dublin the previous day. When the document was completed they handed it to Griffith. Having glanced at it, he astounded them by announcing that he would not present it—or, in fact, any other counter-proposals—at Downing Street. They looked at Collins. He shook his head. He, too, refused to go; let those who wanted to break with the British present the document. Duggan took the same stand.

What had happened since the delegation's departure from Dublin to bring about this extraordinary position? Obviously, Griffith and Collins had talked together during the journey to London and had reached a decision or, at any rate, an understanding. The answer to the puzzle might very well be found in the minutes of the meetings of the Irish Republican Brotherhood, if, indeed, that secret oath-bound body ever kept such things as minutes. For, in spite of its name and its tradition, this self-constituted, subterranean and entirely unrepresentative body had, for reasons which will probably never fully be known, decided to support the signing away of independence. De Valera and Brugha were not amongst its members; they were opposed to secret societies on principle and they strongly resented the use of the hidden hand in the affairs of the nation, more than ever now that the nation had its own Parliament and Cabinet. But the power of the Irish Republican Brotherhood was immense. It had placed its members in key positions in the Army and the Civil Service and it had its own intelligence corps. Collins was a member of its Supreme Council and was in constant communication with it when he visited Dublin during the period of the negotiations. He was thus in a position to be able to assure Griffith that, in accepting the British terms, he would be powerfully supported by the Irish Republican Brotherhood. On no other hypothesis is it easy to find an explanation of the scene in Hans Place on that Sunday morning.

In face of the refusal of the other three delegates, Barton and Duffy declared that they would go to Downing Street alone. Then, and only then, did Griffith consent to accompany them, but not until he had weakened the draft proposals by insisting on changing the wording of the Oath from "Association" to "Associated States." Collins flatly refused to go at all and Duggan remained behind with him.

The British, faced with a disunited and truncated Irish team, made short work of the proposals. They were, declared Lloyd George, fundamentally the same as those which had already been rejected. What was the objection to accepting the generous offer that Britain was making? In the most glowing colours he painted the advantages that Ireland would reap with a minimum of delay if the Treaty were signed. British troops would be withdrawn, Dublin Castle would be handed over, an Irish Parliament would be set up immediately. Griffith replied with one of the best efforts of his career. The man who, an hour before, was refusing to have hand or part in even presenting the Irish proposals, and who had no belief in the possibility of their acceptance, now defended them as eloquently as if his words were sprung from passionate conviction. The British listened respectfully, but they were not impressed. They knew that their hour was at hand. It came a moment or two later when Gavan Duffy put the arguments that the Irish had been using for two months into a sentence: "Our difficulty is coming into the Empire." At once Chamberlain jumped up. "That ends it!" he exclaimed. The other British Ministers rose to their feet as well, indicating that all was over. But the finality of the gesture may not have been as real as it seemed. It is difficult not to suspect histrionics. One can safely assume that the British had heard about that Irish difficulty before.

(VII)

Where was Collins? That was the question that occupied the British after the Irish had left. Why had he absented himself from the Conference? By this time Lloyd George had a pretty shrewd idea not only of the split in the Irish team, but of the divergent views of the two sections. He must, he decided, see Collins. The break seemed final and unmendable, but Lloyd George was a man who had supreme faith in his own ingenuity. He had an instinct, too, that victory was within his grasp.

Collins was with him—alone—at half-past nine next morning. The Prime Minister told him that the British Cabinet was meeting at noon, that news of the break would at once be published to the world, and that it would be made clear that the break was on the question of "within or without" the Empire. Collins mentioned "Ulster," and pointed out that on this all-important matter the British had elicited no definite reply from Craig. Lloyd George countered with a reference to the proposed Boundary Commission. He said, in effect, that what Craig decided to do or not to do was of no real importance. The Boundary Commission would take care of that. If the Treaty were accepted, "Ulster" would be forced into a united Ireland. Collins was impressed. De Valera had said on Saturday that he could understand Griffith sacrificing independence for unity, but that he was getting "neither this nor that." Well, thought Collins, unity is safe now. (Had he forgotten, one wonders, that six days before Craig had announced publicly that Lloyd George had given "Ulster" a pledge to the opposite effect?) It was arranged that Collins should ask his colleagues to return to Downing Street in the afternoon. The break might not be final, after all.

When the Conference re-assembled at three o'clock Lloyd George had his last strategic moves carefully prepared. Griffith, still fighting gamely, brought up the Ulster question once again. He wanted a reply from Craig either accepting or refusing unity. Without that, there could be no assurance. "You promised not to let us down on this," cried Lloyd George. "I've never let down a friend or an enemy on an undertaking," retorted Griffith with heat. There was an interval during which the British Delegation retired. When they returned, Lloyd George had a long envelope in his hand with its contents partly withdrawn. Griffith had given him a pledge: there was a letter . . .

"Now it was full steam ahead. Smash Griffith's attempt to break on Ulster, extend a few concessions, represent them as open for a few hours only, demand an immediate verdict on Dominion status, win over one man, Griffith probably, press on him an ultimatum with immediate war the alternative to refusal, paint war in all its horrors, and fasten on the delegation, man by man, the responsibility for imposing it on Ireland." (Pakenham).

Such indeed was the strategy. In face of the letter—containing Griffith's Park Lane pledge of which his colleagues knew nothing—all the fight went out of the Chairman of the Irish Delegation. Now there could be no break on Ulster. Griffith had, as Dorothy Macardle puts it, "sawn through the branch on which he had wanted to climb."

Lloyd George proceeded to deliver his hammer blow. He had, he said, promised to let Craig know the result of the negotiations that night. The messenger—Mr. Geoffrey Shakespeare—would have to start soon. The British could concede no more and would debate no further. The Treaty must be signed or else . . .

Griffith surrendered. "I will give the answer of the Irish Delegation at nine to-night," he said; "but Mr. Prime Minister, I will personally sign this agreement and recommend it to my countrymen." "Do I understand, Mr. Griffith, that though everyone else refuses, you will nevertheless agree to sign?" "That is so," replied Griffith.

Lloyd George, inwardly jubilant, outwardly grim, turned to the other Irish Delegates, asking them where they stood. He got no reply. "Every delegate must sign," he exclaimed sharply, "or there can be no agreement." Collins and Barton still remained silent. Lloyd George snatched two letters from the table and held them up. "Here," he said dramatically, " are two documents, one containing Articles of Agreement reached by His Majesty's Government and yourselves; the other saying that the Sinn Fein representatives refuse to come within the Empire. If I send the latter it is war, and war within three days. The train is ready with steam up at Euston. Mr. Shakespeare is waiting. Which letter shall I send? I must have an answer by ten p.m. to-night."

The Irish Delegates left, weary, beaten, heavy-hearted. Churchill observed that Michael Collins "looked as if he were going to shoot someone, preferably himself."

(VIII)

Everything, it is clear, depended on Collins. To Lloyd George's ultimatum—an ultimatum described by Frank Pakenham as one "of which there is no other instance in the diplomatic history of modern times"—he had made no reply. He had merely asked, as he walked out of the doors of 10 Downing Street, for a few hours in which to make up his mind.

But his mind, it would seem, was already made up, for on the way back to Hans Place he announced to his colleagues that he would sign. Barton and Duffy were astounded. That Collins, of all men, should agree to sign away independence, that he, one of the stalwarts of the struggle, should admit himself broken, forswear the Republic and accept something less than Dominion status, appeared an almost incredible happening. But there it was.

In Hans Place the last arguments took place. Griffith, Collins, and, finally, Duggan, pleaded with Barton and Duffy for acceptance of the British terms. They believed in the irrevocability of Lloyd George's ultimatum; they spared no words in painting pictures of the horrors that would follow the resumption of war; they declared that the responsibility for the bloodshed that would ensue was too big a burden for them to shoulder. Barton thought of his oath to the Republic. Duffy refused to believe that the ultimatum was anything more than a gigantic piece of bluff.

For more than two hours the argument went on, angry and restrained by turns, always tense. Collins put the point strongly that the I.R.A. could not sustain a renewed attack (although General Macready declares in his Memoirs that the Irish military position was stronger in December than it had been before the Truce), and there he could speak with authority. Barton's position grew more difficult with every moment that passed. The two chief delegates were determined to sign. A refusal on his part might mean war, and what sort of a war could be waged with two men like Griffith and

Collins declaring for peace? Unity, without which victory could never be achieved, was gone.

Was Dublin forgotten at this most crucial of all moments? Did nobody pause to think of the pledge given to de Valera two days before that nothing would be signed without referring back? If the time-factor were as vital as Lloyd George's ultimatum suggested, was there not a telephone at hand? The answer to all these questions may very well be that given by Pakenham: "Lloyd George, if he had cast no other spell, had obsessed each delegate with a sense of inescapable personal responsibility; he had conjured Dublin off the map."

As midnight approached Collins ended the discussion by getting up and reaching for his coat and hat. Griffith and Duggan followed suit. Whatever Barton and Duffy might do, these three were going to sign. It was the end. Barton, after one further moment of anguished hesitation, gave way. He, too, would sign. There was only Duffy left and, obviously, it was not easy for him to make a lone stand. The five delegates left for Downing Street.

At half-past one the Treaty was signed.

CHAPTER EIGHT

The Great Debate

And Discord, with a thousand various mouths . . .
—MILTON, *Paradise Lost.*

(I)

ON Monday night, December 5th, de Valera was speaking in Limerick City. He warned the people to be prepared for the worst.

"We are not bluffing," he declared; "nothing will be accepted that deprives the nation of the essentials of freedom. Our resistance may not be sufficient to drive the English out of Ireland, but it will be sufficient to prevent them ruling Ireland. This is a separate nation, and never to the end of time will they get from this nation allegiance to their rulers." He ended on a note which lifted the controversy high above the realm of common political issues. "Contests like this," he said, "go in the end to the spiritual forces, even though it takes a long time."

Next morning he heard, much to his surprise, for his hopes had been gradually dwindling, that an agreement had been reached. The British, he concluded, must have been playing a game of bluff and must have suddenly decided, in face of the prolonged and determined Irish stand, to yield on the outstanding issues. "I did not expect them to give in so soon," he remarked.

But as he travelled back to Dublin, where he was to preside that same evening at a Dante Centenary celebration arranged by the Ministry of Fine Arts, he began to grow anxious. Beyond the fact that an agreement had been signed he had heard nothing. Supposing it was the Irish Delegation that had given in? It was almost unthinkable, in view of what had happened on the Saturday, but yet . . .

The car in which he had travelled from Limerick took him straight to the Mansion House, and there, in the Lord Mayor's room, he found Brugha and Stack waiting. "Any news?" he asked Stack. "Yes," Stack replied. "Good or bad?" "Bad." Stack handed him an evening paper containing a rough outline of the Treaty provisions. He read it in silence, but his lips tightened and his face went white. Outside in the big Round Room an audience was waiting; it was past the hour for the Dante function to begin. He asked for his University gown, donned it, and was about to lead the way into the meeting, when Duggan, who had travelled hurriedly from London, entered and handed him an envelope. "What is this?" said de Valera. "The Agreement," replied Duggan; "it has been arranged that it be published in London and Dublin simultaneously at eight o'clock." It was eight o'clock then. "Do you mean that it is to be published whether I have seen it or not—whether I approve of it or not?" asked the President. Duggan, very uncomfortable, replied: "Oh well, that's what was arranged."

De Valera stuffed the envelope into his pocket and walked out into the corridor. As he entered the Round Room there was a burst of applause, but it was noticeable that the atmosphere of the meeting was one of tension rather than relief. Not more than a handful present could have known of the impending split in the Cabinet, and nobody, save Duggan, knew of the circumstances in which the Treaty had been signed; but there were hundreds in the packed room who regarded it as an ignominious surrender. Amongst them were a few high Army officers who had even proposed arresting the delegates and charging them with treason.

De Valera made no reference whatever to the Treaty during the function. Apart from the few formal words in which he introduced the speakers, he said nothing. He sat there, stonily impassive, his heart like a stone, in profile bearing a striking resemblance to the great Florentine whose memory was being honoured.

(II)

Next day, December 7th, the President held a meeting at which Brugha, Stack and Cosgrave were present, and it was decided to summon the absent Ministers by telegram "to consider the circumstances under which the Plenipotentiaries had signed the Agreement in London." Desmond Fitzgerald, who was in charge of publicity, and to whom this message was given for publication, suggested an alteration in the wording. "It reads, Mr. President," he said, "as if you were opposed to the settlement." "That," said de Valera sharply, "is how I intend it to be read."

There were no bonfires in Ireland on December 7th; the feeling was one of mingled relief, bewilderment and anxiety. The morning papers on both sides of the Channel, it is true, acclaimed the signing of the Treaty as a triumph and a blessing. "A splendid consummation of patient statesmanship"—"An unhoped-for victory"—"This glorious achievement"—"Ireland's great day"—"An historic event": such were the headlines that the citizens of Britain and Ireland read at breakfast. It was, said the *Morning Post,* a "finely orchestrated chorus." King George congratulated his Prime Minister; the President of France congratulated King George; the Archbishop of Canterbury offered up thanksgiving; the Dominion Premiers joined in the ever-swelling chorus of praise and thankfulness; Sir John Simon declared that the moment had come to write Emmet's epitaph. But in Dublin there was a feeling of impending disaster. Nobody who had read the speech de Valera delivered in Limerick whilst the final scenes were taking place in London—"never to the end of time will they get allegiance from this nation"—could be in any doubt about his attitude to the document which had been signed.

A divided Cabinet met and talked for seven hours on the following day. The atmosphere was one of gloom rather than of anger or recrimination. The main question before the meeting was—how had the surrender come about? Griffith was dour and defiant. He refused to admit that there had been any surrender. Already, before leaving London, he had cabled a personal "victory message" to America in which he declared that "we have won liberty after the struggle of centuries." Stranger still, he refused even to admit duress. Collins admitted "the duress of facts." But Barton and Duffy made no bones about it. They had signed reluctantly and unwillingly, and solely on account of the threat of "immediate and terrible war." The meeting lasted late into the night, de Valera, Brugha and Stack urging the others not to press the document on the Dail. But the gulf had become unbridgable. When the vote was taken, four—Griffith, Collins, Barton and Cosgrave—were for acceptance, and three—De Valera, Brugha and Stack—against.

As soon as the Cabinet meeting was over the President issued a Proclamation to the people in which he said: "You have seen in the public Press the text of the proposed Treaty with Great Britain The terms of the Agreement are in violent conflict with the wishes of the majority of the nation as expressed freely in successive elections during the last three years. I feel it my duty to inform you immediately that I cannot recommend the acceptance of the Treaty either to Dail Eireann or the country. In this I am supported by the Ministers for Home Affairs and Defence. A Public Session o Dail Eireann is being summoned for Wednesday next at 11 o'clock. I ask the people to maintain during the interval the same discipline as before . . The great test of our people has come. Let us face it worthily without bitterness and above all without recrimination. There is a definite constitutional way of resolving our differences."

Had this repudiation of the Agreement been issued two days before—and it would have been had not de Valera yielded to Cosgrave's plea that the delegates should first be heard in their own defence—it would undoubtedly have proved more effective. But now, as Austin Stack wrote afterwards, the Press of the two countries had "carried the people off their feet in favour of the 'Treaty and peace.'" Other forces, too, were being rapidly mobilised. On the very day that de Valera issued his Proclamation, the *Irish Independent* published the views of fifteen members of the Hierarchy—all in favour of the Treaty. Behind the scenes the Irish Republican Brotherhood was working feverishly and a majority of its Council was backing Collins. Simple-minded soldiers like Commandant MacKeon, whose prestige in the Midlands and the West was enormous, were being told, "Trust Collins; Mick knows what he is doing." The business elements, for the most part, who badly wanted normal trading conditions to be restored, also favoured the settlement. With every day that passed the Republican position was being undermined and the obstacles that de Valera had to face were becoming more formidable.

In London, on December 9th, Sir James Craig visited Lloyd George to inquire about the probable operation of the Boundary Commission. The Prime Minister gave him an assurance that was in direct conflict with his pledges to Griffith and Collins. Only "a slight readjustment" of the Border was intended, said the Prime Minister. But even this was unacceptable to Craig. "Not an inch!" was still his slogan.

(III)

De Valera, with the tenacity which has always distinguished him and which has never been more in evidence than at moments of crisis, still clung to the hope that the position might be retrieved. Five men had been bullied—or tricked—into signing a dictated Treaty and the Cabinet was hopelessly split. But if the Dail and the country could be held together, a united front could still be shown to Britain and the Republic might yet be saved. Patiently and laboriously he set about re-drafting the Irish proposals, shaping them into a form which would emphasise even more strongly the safeguards offered to Britain, and using language calculated to soothe British opinion. There was to be no compromise on independence or unity, but in every other respect the plan of External Association was to be made as attractive as possible. The "sugar coating" was laid on thickly.

The Dail met on December 14th, it went into Secret Session on the 15th, and it reassembled in public on the 19th. During the Secret Session de Valera produced his new draft proposals—which came to be known as "Document No. 2"—explaining that he intended them to be no more than a basis on which a new offer to Britain might be constructed. Griffith and Collins flatly refused to consider the new document. For them there was no longer any alternative to the Treaty they had signed; by that Treaty they would stand or fall. The die was irrevocably cast. It only remained now for Dail Eireann and the people to make their decision.

The historic Dail debate lasted a fortnight, with an adjournment half-way through owing to the Christmas holiday, and it unloosed a deluge of oratory such as Ireland had never known. Every

Deputy regarded it as a duty to speak as well as to vote. One spoke for nearly three hours, another for less than three minutes. There were many wearisome repetitions; there was occasional anger; there was pathos; there was even humour. But, taking it all in all, the great Treaty Debate—of which the echoes can still be faintly heard to-day—was one of which Ireland has no reason to be ashamed. Dignity was not lacking; neither was sincerity. There was hardly a Deputy who was not aware of the solemnity of the occasion, who did not realise that the decision about to be taken was one of the most momentous in the country's history; and so for the most part they responded well to the President's plea for calmness and reasoned discussion.

Griffith moved approval of the Treaty in a speech that was earnest, forthright, and almost entirely free from passion. From beginning to end it was pitched in the same unemotional key. One point he emphasised many times over. " The issue is not one between an independent Republic and Dominion status; rather is it between two forms of Association with the British Empire." " Document No. 2"—which, being tentative and uncompleted, the Dail had agreed to regard as confidential—was beginning to rear its head. The fight, suggested Griffith, was concerned now with shadows rather than substance. " We have brought back the flag; we have brought back the evacuation of Ireland after 700 years by British troops and the formation of an Irish Army. We have brought back to Ireland her full rights and powers of fiscal control."

When Commandant MacKeon—the far-famed

Blacksmith of Ballinalee—had seconded the motion in a short, simply-phrased, soldierly speech, de Valera rose. "He was," wrote the special representative of the *Irish Independent*, "in magnificent form—mentally and physically. Unquestionably his speech electrified the Assembly. His blinding sincerity so impresses you that you find yourself listening dazzled and profoundly moved. Every word came with rugged clearness."

Leaning over the half-moon table on the left of the Speaker in the long, low-ceilinged chamber in University College, de Valera went straight to the heart of the problem in his first sentence. "Did the Irish people think we were liars?" Then, after a pause, rapping the table with his knuckles to emphasise every word, he said slowly: "I am against this Treaty because it does not reconcile Irish national aspirations with association with the British Empire. I am against this Treaty, not because I am a man of war, but because I am a man of peace."

This Agreement, he declared, would not bring peace with England; it would not even bring peace in Ireland. The unanimous proposals of the Cabinet had been turned down at the point of the pistol and immediate war threatened on the Irish people. Was that an honourable method of dealing between nations?

"When I was in prison in solitary confinement our warders told us that we could go from our cells into the hall, which was about 50 feet by 40. We did go out from the cells to the hall, but we did not give our word to the British gaoler that he had the right to detain us in prison because we got that privilege.

"Does this assembly," he asked in ringing tones, "think the Irish people have changed so much within the past year or two that they now want to get into the British Empire after seven centuries of fighting? Have they changed so much that they want the British King as their monarch? It is not King George as a monarch they choose; it is Lloyd George, because it is not the personal monarch they are choosing; it is British power and authority as sovereign authority in this country."

In other years Arthur Griffith had joined hands with Connolly and Maud Gonne in hoisting black flags in Dublin on the occasion of the visit of a British monarch. De Valera had not forgotten the incident. "I tell Mr. Griffith, if this Treaty is approved, and if Mr. Griffith thought it wise to ask King George over to open an Irish Parliament, he will see black flags in the streets of Dublin. Do you think that would make for harmony between the two peoples?"

The tension grew as the President proceeded. Deputies strained forward as if fearful of missing a word. Collins sat with chin thrust out, clenching some papers in his hand, occasionally shaking his head in violent disagreement. Erskine Childers, pale and sad-faced, looked up every now and then to nod approval. The mother of Padraig Pearse looked on with calm intensity. When de Valera declared that "under this Agreement the Ministers of Ireland will be His Majesty's Ministers, the Army that Commandant MacKeon spoke of will be His Majesty's Army," the Commandant uttered a startled

"No, No!" Only Griffith remained outwardly unmoved and impassive. And it was to Griffith, to whom he pointed across the table, that de Valera addressed his final words, the words that Parnell had used nearly forty years before: "Time will tell whether this is a final settlement; you are presuming to set bounds to the march of a nation."

There was a burst of applause when the President sat down. "It was," said the *Irish Independent's* descriptive writer, "a great speech, spoken straight from the heart of the man."

(IV)

Words, words, words! Day after day the torrent of oratory drove on, threatening to submerge the army of Pressmen whose minds and pencils were moving ever more listlessly and mechanically. "You may sneer at words," de Valera had said earlier on, "but I say that words mean something, that words in a Treaty mean something, else why should they be put down? They have meanings behind them and great realities that you cannot close your eyes to." It was true, but words were powerless now to undo other words that had five Irish signatures beneath them.

Once in a while the great debate was enlivened by an angry interruption, a gleam of humour, a moment of drama.

"I have said no hard words about anybody, but I have been called a traitor," Collins rasped out during the first session. "By whom?" asked de Valera quietly. That scene passed as quickly as it had arrived. . . . Fionan Lynch, supporting the

Treaty, said: "I can speak for the people of South Kerry——" "No!" The shrill, dissenting voice was that of a lady in black sitting in the body of the hall. "With one exception—an Englishwoman!" said the Deputy, bitingly. The lady was asked to leave. She was the Honourable Albinia Broderick, sister of a British ex-Cabinet Minister. Anglo-Irish, not English, she had been a fervent supporter of Ireland's cause. . . . William Cosgrave was comparing the Treaty and "Document No. 2." "Now, if *x* were absolute independence," he said, "and if *y* be the independence we are told we are abandoning, what is the relative value of *x* and *y?*" De Valera, the one-time Professor of Mathematics, began to look interested. "And if," continued Mr. Cosgrave, "you add £40,000,000 to *x* and 60,000 troops to *y*——." It was too much even for a mathematician. The House broke into general laughter and the President laughed as heartily as any. . . . From Robert Barton came a graphic and moving description of the circumstances under which the signing took place. "Speaking for himself and his colleagues, the English Prime Minister, with all the solemnity and power of conviction that he alone, of all men I have met, can impart by word and gesture—the vehicles by which the mind of one man oppresses and impresses the mind of another—declared that the signature and recommendation of every member of our delegation was necessary or war would follow immediately. He gave us till ten o'clock to make up our minds." Then came a *cri de coeur* from a gallant gentleman. "I broke my oath of allegiance to the Republic, to me the most sacred bond on earth; my signature is a proof of that. I broke it because I judged it to be the lesser of alternative outrages forced upon me" . . . Richard Mulcahy, giving the soldier's point of view, argued passionately against any policy that would lead to a renewal of the war. Major Compton-Smith, a British Officer for whom his captors had entertained a high regard, had been held as a hostage and executed some months earlier as a reprisal for the execution of six Republican prisoners. "Must we," asked the Chief of Staff, "again shoulder the responsibility of killing in self-defence the Compton-Smiths of England?" . . . During the afternoon session of January 5th a Deputy rose to call attention to a leading article which had appeared that morning in the *Freeman's Journal* and in which the writer declared that President de Valera "had not the instinct of an Irishman in his blood." When Gavan Duffy spoke of "this infamous attack" there were cries of approval from all parts of the House. "Member after member," according to the *Irish Independent,* "rose to add his voice to the condemnation and to speak of his faith in and love for de Valera." But Arthur Griffith did not join in the chorus of disapproval. "The Press has a right to say whatever it likes." . . . As the end drew near the strain began to tell. Tempers were frayed and taunts were flung. There were fiery interchanges between Brugha and Collins. Griffith's contributions to the debate grew increasingly bitter. Every Session had its "scene." "I am Chairman of a Board of Guardians——," one Deputy began his speech. There was loud laughter. "And if the Board conducted its business as this

House does," he went on, " I would be ashamed of it." The laughter quickly subsided.

(v)

By a curious irony " Document No. 2," de Valera's last effort to save the Republic—" a supreme effort by the captain of the ship to pull it off the rocks," as Cathal Brugha said later—was turned by his opponents into one of the most deadly weapons used against the Republican position. As we have seen, it was presented in a rough and unfinished draft during the Secret Session of the Dail on December 15th, and it was agreed there to treat it as confidential. Since then the President had been working on it, intending to offer it in its completed form as an amendment to the motion approving the Treaty. Meantime, however, it had in the course of the debate been hinted at, referred to, discussed, and entirely misrepresented. It was said to include allegiance to the British Crown, to accept Partition, and to permit permanent British occupation of the Irish ports, none of which was true. As between it and the Treaty signed in London there was, the public were told, nothing to choose. It was all " a quibble of words."

Suddenly, Griffith did one of the few things in his career which it is difficult to defend. He handed a copy of the early rough draft of the President's proposals to the Press, and it appeared next morning, with carefully worded headings, on the front page of every daily newspaper in the two islands, side by side with the completed document. From the latter, six clauses had been omitted—

those dealing with the Partitioned area—because the President felt that the "Ulster" question was one for Ireland only, and should not be made the subject of negotiations with an outside Power. Great play was made in the Dail and the Press with regard to the omissions. Sharp practice on the part of the President was suggested, and though he protested vigorously against the publication of something which was never intended to be anything more than the foundation on which an alternative to the Treaty might be built, the harm was done. The Irish public grew more and more bewildered. But interested observers who gave "Document No. 2" serious study were quick to see that there was a fundamental difference between its provisions and those of the Treaty. The London *Times* described it correctly as a plan which would make Ireland "an independent State in loose Treaty association with this country." The difference, in fact, was big enough to cause the British Government to threaten to wage "immediate and terrible war" on Ireland rather than accept it.

Next day the President offered his resignation to the Dail. He felt he could not go on any longer. The Cabinet, he said, had become completely, irrevocably split. If he were to defend the Republic he would require a free hand, unhampered by divisions. Never did he speak more passionately than on this occasion. He read a passage from the Constitution of Sinn Fein which denied the right of any foreign Power to claim allegiance from the Irish people. When he had finished he threw the document on the table and declared vehemently that he, at least, would never become a British subject. "I believe I know what the Irish people want. I have been brought up among the Irish people. I was reared in a labourer's cottage here in Ireland." That was his answer to those who doubted his Irish blood, his Irish instincts. "If there was one," said the *Irish Independent* report, "to doubt the sincerity, the transparent honesty of the Irish leader, that doubt would pass with one glance at the man as he stood before his colleagues."

But there were some who raised doubts. Griffith and Collins protested angrily against the step the President proposed taking. His proffered resignation was a trick—a "Tammany Hall trick." The President rose again. "I am sick and tired of politics," he said wearily, "sick to the heart. I have only seen politics within the past three weeks." He agreed to withdraw his resignation, but only on condition that the division on the Treaty motion would be taken within twenty-four hours.

(VI)

When the roll was called at Earlsfort Terrace on January 7th, one hundred and twenty-two Deputies answered to their names. De Valera looked worn and haggard, as if he had not slept. Collins looked even more pugnacious than usual. Griffith appeared a little flushed, but his countenance was as calm and inscrutable as that of a Chinese idol.

The oratory was still unfinished. There were no less than twelve speeches during the morning Session. In the late afternoon Cathal Brugha rose to deliver a final condemnation of the Treaty. Griffith had declared the differences between de Valera's External Association plan and the Dominion Status offered in the Treaty as "no more than a quibble." "To me," said Brugha, "it is the difference between a draught of water and a draught of poison." Acceptance of the Treaty document he regarded as "national suicide." In a memorable passage he declared: "England's position is weak; Ireland's is strong. Why, if instead of being so strong, our last cartridge had been fired, our last shilling had been spent, and our last man was lying on the ground, with enemies howling round him and their bayonets raised ready to plunge them into his body—that man should say, true to tradition, if he were asked, 'Will you come into the Empire?'—he should still say, 'No, I will not!'" He reminded Griffith how, by stepping down from the Presidency of Sinn Fein in 1917 in favour of de Valera, he had won universal respect, and he appealed to him now to make as great a sacrifice and refrain from voting for the Treaty.

Griffith wound up the great debate. He showed himself unmoved by Brugha's appeal and there was much bitterness in his words. Tactically, it was a masterly speech and one that won rounds of applause from the Treaty supporters. Michael Collins he described—as if contemptuously disposing of Brugha's record—as "the man who fought the Black-and-Tan terror," a phrase that brought loud protests as well as cheers. "He is playing Mick for all he is worth," was an audible comment from one of the public seats. When, a little later, he said with emphasis: "There is no more finality in this Treaty than we are the final generation on earth," he scored his best point. It was an uncompromising speech and one that was calculated greatly to heighten the partisan atmosphere in which the last scene was enacted.

When he sat down the vote was taken. The Council Chamber was packed to the doors. The black coats of the clergy were conspicuous in the body of the hall and there was a sprinkling of Volunteer uniforms. The Lord Mayor of Dublin and the Standing Committee of Sinn Fein occupied front seats. The poet "A.E.," red-faced and black-bearded, peered curiously at the assembly through strong-lensed spectacles. Beside him sat a coloured student from Trinity College. Behind was an army of Pressmen drawn from many countries, weary of it all and thankful that the end was near. Outside in the street, braving the cold and fog of a January evening, a vast crowd waited for the result.

Diarmuid O'Hegarty began the roll-call. There was dead silence save for the answers, which were given in Irish. The first name called was that of the Deputy for County Armagh, Michael Collins. "Is toil" ("for") came the answer, in a strong Cork accent. A few seconds later the name of the Deputy for County Down was reached. "Eamon de Valera——?" "Ni toil" ("against"). Three minutes more and it was all over. The Speaker, Eoin MacNeill, called out the figures: 64 for, 57 against. The Treaty had been approved by seven votes.

De Valera, looking deadly pale, rose to his feet. Speaking in low, level tones he said: "The Republic goes on until the nation has disestablished it." Then: "I should like to say my last words. We have had four glorious years of magnificent discipline in our nation. The world is looking at us now——" Overcome by emotion, he was unable to go any farther and, sitting down, buried his head in his hands.

From the street came the mingled sounds of cheering and boohing.

CHAPTER NINE

Chaos

In all disputes, so much as there is of passion, so much there is of nothing to the purpose.

—SIR THOMAS BROWNE, *Religio Medici.*

(1)

LESS than a year had passed since, during the Summer Session of Dail Eireann in 1921, de Valera had spoken of " the fundamental rock of right and justice," and had declared, amidst crashing applause, that " the moment we get off that rock we have no case whatever."

What was going to happen now? With the rock swept by a sea of dissension, where was the Republic to find a foothold? Something more than unity, he realised, had been lost in the Council Chamber of University College. The pure, high note sounded in Easter Week—the note that was music in the ears of Young Ireland—had been drowned in a tumult of discordant voices. The crusaders had, as it were overnight, become politicians. In the eyes of the world, and what mattered infinitely more, of the Irish people, their stature had been reduced. No longer could he, the leader, appeal to all generous minds in other countries to lend their suport to a small nation fighting unitedly for an ancient and a righteous cause.

He thought seriously of retiring into private life.

He was, as he had told the Dail, sick and tired of politics. "I have only known politics within the past three weeks," he had said. From now onwards he was to know them in all their bitterness, their tyranny, and their disillusion, because, after a short period of hesitation, he decided to carry on the fight. The Republic, after all, had not been disestablished, and could only be disestablished by the people who had brought it into being. Once again, his guiding motives were faith in the people and the cause. The people, he knew very well, were weary of the struggle and were being offered a peace which, on the materialistic side, was being presented with an almost irresistible appeal. A local Parliament, a native army, fiscal autonomy—these were no small gains. Dublin Castle—Britain's seven hundred years old fortress-prison—was being evacuated. The Irish Bastille had fallen. The victory had been painted in glowing colours by the Treaty supporters, and de Valera and his followers had not a single newspaper at their command in which to present the other side. "Don't go rainbow-chasing," the people were told. "Don't sacrifice the substance for the shadow. The Treaty gives you a Republic in all but the name. It is a victory, not a surrender. Besides, it can always be used as a stepping-stone to higher things." Such were the arguments poured into the people's minds, in the Press, on the platform, from the pulpit.

The real truth was revealed only in the British Parliament, through which the Treaty had been rushed in forty-eight hours. There, the very definite status of inferiority which it had imposed upon Ireland was made sufficiently plain. Lloyd

George stressed the fact that there had been complete acceptance of allegiance to the British Crown and that what had been granted by Britain was not even Dominion Home Rule. Under the Treaty Ireland was committed to participating in all England's wars. "The first thing we provided for," said the British Prime Minister, "was that in the case of war we should have free access to all the Irish harbours and creeks. If there is war we cannot wait for discussion between Governments as to whether you can send your ships here or land men there." Winston Churchill was equally emphatic. The provisions of the Treaty, he told the House of Commons, included "allegiance to the Crown, partnership in the Empire, facilities and securities for the Navy, and complete option for Ulster." But the Irish newspapers, unanimous in their support of Griffith and Collins, only stressed the gains. More and more they directed their assaults towards de Valera. The man who had, by common consent, led the national struggle for four strenuous years with incomparable skill, courage and tenacity; who had, during the days of terror and bloodshed, always been a steadying and moderating influence; and who desired nothing more passionately than a just and lasting settlement between the Irish and English peoples, was suddenly presented to his own people as an "extremist," a "quibbler," a "rainbow-chaser." It required the passing of many years, many dissensions and many prejudices before the bulk of the Irish nation came to agree with the verdict of a distinguished Oxford historian—that if de Valera had acted otherwise than he did at the time of the Treaty crisis he "would have been a traitor to all he believed in."

(II)

No Irish writer will care to linger over the period that elapsed from the passing of the Treaty in January, 1922, to the outbreak of the Civil War six months later. It represents a dark, inglorious, confused and melancholy episode in Irish history. But the biographer of Eamon de Valera must take note of some of its happenings, for out of it emerged a legend, sedulously cultivated and skilfully expanded, by which de Valera was held up to the opprobrium of the world and of his own people as the Man Who Was Responsible for the Civil War. The charges hurled at Lincoln by infuriated Southerners in 1862 had their counterparts in those brought against de Valera by his critics in 1922.

Looking back from a distance of twenty-two years one sees that although what happened might possibly have been averted, it was in a sense inevitable. Forces had been set in motion which in the end defied all restraint and which moved blindly and ever more swiftly to the culminating tragedy. Cathal Brugha had pointed out the danger to Griffith at the last fateful meeting of the Cabinet before the signing when he said prophetically: "Don't you know if you sign this thing you will split Ireland from top to bottom?" And Griffith had not expressed dissent.

But if there was inevitability about the coming of the war between brothers, it was not, as has sometimes been suggested, on account of some inherent weakness in the Irish character, some fatal inability to settle major differences without having recourse to violence. The politicians could, and probably would, had they been left to themselves, have succeeded in preserving peace. "There is," de Valera had told the people in his Proclamation of December 8th, "a definite constitutional way of settling our differences," and in the Dail on January 9th, when a Deputy spoke of "fratricidal strife," he had said, "I hope nobody will talk such nonsense; we have a nation that knows how to conduct itself."

The real peril did not lie in the cleavage in the Cabinet, the Dail or the people. The Army was the danger-point. So far as numbers went, it showed a division of roughly half and half. It was still the Army of the Republic, and General Mulcahy, after the Treaty vote, declared in the Dail that it would remain so. But, clearly its position was equivocal. Already its two sections were being labelled "Free State" and "Republican." Cathal Brugha, Minister for Defence before the setting up of the Provisional Government; Austin Stack, Deputy Chief of Staff; Liam Mellowes, Director of Purchases; Rory O'Connor, Director of Engineering; Oscar Traynor, Commandant of the Dublin Brigade, and several more were against the Treaty. Richard Mulcahy, new Minister for Defence; Michael Collins, Director of Intelligence; Eoin O'Duffy, new Deputy Chief of Staff, and Diarmuid O'Hegarty, Director of Organisation, amongst others, supported it. To a certain extent the division was one of personalities rather than of principles. The majority of the men who had been closely associated with Collins during the Terror remained loyal to him, and similar loyalty was given by other Army units to other popular officers. Most uncompromising of all in their opposition to the Treaty were the single-minded soldiers who regarded the Republic as the symbol and only true expression of independence and who proclaimed passionately that they would never have gone through the hell of the Black-and-Tan war for the poor measure of freedom which the Treaty represented. These men felt they had been deceived and they did not hesitate to fling the word " traitor " at Collins and Mulcahy. It was nonsense, of course. Men who were heroes on December 5th, men who had risked a horrible death a hundred times during the struggle, did not become traitors on December 6th. But, as in all such conflicts, men's minds were too clouded by passion and bitter dejection to permit of the exercise of logic or clear thinking. The one great issue at stake—whether a minority had the right to continue the fight for full independence in face of the acceptance of something substantially less by the majority—became hopelessly obscured by a welter of disputation, recrimination, and discord.

Yet it needed even more than the splitting of the people, the Dail, and the Army to produce the circumstances in which civil war finally became " inevitable." The weight that in the end overbalanced the scales came, as we shall see, from without, not from within. The British Government were determined that there should no longer be any tolerance for the Republican Movement, and they were equally determined to interpret and implement the provisions of the Treaty regarding " Ulster " to their own advantage. Their pressure on Griffith and Collins was remorseless and unrelenting, and it ended in an ultimatum which precipitated the final collision.

(III)

When the Dail reassembled after the approval of the Treaty, de Valera resigned, but intimated his willingness to take office again if re-elected. He made his position perfectly clear. He stood by the Republic, but would, if elected, put his personal antagonism to the Treaty aside and refrain from taking any active steps to oppose the Provisional Government so long as that Government did not exceed its powers.

> "I am thinking," he said, "only of the best way to do two things—to carry over the interim period and to do what I told this House several times I would like to see done. We came together to a certain bridge. At that bridge I thought for years we might part. I, at least, am anxious that we should never be driven back beyond that bridge; that we should entrench ourselves there and leave the final decision to the Irish people; and that in fairness to the Irish people we do not play party politics now any more than in the past. In fairness to the Irish people we will present them with an issue which will be so clear-cut and definite that they will not have any doubt about it."

It was a moderate and transparently sincere speech and its effect was seen in the division which followed. Fifty-eight Deputies voted for de Valera's re-election, sixty against. The narrowness of the majority indicated that even some of those who favoured the Treaty were loth to part with a leadership which they had always admired. Even Griffith was moved to emotion. "There is scarcely a man I have met in my life whom I have more love and respect for than Mr. de Valera," he said. "We want him with us." But on the Treaty, de Valera made it clear, there could be no co-operation. "You," he said to Griffith, "acting for the majority—and I suppose for Ireland—have to do certain work. Even to get through that portion of the work you will need us. We will be there with you against any outside enemy at any time. I am against this Treaty on one basis only; that we are signing our names to a promise that we cannot keep. We will not interfere with you except we find that you are going to do something that will definitely injure the Irish nation."

There was no "extremism" in such an attitude. The words de Valera spoke were the words of a man who was keeping his eyes on realities, who recognised that a momentous new factor had come into the life of the Irish nation, and who was sincerely anxious not to use the situation thus created for any personal or party purposes. When Griffith was proposed for the Presidency—having given a pledge that "the Republic of Ireland would remain in being until the Free State came into operation"—de Valera pointed out the anomaly that was bound to arise. "Mr. Griffith," he declared. "will be supposed to maintain the Republic with his right hand and to knock it down with his left." And that, precisely, was what happened. The new Government began to act as if the people had spoken and as if the Republic were already disestablished. A new Army was being recruited—and armed with rifles supplied by the British Government. A new Police Force was being set up. The Civil Service was no longer controlled by Ministers of Dail Eireann, but was taking its orders from Ministers of a Government subordinate to the British Crown.

It may be that in a difficult time of transition something of the sort was bound to occur. There were conflicting loyalties on every side and, in the popular mind, at any rate, there was no clear conception of where fundamental authority lay. If the "constitutionalists" were acting unconstitutionally the fact was not always clear to the man in the street. He was given only one side of the case and it is little wonder if he said to himself: "The Dail has accepted the Treaty and a new Government has been set up; it is my duty to accept and obey that Government." Erskine Childers, it is true, watchful as ever and jealous of the honour of the Republic, was pointing out week after week the rapid undermining of the Republican position and the unconstitutional things that were being done, but the voice of his small journal had little chance of making itself heard amidst the thunders of the daily Press. Griffith, in a regrettable moment of anger, called him "a damned Englishman," but there was no man who was performing more necessary or more disinterested work and none who had a greater love both for the land of his birth and the land of his adoption.

(IV)

The "maintaining of the Republic with the right hand and the knocking it down with the left" proceeded steadily during the spring. The Irish representatives in Washington and Paris, for example—Harry Boland and Sean T. O'Kelly—were dismissed on account of their anti-Treaty views, yet Harry Boland's successor, Mr. Smiddy, was given his credentials by Arthur Griffith as "Envoy Extraordinary from the Elected Government of the Irish Republic to the United States of America." Griffith and Collins, in fact, were attempting to do what the British Government had no intention of permitting—preserving a shadowy symbol of the Republic as well as carrying out the provisions of the Treaty. Many of his supporters believed that Collins, using I.R.B. methods, was throwing dust in the eyes of the British and that when an appropriate time came he would prove himself as good a Republican as ever. When summoned to London, however—and soon summonses began to arrive with embarrassing frequency—he succeeded, apparently, in convincing British Ministers that they had nothing to fear. They were left under the comfortable impression that, if dust was being thrown, it was in the eyes of Collins's own countrymen.

When the Ard-Feis of Sinn Fein, of which de Valera was still President, met at the Mansion House in Dublin in February there was none of the three thousand delegates present who did not recognise the gravity of the situation that had arisen. Sinn Fein was still the Grand Council of the nation; its prestige was enormous; it controlled funds and election machinery. In its ranks were Ministers, members of the Dail, Army Officers, I.R.B.-men, and even clergymen. Left, Right and Centre were represented on its platform, and if a vote hostile to the Treaty emanated from it, the effect on opinion in the country would be far-reaching. Such a vote was not unlikely, and at an early stage of the proceedings Michael Collins declared openly that Republican feeling in the hall was intense and that there was a majority against the Treaty. The Six-County delegates, in particular, who had little faith in the Boundary Commission, and who had come from an area where an intensified anti-Catholic pogrom had been in operation for several weeks, were bitter in their opposition. De Valera, in an earnest speech, asked for continued support for the principles and ideals of the organisation, and appealed to Sinn Fein "in God's name not to give a British monarch a democratic title in Ireland." A vote on the Treaty issue, however, would only serve to widen further the divisions which already existed in the country, and after a long discussion, in which the strength and endurance of Republican feeling were demonstrated again and again, an agreement was arrived at between de Valera and Griffith. It provided that no election would take place for at least three months, that before any election was held a Constitution drafted by the Signatories of the London Agreement—a Constitution which Collins promised would be a "Republican Constitution"—would be placed before the people, and that in the meantime Dail Eireann should continue to function as before in all its departments. These proposals received the unanimous approval of the Ard-Feis, and they were ratified a few days later by the Dail.

There was relief in Ireland, but anger in London. Churchill summoned Griffith to the Colonial Office and demanded an explanation. The assurances he received were apparently satisfactory, and he was able to report to the House of Commons that "the Irish Ministers have in no respect weakened . . . their opposition to the Republican Party remains unabated." Where the Irish Republican Army had defied the Provisional Government, he informed the House, appropriate action had been taken. "In the case of Limerick the Provisional Government have turned out the Republicans and put in their own men, and," he declared, "Tipperary will have to be treated in the same way."

Republican soldiers were angered and disgusted at the spectacle of an Irish Minister taking orders from Whitehall and at the abrogation of the functions of Dail Eireann by the Provisional Government. The Ard-Feis agreement had succeeded in postponing the elections and in providing time for the drafting of the Constitution, but it had not brought peace. The Army situation continued to deteriorate. Minor clashes between units of the two sections became more and more frequent; there were raids, arrests, and counter-arrests. Serious fighting was narrowly averted at Limerick in March and at Kilkenny in May. An Army Convention, requested by prominent Republican Officers, was at first agreed to by General Mulcahy, and later prohibited. The Convention was held, nevertheless, and it resulted in an act of open defiance of the Provisional Government. Led by fifty senior Officers of the Army, including Rory O'Connor, Liam Mellowes, Liam Lynch, Ernie O'Malley and Oscar Traynor, the Republican section of the Army broke away and repudiated the authority of the Dail. In an interview with the Press, Rory O'Connor made no attempt to conceal the seriousness of what was being done or its purpose. "Dail Eireann," he said, "has done an act which it had no moral right to do. The Volunteers are not going into the British Empire; they stand for Irish liberty."

O'Connor, no doubt, was speaking for a majority of the men who had endured the horrors of the Black-and-Tan war, men who had seen their comrades slain or tortured in the terrible days of 1920 and 1921, men who had believed with a passionate conviction that they had been fighting for a Republic. But what he was attempting to set up now was suspiciously like a military dictatorship, and there were many Irish democrats, sincerely attached to the Republican cause, who disapproved. Rory O'Connor himself admitted that de Valera, who was able to see more clearly than most the fundamentals underlying the bewildering complexities of the time, had asked the anti-Treaty section of the Army to obey the existing G.H.Q., but, he said, "the Army for which I speak cannot, because the Minister of Defence has broken his agreement that the Army should be maintained as the Army of the Republic." Why did not de Valera openly repudiate or denounce Rory O'Connor and his followers—who presently formed a G.H.Q. of their own, and occupied the Four Courts in Dublin and many other buildings? The question was asked at the time and has often been repeated since. The answer may very well be the same as that which Parnell gave to Gladstone in the days of the Land War when things were done of which the Irish leader did not approve: "I will not become England's policeman!" Besides, at that moment of chaos, de Valera was no longer leader. He still possessed influence, but his position of authority was gone. In private, he employed counsels of moderation and in public he gave repeated warnings as to the dangers of the situation that had arisen.

Two utterances of the period may be taken as indicating how he viewed that situation. The first—from what is probably the most publicised and misrepresented of all his speeches—was made at Thurles on St. Patrick's Day. "If they accepted the Treaty," he declared, "and if the Volunteers of the future tried to complete the work the Volunteers of the last four years had been attempting, they would have to complete it, not over the bodies of foreign soldiers, but over the dead bodies of their own countrymen. They would have to wade through Irish blood, through the blood of the soldiers of the Irish Government, and through, perhaps, the blood of some members of the Government, in order to get Irish freedom." In comparable circumstances Abraham Lincoln had used almost identical words. "We are in a trying time," he told the first Republican State Convention of Illinois in 1856, "and this movement to call a halt and turn our steps backwards needs all the help and good counsel it can get; for unless popular opinion makes itself felt and a change is made in our present course, blood will flow and brother's hand will be raised against brother." Just as Lincoln's opponents misrepresented his speech to show that he wished for a bloody struggle between the States, so the pro-Treaty Press pounced upon what de Valera said and held it up to the public as a cold-blooded incitement to civil war, instead of as—in the words of Erskine Childers—"a fair, just and absolutely necessary warning of what would inevitably happen if the freedom of Ireland were to be voted away." De Valera himself sent an immediate protest against the misrepresentation of his speech to the Press, but his prophetic warning—for that is what it amounted to—continued to be distorted not only during this period, but for years afterwards.

The other statement—one which was given little or no prominence—occurred in a speech made at Dun Laoghaire on April 4th. De Valera was dealing with the charge that the anti-Treaty section was flouting the will of the people. "Everybody," he said, "regards the will of the Irish people as supreme. I do for one. Not merely do I say I hold that this nation, taking away all force, should have the right to do with itself what it wants, but I would say further, that even in the circumstances of the moment, even with the threat of war, the Irish people would have the right, if they wanted to, to avoid war by taking another course."

That utterance, at any rate, was not open to misrepresentation. Re-reading the speeches that de Valera made during this period, one gets the impression of a man moving steadfastly along a predetermined road from which he refused to be diverted by the excitements and passions of the time. His position was one of extraordinary difficulty. He could not accept the Treaty and he felt himself impelled by his innermost convictions to urge the people to reject it. The Republic had not been disestablished, and he knew that, if the threat of war were removed, the people's loyalty to it would be unshakeable. But the Dail had, however reluctantly, approved the Treaty, and it was highly probable that a war-weary people would acquiesce in that decision. Nevertheless, as leader of the anti-Treaty minority—and it was a very large minority—he was bound to carry on the fight for the Republic and to keep the basic issue before the people's minds until they had spoken. At the same time, he had to take note of the difficulties of those who were putting the Treaty into operation; to try and lift the whole controversy above the plane of party politics; to prevent ideals from becoming soiled and vulgarised by wordy squabbles; and to restrain, as far as lay in his power, the men who had little belief in anything save physical force. There was, as he had said, a constitutional way of resolving the political differences that had arisen, and he, for one, was determined to find it.

(v)

There were two problems of immediate urgency to be dealt with: the General Election and the Constitution. The two were closely connected, for the Constitution that emerged from the Treaty Agreement would prove an infallible test of the worth of that Agreement. If the Treaty gave Ireland—as its supporters never tired of declaring—"a Republic in all but the name," the Constitution could not fail to reflect that fact.

The British were pressing for an early election. They saw resistance to the Treaty hardening, as the full truth about the circumstances under which it came to be signed sank into the minds of the people. They wanted an end of Dail Eireann, an end of Republicanism, an end, in fact, of the whole movement that had lasted from Easter Week onwards, and they called on Griffith and Collins to act, and to act swiftly. "The issue," said Winston Churchill in the House of Commons, "is about to be put before the Irish people so that they can choose freely between a Republic and a Free State." How "freely" they were to be allowed to choose was made evident by Mr. Churchill in the same speech when he declared that, on the part of Britain, "there could be no question of any accommodation on the subject of a Republic, none whatever." Lord Birkenhead, speaking on the same day in the House of Lords, declared that he looked "with infinite pleasure on every illustration from Ireland that Mr. Collins and Mr. Griffith are attempting to place themselves, under great difficulties, at the head of such forces as are available in order that they may restore law and order. And," he added, "I, as an Englishman, rejoice to see them making this effort. If there are to be struggles and fisticuffs, and if blood is to be shed, then in the first place it ought to be Irish blood and Irish fisticuffs that are expended . . . If the task is effectively carried out by them, the fact that it should be done by them and not by us will have resulted in an economy of English lives." A declaration like this, coming from the Lord Chancellor of England, left no doubt as to the quarter from which the strongest incitements to civil warfare were coming. Birkenhead—the "Galloper Smith" of 1912, the man who boasted that he would defy every law of the land in his opposition to Home Rule—made many cynical speeches in his time, but none so blatantly cynical as this.

De Valera, for his part, was determined not to

play into the hands of the British. The idea of Irishmen shedding the blood of Irishmen was abhorrent to him. He continued to use his efforts for peace, and when attempts were made by Republicans to prevent meetings addressed by Griffith and Collins from being held, he expressed strong disapproval. But he found that co-operation with the Treaty Party was becoming increasingly difficult. Under pressure from Whitehall, the Provisional Government was gradually usurping the functions of Dail Eireann and acting as if the Articles of Agreement had been submitted to and approved by the electorate. In an interview with a representative of the *Chicago Tribune* de Valera said: "Had the majority party in Dail Eireann continued legally to function as the Government of the Republic there would have been no objection. It was when Ministers proceeded to abdicate their functions in favour of a so-called 'Provisional Government' operating under British law, and were allowing the Departments of the Dail to lapse into a mere nominal existence that objection was made. The Army of the Republic was the first to object. If the Irish people were allowed a free choice they would choose by an overwhelming majority exactly what those armed forces desire." When the *Irish Independent*, commenting adversely on this statement, asked: "What then becomes of the free choice of the Irish people?" de Valera answered: "It does not exist."

As the three months' period fixed as the term of the Ard-Feis Agreement neared its end, fresh efforts were made to find a way out of the chaos in the interests of peace and order. The Republican

Party were strongly opposed to the holding of an election on the Treaty issue at a moment when the calm atmosphere necessary for the making of such a momentous decision could not be secured. They wanted to avoid, at all costs, a panic vote that might leave the national claim irretrievably compromised. At a Conference held in the Mansion House at the end of April de Valera proposed postponing the election for six months, in order that "time may be secured for the present passions to subside, for personalities to disappear, and for the fundamental differences between the two sides to be appreciated." Griffith refused and the Conference ended in failure. The British had given him his instructions and these included the holding of an election or plebiscite on the Treaty issue not later than June. A Committee appointed by the Dail early in May failed equally to find a way out.

The situation grew more and more precarious, but the friends of peace did not give up hope. Groups of army officers, representative of both sections, began to hold private conferences and their efforts resulted in a military "truce" being declared. Amongst the politicians support was growing in favour of a proposal which was being canvassed for an "agreed" election, and when Collins in the Dail on May 17th used words which suggested that he favoured a Coalition "to carry out the advantages of the Treaty and to consolidate their position, having in view the unity of Ireland," it appeared that an avenue to peace might be found. De Valera's response was immediate. Stable government, he said, was the need of the moment, and he offered, speaking for the minority party in the Dail, to render any assistance that he felt he could give in that direction. His offer was received with approval by both sides of the House and he and Collins were appointed to investigate the possibility of an agreement. The result, which was announced to a cheering Dail three days later—May 20th—was the historic Pact.

(VI)

It had required all de Valera's persuasive powers to bridge the ever-widening gulf. Collins's position was, admittedly, one of extreme difficulty. The Dail and the country, it was evident, would welcome a Coalition as the only instrument capable, in the circumstances of the moment, of safeguarding peace and yielding stable government. But Downing Street was watching every move that Collins made with cold, scrutinising eyes. And then there was Griffith to be considered: Griffith who all along had shown himself opposed to any compromise, who, almost alone even in his own Party had refused to admit that there was anything of the nature of a surrender in the Treaty, and who, the very day before the Pact was signed, had made a bitter attack in the Dail on those who wanted the elections postponed. Time and again the talks between de Valera and Collins had appeared to be on the point of breaking down, and it was only by the exercise of infinite patience that an arrangement was finally reached.

The terms of the Pact provided that an election should be held in June with a view to establishing a National Coalition Government, "on the ground that the national position requires the entrusting of the Government of the country into the joint hands of those who have been the strength of the national situation during the last few years, without prejudice to their present respective positions." The Sinn Fein organisation was to put forward a panel of candidates, 66 nominated by the Treaty Party, and 58 by the Republican. Other interests, however, were to be given freedom to contest the election. After the election a Coalition Ministry was to be formed consisting of five Treaty and four Republican members, with the addition of the President, who would be elected by the Dail, and a Minister for Defence, elected by the Army. Partition was not overlooked. Clause 5 of the Pact provided for the representation of the Six-County area "by their present Deputies"; in other words, the new Dail would be an all-Ireland assembly. The Treaty was not to be made an issue, and it was understood that both sides would use their influence to have the elections carried out in the spirit of the agreement.

Such, in its main features, was the Pact that the Dail applauded and that a dissension-ridden country welcomed with a sigh of relief. De Valera's "constitutional way out" had, it seemed, been reached; his genius for negotiation had never been exercised to better purpose. Arthur Griffith alone refused to look upon the Pact either as a stroke of statesmanship or as the best possible solution of a problem the gravity of which no one was likely to underestimate. Perfectly content from the beginning with the position which the Treaty—*his* Treaty more than any other man's—had created, he had become more and more hardened in his hostility not only to those

 (D1238)

who opposed it, but even to those who held that its acceptance should not be presumed before the people had spoken. For him the Treaty was a *fait accompli* and the Provisional Government rather than the Dail *the* Government of the country. But in face of the unanimous welcome given to the Pact in the Dail, there was no other course open to him short of resignation than to amend his motion for a June election and to bring it into conformity with the terms of the Pact. He made no secret, however, of the fact that he strongly disapproved of what was being done.

Speaking at the Ard-Feis of Sinn Fein on May 23rd, where the Pact was ratified with only one dissentient, de Valera said that those who made it and those who approved it regarded it "not as a triumph for one section or the other, but as a great triumph for the Irish nation." Michael Collins spoke in a similar strain, and he gave the assembly the impression that he was taking his courage in both hands and putting the interests of peace and the national well-being before all other considerations. When he said that the Pact would bring about stable conditions in the country, "and if those stable conditions were not more valuable than any other agreement, well, then, they must face what those stable conditions would enable them to face," the delegates were quick to grasp the challenge that underlay his words and they were in no doubt as to the quarter towards which the challenge was directed. The attempt of British Ministers to force the pace and to weaken the Republican position in advance of the people's decision was being frustrated. The Government that would result from the

Pact election would be the Third Dail and would retain its Republican status. The Army would continue to be the Army of the Republic. In the event of differences in the Government obliging it to dissolve later on, the Treaty would, under the terms of the Pact, be put before the people at another General Election. But by that time the Constitution would have been published, adult suffrage established, and a peaceful atmosphere created.

(VII)

The ink of the Pact was hardly dry before Griffith and Collins were peremptorily summoned to London and asked for an explanation. Griffith was quite frank about his own position: What had been done had been done against his will. Collins, on the other hand, according to Winston Churchill, appeared "half defiant, half embarrassed." At Westminster the two Irishmen, sitting in the Distinguished Strangers' Gallery, listened to a stormy debate in which one Unionist member after another denounced what they called "the violation of the Treaty." They heard Churchill tell the House that if the Pact became effective the Treaty was thereby broken and that, in such an event, the Imperial Government would consider itself bound to take such measures as it considered "appropriate to the gravity of the breach." A naval force, the Colonial Secretary added, had already been dispatched to Belfast, the evacuation of British troops from the Twenty-Six Counties had been suspended, and supplies of arms to the Provisional Government had been stopped from the date of the Pact. In the

House of Lords, Lord Birkenhead—using the same words that Gladstone had hurled at Parnell forty years earlier—declared that "should a crisis arise the resources of our civilisation are by no means exhausted."

At home preparations for the election, fixed for June 16th, began. At once it became obvious that certain pro-Treaty elements were working against the Pact. Darrell Figgis, a member of the Standing Committee of Sinn Fein, attended a meeting of farmers and business men and urged them to put forward pro-Treaty candidates in constituencies where Republicans would otherwise be returned. Election posters were issued telling the public that the way to get a Republic for Ireland was "through the safe and sure method of the Treaty." Lord Midleton, leader of the Unionists in the Twenty-Six Counties, told Churchill that Michael Collins was already afraid of the consequences of the Pact and that pressure should be brought to bear upon him "to make him break down."

But when the opening meeting of the election campaign took place in the Mansion House in Dublin on June 9th, there did not seem to be any danger of a serious breach of the agreement. Michael Collins stood beside de Valera on the platform and both of them appealed to the people to support the Pact in the letter and the spirit. Collins declared that none but the enemies of Ireland were hostile to the Pact. Once again his words seemed to hold a challenge to Britain.

Three days later—on June 12th—he was back to London, where Griffith, who had brought over the draft Constitution, had preceded him. On June 13th he had an interview with Winston Churchill. On June 14th he spoke in Cork. There he said:

> " You are facing an election here on Friday and I am not hampered now by being on a platform where there are Coalitionists. I can make a straight appeal to you—to the citizens of Cork, to vote for the candidates you think best of, whom the electors of Cork think will carry on best in the future the work they want carried on. When I spoke in Dublin I put it as gravely as I could that the country was facing a very serious situation. If the situation is to be met as it should be met, the country must have the representatives it wants. You understand fully what you have to do, and I depend on you to do it."

The " half-defiance " that Churchill had noticed in Collins had vanished and in its place there was complete submission. The Pact had been thrown overboard, suddenly, completely, unceremoniously, by one of its co-architects. What had happened between June 9th, when Collins declared in Dublin that nobody save " the enemies of Ireland " were displeased with the Pact, and June 14th, when he appealed to the electors of Cork to ignore it? Is it entering too far into the realm of speculation to assume that once again he had yielded to a British ultimatum? On the face of it, no other explanation seems adequate.

On the same day that Collins repudiated the Pact de Valera was addressing election meetings in other centres. He urged the people everywhere to vote for the Panel candidates, and asked those who favoured the Republican programme to vote also for the candidates of the pro-Treaty Party. " I hope," he said, "that those who stand for the Treaty will be equally honest in voting for candidates who are not on their side."

Next morning, to his dismay and bewilderment, he saw Collins's Cork pronouncement printed with flaming headlines in the *Freeman's Journal.* The Pact was no longer worth the paper on which it was printed.

Whilst Collins at home was repudiating the Pact, Griffith was making still another surrender in London. The draft Constitution which he had brought over with him was indignantly rejected by British Ministers and another one dictated.

The Constitution was the touchstone by which the measure of freedom conferred upon Ireland by the Treaty would be tested. If the Treaty gave Ireland "a Republic in all but the name" the fact would be evident in every article of the Constitution. The Committee set up by the Provisional Government to draft the Constitution had, indeed, striven hard to make it a document that would conflict as little as possible with Ireland's national claim. The traditional formalism found in similar documents of an Imperial character was carefully avoided. In it, the King of England was, in Gavan Duffy's phrase, "relegated to the exterior darkness," and an effort was made to shape it in such a form as might help to render acceptance of the new regime easier to the Irish people. But British Ministers would have none of it. They insisted on a new text which reduced the Constitution to an inferior instrument, in which, as the *Sunday Times,* acclaiming an "English victory," put it, "everything which left the question of the Imperial connection in doubt in the Irish draft has been positively and successfully restored."

This emasculated Constitution, which was deliberately withheld from the Irish people until the morning of polling day, was the final blow at co-operation between the Republican and the pro-Treaty Parties. No Republican, obviously, could ally himself with a regime operating under a Constitution which was aimed directly at destroying Republicanism. De Valera's best efforts were undone; in the circumstances, the Pact election could be nothing but a farce.

What, it may be asked, could Griffith and Collins have done, in view of their commitments to Britain? They could, as Gavan Duffy, who tendered his resignation as soon as he saw the published draft of the Constitution, said, have temporised; they could have assembled the Dail and have published to the House the diplomatic situation of which no one outside the Cabinet was aware; they might have called in aid the compulsory arbitration of the League of Nations; they might have appealed to the Dominions; they might have resigned and left the British Cabinet face to face with de Valera and the opponents of the Treaty. . . . They took none of these courses. Yielding once again to pistol-point persuasion, they gave in.

CHAPTER TEN
Into the Abyss

"Now we are engaged in a civil war, testing whether this nation, or any nation so conceived and so dedicated, can long endure."

—ABRAHAM LINCOLN.

(I)

ON June 24th the results of the election became known. 94 Panel candidates were returned, 58 pro-Treaty, and 36 Republican. Of the remaining 34, 17 were Labour, 7 Farmers' Party, 6 Independents, and 4—representing Trinity College—Unionists. De Valera was returned for his old constituency, East Clare.

If the election were to be regarded as implementing the Pact, there could be no doubt that the country had voted for a Coalition. The Panel candidates had secured a majority of 73 per cent. and the 17 Labour candidates were supporters of the Pact. But the Treaty Party refused to view the results in that light. In spite of the fact that it had been agreed to relegate the Treaty issue to a later decision of the people, the result was proclaimed by members of the Provisional Government as a party triumph. If there was any intention on the part of Griffith and Collins of forming a Coalition Cabinet in which Treatyites and Republicans would sit side by side it was not disclosed. No word reached de Valera from Collins.

But even if an invitation had been issued it is difficult to see what could have been done. As a consequence of the repudiation of the Pact and the acceptance by the Provisional Government of a dictated Constitution, co-operation between the two Parties had become virtually impossible. The Constitution was subordinate to the Treaty; it vested all executive authority in the Irish Free State in the British monarch; it gave the King the power of veto over all Irish legislation: and it laid down that no member of either House of the Oireachtas could take his seat without subscribing to the Oath of Allegiance to the British Crown laid down in the Treaty.

Out of such a position how could a Coalition emerge? Was it at all likely that Republican stalwarts like Brugha and Stack would take the repugnant oath as the price of admission to a Parliament subordinate to that of England? And what about the Army? The Pact fiasco, the humiliating Constitution, the failure of the Provisional Government to meet threats from Britain with anything but repeated surrenders—such happenings as these were rendering its Republican section more and more impatient. With every day that passed the portents grew darker.

(II)

The British had been waiting for a pretext to force the hands of the Provisional Government. They were given one, suddenly and sensationally. On June 22nd Field-Marshal Sir Henry Wilson was shot dead on the doorstep of his house in London.

The men who fired the shots were two Irishmen who had served with the British Army in France. One of them, Joseph O'Sullivan, had lost a leg at Ypres. The other, Reginald Dunne, in a speech that he had prepared, but was not permitted to deliver from the dock, said: "The same principles for which we shed our blood on the battlefields of Europe led us to commit the act we are charged with . . . You can condemn us to death but you cannot deprive us of the belief that what we have done was necessary to preserve the lives and happiness of our countrymen in Ireland."

There were few tears shed in Nationalist Ireland over the passing of Wilson. "A born and unscrupulous intriguer"—to borrow a fellow-general's description of him—he had tried by every means in his power, from the time of the Home Rule crisis in 1912 onwards, to impede Ireland's march to freedom. From within the walls of the British War Office he had given secret support to the British officers who had mutinied at the Curragh in 1914. During Carson's campaign he had demanded "belligerent rights" for the Ulster Volunteers; the Irish Volunteers he never referred to otherwise than as "murderers." In 1918 he had badgered and bullied British Ministers into passing legislation to conscript Irishmen. Early in 1922 he became Military Adviser to the Six-County Government, and was given a promise by Craig that any measures he proposed would be carried out "regardless of the consequences or the cost." His amazing diaries when published in 1927 created a sensation. Their publication, according to a distinguished Scots-Canadian writer who has faithfully analysed them in a brilliant volume [Sir Andrew MacPhail, *Three Persons*, 1929], was "an act of cruelty" which exhibited Wilson as "a public spectacle" and as "a Playboy of the Western Front"; their only coherency was "a single dark thread, hatred of Ireland."

Popular opinion credited this strange and sinister figure with responsibility for many of the horrors which were turning Belfast into a city of dreadful night. There the pogrom which had continued intermittently for nearly two years had become under Wilson's regime greatly intensified. Collins, who had made an Agreement with Craig in March with the object of saving the lives and property of Catholics, was forced a few weeks later to protest against the "abominations" which were of daily occurrence. In the British House of Commons Joseph Devlin made an impassioned protest against the barbarities practised by the "Specials" whom Wilson was busy recruiting. "If Catholics have no revolvers to protect themselves they are murdered," he said. "If they have revolvers they are flogged and sentenced to death." The Catholic hospital in Belfast, Dorothy Macardle records, "was like a war hospital in the first week in June. The wards, even the children's wards, were filled with bullet-wound and shrapnel-wound cases; fifty children under sixteen years of age had been treated there for wounds since February, when the bombing and sniping of children had become a part of the expulsion campaign. On the night of June 4th the hospital was surrounded by an armed mob who fired through the windows with rifles and revolvers." Over 20,000 Catholics had been driven from their homes and train-loads of refugees were arriving in Dublin day after day. Others sought refuge in Britain. Glasgow gave shelter to nearly a thousand.

Responsibility for the pogrom was laid, rightly or wrongly, on Wilson's shoulders. He could, at any rate, have ended it with a word. De Valera, when asked for a statement with regard to the shooting, expressed what was undoubtedly the feeling of the vast majority of Irish people on the subject. Assassination as a political weapon had always been abhorrent to him, but at the same time he was perfectly aware that a desperate position might at any time produce desperate acts. He said:

> "The killing of a human being is an awful act, but it is as awful when the victim is the humble worker or peasant, unknown outside his own immediate neighbourhood, as when the victim is placed in the seats of the mighty and his name is known in every corner of the earth. It is characteristic of our hypocritical civilisation that it is in the latter case only we are expected to cry out and express our horror and condemnation.
>
> "I do not know who they were who shot Sir Henry Wilson or why they shot him. I know that life has been made a hell for the Nationalist minority in Belfast and its neighbourhood for the past couple of years. . . . I do not approve, but I must not pretend to misunderstand."

Griffith's condemnation of what he called "this anarchic deed" was as strong as he could phrase it.

Everything is paid for, says the old proverb, and somebody had to pay for the killing of a British Field-Marshal. To a House of Commons "hungry with anti-Irish fury" Lloyd George stated that he had sent a "communication" to the Provisional

Government, but he did not disclose its terms. It was, in fact, of the nature of an ultimatum, and it insisted that the men in the Four Courts should be driven out without further parleying or delay. "Documents," he alleged, "have been found upon the murderers of Sir Henry Wilson which clearly connect the assassins with the Irish Republican Army." It was untrue, and when asked by Collins that the information in his possession should be placed at the disposal of the Provisional Government Lloyd George refused. The truth was that he had nothing to disclose. Even the Commander-in-Chief of the British Forces in Ireland, General Macready, was unable—as he stated afterwards in his Memoirs—to connect the shooting with Rory O'Connor and his men. The Chairman of the Provisional Government, in fact, could have given Lloyd George more information about the crime than the British Prime Minister could have given him, for it had been ordered and carried out by the I.R.B. Michael Collins was deep in the counsels of that organisation.

The Provisional Government, then, was being called upon by the British to punish a section of their own countrymen for a deed of violence in which the Chairman of that Government knew they had had neither hand nor part.

(III)

Collins was caught in the web he had woven. All his instincts and sympathies were with the Republican movement for which he had laboured so untiringly and heroically. He declared himself to be—and there was no doubting his sincerity—as staunch a Republican as ever. If he differed from those who opposed the Treaty, the issue was one of methods rather than of principles. Unlike Griffith, he would, if he could, have undone the fatal work of the night of December 6th. But what was he to do now? The British, to whom he had committed himself, were holding a pistol at his head and ordering him to attack some of his former comrades in arms. Griffith and the inner council of the I.R.B. counselled obedience. Neither appeared to realise the inevitable consequences of an attack by Irish soldiers upon Irish soldiers. The capture of the Four Courts, they seemed to imagine, would be no more than an "incident" which would soon blow over.

Griffith's attitude can be understood. The gains which the Treaty conferred were, in his view, weighty enough to outbalance all other considerations. He had achieved as much as he had hoped for, and he wanted the Treaty position and the authority of the Provisional Government established without further delay. The Four Courts garrison was a stumbling-block that had to be got rid of.

The attitude of the I.R.B. is less comprehensible. When one considers its origins, traditions and purpose, its part in the Treaty episode cannot be considered as otherwise than a curious one. From its foundation in the eighteen fifties it had generally been regarded as the most extreme organisation in Irish nationalism. It had created the modern Irish Republican movement. It had been the driving force behind the events leading up to Easter

Week. It had helped to depose Griffith, whose Republicanism was in doubt, from the Presidency of Sinn Fein and had put de Valera in his place. It had, until December, 1921, strenuously resisted all attempts to dilute the full Republican claim. It had condemned Sir Henry Wilson to death.

Yet during the critical months from December to June it had watched one surrender after another with complacency, if not with approval. Its whispered motto, to be sure, was: "To fool the British, not to serve them." Accept the Treaty, consolidate the advantages that it brought, stage a come-back to Republicanism at a riper moment—that was the plan. If Republican soldiers who had no belief in secret society methods stood in the way of the plan, then they must be dealt with firmly, even drastically. Collins was their man and their instrument, and they would support him even to the extent of attacking their own countrymen.

There was no doubt that a decision would have to be made and made quickly. If Collins had been bluffing the British, their ultimatum had called his bluff. But his old loyalties were still strong and he could not make up his mind. Those in close touch with him at this juncture remember him as a man at war with himself: silent, morose, and generally unhappy.

(IV)

Those last days of crisis were a time of infinite confusion. No section appeared to know what any other section was doing, or about to do. The full gravity of the situation was recognised only by those who were aware of the British ultimatum.

These did not include either the Republican soldiers or politicians.

A Coalition Army Council composed of pro-Treaty and anti-Treaty officers had been in existence since the date of the Collins-de Valera Pact, and by its efforts had so far succeeded in maintaining peace. The Four Courts section of the Republican Army Executive, however, were becoming impatient of conferences and pourparlers that seemed to lead nowhere. Time was passing and the Republic, they were convinced, was being "sold." Some of them held that the only way out of an impossible position was an open attack on the British, and they proposed that seventy-two hours' notice of the termination of the truce with Britain be given. Its justification, they declared, lay in the pistol-point Treaty, the broken Pact, the dictated Constitution, and the pogroms in the North, for all of which the ultimate responsibility lay at Britain's door. Furthermore, such a course would, in their opinion, re-unite the forces of the Republic, sweep away the Treaty, and cut the Gordian knot of the position that had been created.

At this stage there was no demand on the part of Collins or the Provisional Government for the evacuation of the Four Courts. In fact, when the question was raised at a meeting of the Coalition Army Council, Mulcahy, the Minister of Defence, "laughingly said"—as Rory O'Connor recorded afterwards—"that so long as we [the Republicans] held the place, the war against North-East Ulster would be attributed to us." Mulcahy appears to have left no doubt in O'Connor's mind that Collins, confident that he was bluffing both the British and the Six-County Governments, was conniving at the continued occupation of the Four Courts by the Republican forces.

The incident reveals the equivocal position into which Collins had steadily been forced. In March he had made a " peace pact " with Sir James Craig, with the hope of ending the pogroms in the North, and had called off the boycott of Belfast goods which had been in operation since the beginning of the War of Independence. But it had proved to be an illusory peace. Under Sir Henry Wilson's regime persecution of the Catholics had continued unabated and Collins found himself impelled to give secret assistance to the Northern divisions of the I.R.A. who were carrying on a " little war " against Craig's Government. Not only that, but at the very moment that the British were giving him orders to attack the Four Courts, his G.H.Q. was conferring with the garrison there with a view towards taking concerted action in the North, where it was feared that heavy reprisals would be taken against the Catholic population as a result of the shooting of Wilson. The Provisional Government was not to be involved. The arms which Macready had provided were not to be used, lest they should be identified. Instead, an exchange of rifles was effected between Collins's G.H.Q. and the Four Courts, and soon preparations were well advanced for a joint expedition to the North.

Griffith, who almost certainly would have disapproved, was not informed of what was taking place. He, as impatient now as any British Minister, demanded that Rory O'Connor's men should be cleared out without further delay and called upon

(D1238)

Collins to take action. Collins, having no love for the task, and still hopeful that his own prestige and popularity would help to avert strife, was slow to be persuaded, and for a time it looked as if he would break with Griffith. When the rest of the members of the Provisional Government had decided to obey the British ultimatum, Collins was still holding out.

De Valera, with his authority gone, was almost sunk in despair. No longer did "a constitutional way out' present itself. The politicians were being by-passed and control of events was passing more and more into the hands of the soldiers. In a few days' time, it was true, the new Dail was due to meet, but there was only a slender hope of peace in that direction. The Coalition was dead.

At the same time he was opposed to any violent or precipitate action. During six years of struggle and tension the connection between philosophy and political reality had scored itself deeply on his mind. He did not lose sight of his ideals, but he thought of the people. They, the inarticulate mass, would have to bear the brunt of a renewed war, a war that, with the nation's morale at a very low ebb, could have little or no hope of success. He counselled patience and caution. With the leaders and the Army divided, a resumption of the war against the British was a course which he could not regard as other than reckless. Besides, he was not yet convinced that the situation, desperate though it was, was altogether irretrievable. When the people's assembly met he would make one more effort for peace. De Valera knew nothing about the British ultimatum.

P

(v)

When an outraged Government, backed by the might and prestige of Empire, decides to strike at a subject people, it generally does so blindly, swiftly and remorselessly, and the resultant blow is often a greater outrage than the one that provoked it. The first impulse of the British Cabinet after the shooting of Wilson was to let loose their big guns on the Four Courts. But General Macready, who had been hastily summoned to London, was strongly opposed to such a measure. A British attack on the Republican Headquarters would, he pointed out, almost inevitably have the effect of driving the pro-Treaty forces into an alliance with the militant Republicans. The thing could be done in another way—a way that would ensure "an economy of English lives." After some hesitation his advice was taken and the General, as he records in his Memoirs, never afterwards "ceased to congratulate himself on having been an instrument in staving off what would have been a disaster." The disaster was to be Ireland's, not Britain's.

How it finally came can best be appreciated if the events of the last fatal week are set out in chronological order:

June 22. Sir Henry Wilson assassinated. General Macready summoned to London. Ultimatum dispatched by British Cabinet to the Provisional Government.

June 23. Reply sent by Provisional Government to British Cabinet asking that information which the British claimed to have in their possession with regard to the shooting of Wilson should be placed at their disposal. Griffith holds conference in Dublin with British officials and military officers "to consider the continued occupation of the Four Courts by Irregulars under General Rory O'Connor."

June 24. General Macready returns to Dublin. British refuse to give the Provisional Government the information requested, on the ground that it is of "a highly secret character." Macready ordered by telegram to bombard the Four Courts.

June 25. Macready informed that the British Cabinet has reconsidered its decision and instructed not to take any action against the Four Courts. Republican Headquarters, fearing punitive measures against the Catholics in Ulster as a result of the Wilson murder, decides to send an expedition to the North immediately.

June 26. Winston Churchill in the House of Commons describes the presence of Republican forces in the Four Courts as "a gross breach and defiance of the Treaty," and declares that "if through weakness, want of courage, or even some less creditable reason, it is not brought to an end, and a speedy end . . . we shall regard the Treaty as having been formally violated . . . and shall resume full liberty of action in any direction that may seem proper." Republican Headquarters seize sixteen motor-cars recently imported from Belfast by a Dublin firm, with the purpose of providing transport for the convoy going North. Leo Henderson, the Republican officer in charge of the raid, arrested by pro-Treaty forces. General J. J. O'Connell, pro-Treaty Deputy Chief-of-Staff, arrested by Republican forces as a reprisal.

June 27. Statement appears in Dublin morning papers from the Provisional Government commenting on the arrest of General O'Connell, and declaring that "the Government is determined that the country shall no longer be held up from the pursuit of its normal life and the re-establishment of its free institutions." Calls upon all citizens "to co-operate actively with it in the measures it is taking to ensure the public safety and to secure Ireland for the Irish people."

June 28. The Four Courts surrounded in the early hours of the morning. Instructions sent from London to Macready to hand over two eighteen-pounder field-guns to the Provisional Government. At 3.40 a.m. a note delivered to the Four Courts garrison on behalf of the Provisional Government demanding surrender before 4 a.m. At seven minutes past four the Four Courts bombarded with British guns.

Such, in brief, is the catalogue of happenings which took place in the last week of June, 1922. Nobody believes any longer that civil war came about because a pro-Treaty military officer was arrested by Republican troops on June 27th (a member of the Provisional Government admitted at the time that the decision to attack the Four Courts had been "practically taken" before that incident occurred), nor does it seem, looking back over a distance of twenty-two years, that there was any "inevitability" in the tragedy. All the elements that make for a civil conflict were present, it is true, and had been present from the moment the Treaty had been signed, but without outside pressure the explosion could have been avoided. It needs more than chaos and confusion, more even than a divided Army, to impel men, all of whom professed to have the same goal in view, to fly at one another's throats. The issue, clouded by passion and propaganda when it arose, is clear enough to-day. One section of Irishmen was given orders by a foreign Government to attack another section. The civil war was fought in a gallant attempt to ensure that the position which rendered such a happening possible would be swept away for ever and that the Irish nation would be left free to work out its own destinies unhampered by outside interference.

(VI)

De Valera, anxious and depressed, was driving from his home in Greystones to Dublin on the morning of June 28th. Before he had travelled many miles he was recognised by a farmer, who raised his hand to stop the car. "I wouldn't go into Dublin if I were you, sir," he said. "The Free Staters are shelling the Four Courts."

De Valera received the news in stunned silence. Then he shook his head. "Nonsense," he said. "I cannot believe it."

How true it was, how horribly true, he was soon to learn. That sunny June day in 1922 was the most tragic that he has ever known. It witnessed his descent into the inferno. The edifice to which the best and most generous minds in the country had given six years of patient building was going up in flames. One of the greatest disasters that can happen to a country had overtaken Ireland. The attack on the Four Courts meant civil war, the war between brothers with regard to the danger of which he had issued a prophetic warning. All the conferences, pacts and concessions of the previous six months had gone for nothing. Another surrender, a surrender infinitely worse than that of December 6th, had taken place, a period of renewed horror was opened up before the eyes of a stupefied people, and a cleavage was begun in the nation's ranks which would require the passing of many years to heal.

Many a man in his position would have stood aside from the conflict. He had been deposed from leadership and, even on the Republican side, control of events had been taken out of his hands. Some things had been done by men who shared his ideals of which he did not approve. His moderating counsels had not infrequently been rejected. Yet there was no room in his mind for hesitation. Of the ultimate, inescapable issue in the armed struggle that was beginning he had no doubt whatever. It was the same for which all Ireland's wars had been fought. Had the tragedy come from within, he would not, however deeply his sympathies had been engaged, have taken sides. But now he felt that he had no choice. At once he threw his lot in with the men who had been attacked, "the best and bravest of our nation," as he described them in a public statement that he issued.

What agony it cost him to make this decision only

he himself can compute. Less than twelve months before, happy, buoyant, confident, he had been able to say to a united Parliament: "I feel as a boy among boys. It is as a team we have worked and as a team we shall work. With gratitude I turn to you, my comrades and colleagues, who have conferred on me what I believe to be the highest honour that could be conferred at this moment on any human being: because here, at an issue of peace and war, I have been chosen to be leader." That his leadership was gone now was of little import: he could have retained it had he been willing to do the easy thing. What was tragic and terrifying was the blood feud that had begun, sweeping away unity and idealism, shaming Ireland in the face of the nations.

And yet, he must have thought, there were worse shames. If the nation, as a whole, had "sold out" in 1922; if the Republic, the symbol of nationhood for which so many of his comrades had given their lives, had been forsworn at the bidding of England; if sheer materialism had been allowed to carry the day, the shame would have been infinitely greater.

To the people of Ireland he said: "At the last meeting of Dail Eireann an Agreement was ratified which, if faithfully observed, would have given us an opportunity of working for internal peace and of taking steps which would make this nation strong against the only enemy it has to fear—the enemy from outside. At the bidding of the English this Agreement was broken and, at the bidding of the English, Irishmen are to-day shooting down on the streets of our capital brother Irishmen—old comrades in arms, companions in the recent struggle for Ireland's independence and its embodiment—the Republic.

"English propaganda will strive to lay the blame for this war on Irishmen, but the world outside must not be deceived. England's threat of war, that, and that alone, is responsible for the present situation. In face of England's threat some of our countrymen yielded. The men who are now being attacked by the forces of the Provisional Government are those who refuse to obey the order to yield—preferring to die."

Having issued that statement, de Valera immediately reported to his old battalion, the Third, which still contained the bulk of the men who had fought with him in Easter Week. His manifesto was refused publication by the controlled daily Press, but Erskine Childers, who had been given charge of Republican propaganda, rushed out printed copies. The other Republican leaders, including Brugha, Stack, and the Countess Markievicz, were already in the fight. Most significant happening of all was the arrival at Brigade Headquarters in Dublin of Robert Barton, one of the signatories of the Treaty. That sincere and gentle idealist, at least, had no doubt as to which side claimed the allegiance of Irishmen, who had been told during six years of bitter struggle—told by Griffith and Collins as well as by de Valera—that they were fighting for a Republic.

Once again, because de Valera had not taken the easy way out, because he had had the moral courage to do the hard and the bitter thing, he was made the chief target for opprobrium and abuse. He, and almost he alone, was held up to the peoples of the two islands and to the outside world as the man who had plunged Ireland into civil war. He was stigmatised as vain, fanatical and obstinate, as a man who had broken all the rules of fair dealing, as one who should be outlawed forever from the councils of statesmen. In Britain, the old jibe, applied in other years to Parnell and O'Connell, was revived: "He doesn't know what he wants and he won't be happy till he gets it"; and that in spite of the fact that no leader had ever stated what he wanted more consistently or more lucidly. Such attacks were the measure of his enemies' fear. They dreaded lest he should succeed in re-uniting the forces of the Republic and in giving public opinion the sense that resistance to the new oppression was morally right.

(VII)

The biographer of de Valera is not required to linger over the actual period of the civil war. De Valera had tried to prevent its coming and he had failed; he was equally powerless to shape its course.

From the military point of view the issue was hardly ever in doubt. At the outset there was not much to choose in number between the two sides, but the Republicans were badly equipped, they had no means of making good their losses in men or material, and they were the victims of an unceasing onslaught of propaganda to which they could make no effective reply. Erskine Childers's portable printing-press was a poor weapon with which to counter the flood of misrepresentation that flowed from the newspapers of two countries. The Catholic

Hierarchy, wielding an influence as potent now as in the days of the Parnell Split, condemned the Republicans with bell, book and candle; in their eyes the fight for the Republic was banditry, not war.

On the other hand, the Free State Army was receiving shiploads of arms and ammunition from Britain; they alone were equipped with artillery; and they alone had the means of moving troops by sea. Their ranks were rapidly augmented by a Call to Arms, issued by Collins (in the name of the Republic!) which was responded to by British ex-soldiers, R.I.C. men, and thousands of others who had always been hostile to the Republican Movement. The Free State forces were called the "National Army," whilst the newspapers were ordered to refer to the Republican troops as "Irregulars."

All this had its inevitable effect on public opinion. The largest section of the population, civilians set in the midst of a cruel internecine struggle in which life was being sacrificed and property destroyed, had only one desire. They wanted peace. No nation is capable of abstract thought in war time, and very little attempt was made, apart from the fighting men, to weigh the issues. There were, to be sure, angry Dubliners who, as they listened to the shells bursting on the Four Courts, asked why Collins should have taken this desperate step when the new Parliament was due to meet only two days later. But the majority of people, disillusioned and sick to death of dissensions that had lasted for six months and that had brought the whole national cause into disrepute, gave themselves over to gloom and apathy. Kept in ignorance by a strict military censorship of the final events which had precipitated the tragedy, they accepted what the pro-Treaty newspapers told them. And so it came about, by a curious irony, that the men who were responsible for the shelling of the Four Courts were held up as apostles of peace, as guardians of law and order.

The Four Courts fell after a siege that only lasted three days and its garrison surrendered. But the final explosion that shattered its walls and destroyed the records of centuries did not have the effect that its besiegers desired. Collins had made a bad miscalculation when he estimated that the fall of the building and the capture of Rory O'Connor would end hostilities. It was a beginning, not an end. Other leaders of the Republican forces, many of whom had disagreed with O'Connor's methods, were filled with rage at the spectacle of borrowed British guns being turned by Irishmen upon Irishmen and they swore a deep oath of vengeance. Within a few days fighting was general throughout the country.

De Valera made one final effort for peace. Having consulted with Brugha, Traynor and the other leaders at the Republican Headquarters in O'Connell Street, he dispatched not one, but—to make doubly sure—two messengers to Griffith and Collins with peace terms. Let the fighting cease; let the Republicans vacate their positions and go away with their arms; summon Dail Eireann instantly and let the whole matter be settled there once and for all. The offer was refused. One can see now that Collins could not have accepted it without going back on the position he had taken up. In the Dail the shelling of the Four Courts would inevitably have been made the subject of the closest investigation, and the last thing that members of the Provisional Government desired at that moment was a cross-examination regarding the relations between themselves and the British.

The positions in the O'Connell Street hotels, heavily bombarded, soon became untenable and Traynor gave an order for evacuation, leaving Cathal Brugha with a small garrison to carry on resistance as long as possible. Dublin was as good as lost and the plan was to withdraw as many men as possible to the country and organise guerilla warfare. On the fifth day of the fighting Traynor, de Valera, Stack and others made their escape, crossing the river to houses on the South Side. By this time the Gresham and the Granville hotels were demolished and there only remained the Hammam, where Brugha was still holding out. On the sixth day the building went on fire and a peremptory message was sent by Traynor to Brugha ordering him to surrender. But the girl messenger was unable to penetrate the cordon of attackers and no white flag appeared. But when evening came and the roof was seen to be ablaze Brugha called his handful together and told them to leave the building. Outside Collins's men were waiting. The little garrison marched out and gave themselves up, but still there was no sign of Brugha. At last he appeared in the doorway, a revolver in each hand, a little bulldog figure with smoke-begrimed face and defiant eyes, determined neither to give nor ask for quarter. A cry of "Surrender!" came from the troops, and from his own men, now lined up as prisoners, an even more anxious cry, "Cathal, surrender!" The answer was "No—never!" and the little man rushed forward into a hail of bullets from the levelled rifles. He fell, mortally wounded.

So far as Dublin was concerned that was the end, and there was jubilation in London. "They" (the troops of the Provisional Government), said Lord Birkenhead, "have destroyed in the course of their necessary operations some of the most beautiful and historic districts of Dublin. I, for one, rejoice that this task, painful, costly, bloody as it must ultimately prove, is being undertaken by those to whom it properly falls." Churchill spoke to the same effect. There was no note of regret that an imposed Treaty had brought to Ireland not peace, but bloodshed; no prophetic vision to enable British Ministers to see that what was being done so bloodily would some day have to be undone.

It was left to a Unionist and bitterly anti-Republican historian to make the fitting comment. "It is possible to regret," wrote Professor Alison Phillips, referring to de Valera's "Document No. 2, "that the British Government, having once made up its mind to surrender, did not frankly recognise the Irish Republic on some such terms as these. To have done so would not have exposed the Crown to any greater humiliation than it has suffered, nor Great Britain to any dangers from which the actual Treaty preserves her, while Ireland might have been spared the ruin, desolation and bloodshed of another year of fratricidal strife."

(VIII)

By the middle of August the first phase of the civil war was over. At the outset the Republicans were strongly entrenched in the South, where they held the counties of Waterford, Tipperary, Cork, Kerry, and most of Wexford. But they were fighting against great odds and one town after another had to be evacuated. As they retreated they burnt military barracks, blew up bridges and trenched roads. When, on August 11th, Fermoy fell, open warfare came to an end and the Republican divisions broke up into mobile columns, taking to the hills and adopting the guerilla tactics which had served them so well against the Black-and-Tans.

De Valera had joined Liam Lynch and the other Republican leaders in the South after Dublin had fallen and was given a post as Adjutant to Sean Moylan, Director of Operations (now Minister for Lands in de Valera's Cabinet). After the fall of Fermoy he realised that the fight was hopeless and he urged his view on the military leaders, declaring that its continuance would have no other effect than that of greatly aggravating the physical and spiritual wounds which the country had already suffered. His advice, given with all the earnestness he could command, was rejected, and for another eight months the struggle went on, increasing every day in bitterness, fought out to its pitiful end with all the savagery that has characterised civil war in all countries and at all times.

Before it was over many of the men who had led the independence movement had fallen.

Harry Boland, gay, boyish, debonair, close to the

affections of both Collins and de Valera, a *beau sabreur* of the revolutionary movement, fell within the first few weeks. Griffith, greatest name on the pro-Treaty side, first President of the Free State that he had done more than any other single man to call into being, died suddenly on August 12th. The passions and estrangements of the time did not prevent Erskine Childers—the one Republican journalist of his own stature—from paying him the tribute that his life-work deserved.

A little more than a week later Michael Collins, Chairman of the Provisional Government and Commander-in-Chief of the Free State Army, fell in a skirmish on a lonely road between Macroom and Bandon. A couple of days before, in an hotel at Skibbereen, he had confided to a friend that he was sick of the whole tragic business and that he was determined to bring it to a speedy end. "I'm going to see the Long Fellow," he declared (in the Irish idiom de Valera, on account of his many inches, was nicknamed the "Long Fellow" as the stalwart Collins was dubbed the "Big Fellow") "and fix it up." "What about the British?" he was asked. "To hell with the British!" he said. But the Long Fellow and the Big Fellow were fated never to meet again.

With the deaths of Collins and Griffith the civil war took on a more sinister complexion. Their successors had no desire to treat with the Long Fellow. William Cosgrave became head of the Provisional Government, of which Kevin O'Higgins, Minister for Home Affairs, was soon to emerge as the "strong man." Richard Mulcahy, in addition to holding the post of Commander-in-Chief of the

Army, remained Minister for Defence. Under this regime Republicans were outlawed, secret military courts established, and the execution of prisoners begun.

One of the first victims was Erskine Childers, the gentle intellectual, against whom an amazing "hate campaign" had been launched. All through the autumn he had been busy exposing the unconstitutional procedure of the Provisional Government—the abrogation of the functions of the Dail, the setting up of a military dictatorship, the abolition of the Republican Courts, and now he was singled out by Ministers of that Government as a chief target for attack. Referring to him in the Dail as "the Englishman, Erskine Childers," O'Higgins accused him of "steadily, callously, and ghoulishly striking at the heart of this nation." In November he was captured in the house of his cousin, Robert Barton, and executed with indecent haste. The charge against him was that he had been found "in unlawful possession of a Colt automatic pistol" (the pistol in question was a small one which had been presented to him by Michael Collins).

Winston Churchill expressed his joy at the capture of the man whom he termed "that murderous renegade, Erskine Childers," and concluded an amazing reference with the words: "Such as he is may all who hate us be."

Of the many acts of violence employed to suppress the Republic in 1922 the judicial murder of Erskine Childers was, perhaps, the least defensible. Gavan Duffy answered Churchill and O'Higgins when he said that "Childers was a great Irishman, born of an Irish mother, brought up in this country, a man

(D1238)

who consecrated his life in later years to the independence of Ireland." And, speaking as a lawyer, he declared that the execution was "something contrary to natural justice as understood in every part of the world."

Less than a month later Rory O'Connor, Liam Mellowes, Joseph McKelvey, and Richard Barrett—the four senior officers of the Four Courts garrison who had been prisoners of war for five months—were executed as a reprisal for the shooting of a Free State Deputy. Once again Gavan Duffy spoke words which were long remembered. Those responsible for such a deed could not, he suggested, be "in a normal frame of mind." It was, no doubt, true. Entrenched in their heavily-guarded, sandbagged offices in Merrion Street, the seven members of the Free State Executive were waging a war on the Republic as ruthless as anything the country had experienced in the days of the Black-and-Tans. They were refusing their opponents belligerent rights, and the word "rebel," which they constantly employed in their proclamations, was being given a significance never before known in Irish history. Victims of a war hysteria, they were unable, it would seem, to grasp the import of what they were doing or to realise the indefensible character of a campaign from which they had banished not only clemency, but chivalry. Future Irish historians will have for their task the solution of the psychological problem that inevitably confronts the student of the civil war—how a group of men who had fought and worked for the Republican ideal came in time to look upon it as no more than an opium dream and why they branded as outlaws former comrades who had kept the faith.

To de Valera the whole thing was torture. His own life not worth a moment's purchase if captured, he moved with the rest of the Republican leaders from one hiding-place to another in the fastnesses of the South, bearded as a disguise. Oftentimes he would wander, alone with the tempest of his thoughts, among the woods and boulders of the mountainside, seeking a way out where way there was none. The news that reached him was always bad news—reverses everywhere, mounting horrors, the deaths of friends.

Once he risked a visit to Mallow to call upon Wiliam O'Brien, almost the last survivor of the great Parliamentarians, whom he found sympathetic, but critical. "Ah, if you had only gone to London yourself!" said the old man with a sigh.

The cause of all the trouble

(IX)

A week or two before Childers's execution the Republican Army Executive called upon de Valera to reconstitute the Government and to form a Council of State. Unless the Army was to control Republican policy, something of the kind had to be done. On October 25th the Republican Deputies met in secret in Dublin and de Valera was unanimously elected "President of the Republic and Chief Executive of the State." To the Emergency Government which he formed the Army Executive pledged its allegiance, without, however, surrendering its claims to decide the issue of peace or war.

On that issue de Valera continued to concentrate

all his influence. A prolongation of the conflict could, he was convinced, have no other effect than that of plunging the country into deeper ruin. Of a Republican victory in the field there was no longer any hope. The pro-Treaty Party, assured of the support of the British Cabinet, held all the cards in its hands. It controlled administration, propaganda and election machinery. It had a large army and the means of adding to it. From Britain it was able to secure all the supplies of war material that it needed. Its Parliament was in a position to implement all the decrees that it passed, whereas the re-constituted Republican Government, prevented from functioning, could do little more than protest against the seizure of power by the pro-Treaty leaders. Time and again de Valera, fighting strenuously for peace, put the hard facts of the situation before the militant Republicans, but all to no purpose. During several weary months he was compelled to look at what was happening through—as he phrased it himself—" a wall of glass." In a public statement that he issued in January, 1923, he deplored " the ever rising tide of bitterness, the vanishing of the common dreams of regeneration and reconstruction, the lowering of national credit and prestige." But the Republican soldiers still refused to accept defeat and the pro-Treaty Party refused to accept anything short of unconditional surrender.

Before the spring was over, however, the struggle had virtually burnt itself out. In April Liam Lynch, the high-minded and chivalrous Chief of Staff of the Republican Army, was killed in a fight near Clonmel, and the blow took the heart out of the fighting men

To Commandant Lynch, one of the leaders who had striven arduously for peace before the bombardment of the Four Courts, de Valera paid a moving tribute in an address he issued to the Army.

> "Faced in arms," he wrote, "by former comrades who have deserted from your side, your task is a hard one and a sad. It is a task which only heroes would venture. You have to fling yourselves across the stampede of a nation. But it is better to die nobly as your Chief has died, than live as slaves. Your cause is immortal; weariness from the exacting struggle, false teachers, temporary losses and defeats may defer, but cannot prevail against the ultimate triumph."

What was happening was, indeed, "the stampede of a nation." People were crying, "Give us peace, peace, peace at any price!" The country was at the point of exhaustion, physically and spiritually. It craved for a long rest from war, for normal conditions of living, for stable government; and, for the moment, it did not care very much who governed so long as they had the power to impose their will and to restore order.

De Valera was painfully aware of all this. The Republic had been defeated. With the active assistance of Britain a Government subordinate to that of Britain had been established with a jurisdiction over twenty-six Irish counties. It controlled an army which was in possession of every town and every position of strategic importance. It controlled the police, the judiciary, the civil service. More vital still was the fact that it had gained the allegiance of the majority of the people, however reluctantly given.

To continue the struggle any longer would be madness. All that was left of the Republican Army was scattered remnants, ragged and short of equipment, harried from one mountainside to another, denied all the recognised rights of warfare. The jails and internment camps were bursting with prisoners. Executions were an everyday occurrence. The civilian population dared not, even if it were willing, give the Republicans the help and the sympathy bestowed so wholeheartedly in the fight of 1920-21. All the efforts of intermediaries to end the disastrous struggle were summarily rejected by Free State Ministers; even an envoy from the Vatican was received with scant courtesy.

In the end the soldiers yielded to the advice de Valera had so often given them. Months before, in a letter to the Republican Party, he had insisted that the Army Executive should publicly take responsibility for a continuance of the struggle and thus end the pretence of the pro-Treaty propagandists that the politicians—men like himself and Childers—were inciting the Army. Now that the inevitable end had come he put his signature along with that of Frank Aiken—who had succeeded Liam Lynch as Chief of Staff—to a "Cease Fire" order. It took effect on April 30th, the seventh anniversary of the day in Easter Week on which he and his men had surrendered at Boland's Mills.

CHAPTER ELEVEN

In the Wilderness

"No Government can be long secure without a formidable Opposition."

—DISRAELI.

(I)

THE Civil War was over. The defeated Republicans dumped their arms and returned to their homes. The country lay stunned and silent.

In May, de Valera, still in hiding, opened peace negotiations. They broke down on the two questions of the Oath and of the disposal of arms. In the Dail the leader of the Labour Party, Thomas Johnson, strongly supported de Valera's proposals, and declared that his Party, in taking the Oath, regarded it as no more than a formality. Gavan Duffy took a similar line. The Oath clause in the Treaty, he said, must go. There was no enthusiasm for it in any quarter and its retention could have no other effect than that of driving sincere Republicans into "the wilderness of unconstitutional opposition."

But the Free State Government refused to budge an inch. "You will find," said President Cosgrave, "that the party which has promoted disorder is prepared to accept peace only if they are guaranteed a lease of political life. We are not going to guarantee them that lease."

That declaration closed the door to peace with a

bang. The "Cease Fire" order had been obeyed, it is true, but Republicans had no intention of accepting a Pax Britannica. So long as the obnoxious Oath debarred them from using constitutional methods to advance from the status conferred by the Treaty to full independence, there would be no surrender of arms.

In a final message to the Army de Valera said: "Military victory must be allowed to rest for the moment with those who have destroyed the Republic. Other means must be sought to safeguard the nation's rights. . . . Seven years of intense effort have exhausted our people. If they have turned aside and have not given you the active support which alone could have brought you victory, it is because they saw overwhelming forces against them; they are weary and need a rest. A little time and you will see them recover and rally again to the standard."

It was the man of faith speaking. The virtue of a statesman is not that he sees a splendid image which nobody else has seen, but that he sees clearly something which the mass of the people only see dimly. The Republic was defeated, but it was not dead. Once an idea has taken possession of the spirit of a nation it cannot be eradicated by methods so crude as those of brute force. To de Valera the gospel that had been preached, not only by himself, but by men who had seen the light and yet wavered, seemed to be the firmest truth that life contained, and he clung to it with an intensity and an unwavering belief that no logic could shake.

At that moment he was encompassed by disaster—disaster which men of lesser courage regarded as irreparable. A country sunk in apathy and despair, exhausted and disunited, slowly and painfully piecing together the broken fragments of its daily existence; a Government which, in the struggle for its life, had been pushed farther and farther into the arms of the ancient enemy and which was crying halt to the march of a nation; a movement and an ideal discredited; leaders whom the country could ill afford to spare lying in their graves; gaols and internment camps filled with men who believed they had been betrayed; himself the central target in an increasing campaign of odium and vilification—such was the prospect that faced Eamon de Valera in the summer of 1923.

But his courage did not fail him even in that dark hour. The edifice of which he had been the chief architect lay in ruins, but already he was planning a rebuilding.

(II)

In August a General Election took place and de Valera decided to contest it, making use of the Sinn Fein organisation, of which he was still President.

He made his policy clear. If the Republicans were given a majority, they would govern the country on Sinn Fein lines as in 1919, refusing to co-operate with England in any way until England was ready to make such an arrangement as would render a permanent settlement possible. If elected in a minority, the Republican Party would refuse to take any oath of allegiance to the King of England and would meet outside the Dail and act as a separate body. When the cry "A vote for de Valera is a vote for war" was raised by supporters of the Government, he said: "The war, so far as we are concerned, is finished. We intend to devote ourselves to reform and to education and to developing the economic and material strength of the nation."

Sinn Fein entered the campaign under difficulties greater than ever before. Its leaders and organisers were in gaol or in hiding. Its candidates were still "wanted" men, liable to arrest if they appeared in public. Almost the entire Press and the whole of the Catholic Hierarchy were bitterly anti-Republican. The result of the election, keen observers prophesied, would be the virtual extinction of the Republican movement.

Seldom has a prediction been more completely falsified. In spite of all the difficulties of the time the Republicans won 44 seats as against the Free State Party's 63. Everything considered, it was an astonishing result and one with which de Valera had no reason to be dissatisfied. If on the morrow of a civil war that had brought tragedy and disillusionment to the nation, so large a proportion of a war-weary people still had faith in the cause, there could be no doubt about the future.

But by the time the results of the polls were made known de Valera was in gaol. Standing once again for his old constituency, he had declared after nomination that he would go amongst the people of Clare and that "nothing but a bullet would stop him." When it was announced that he would address a meeting in Ennis on August 15th the excitement was intense. More than a year had passed since his last public appearance and now he was an outlaw. What would happen, people asked, if he mounted a platform in the "free" election which Mr. Cosgrave had promised the country?

When Lady Day came every road in Clare led to Ennis. An army of pressmen descended upon the town and the historic market-place was filled with de Valera's supporters. Few amongst them believed that he would succeed in reaching the platform, for every approach was held by Free State troops. But, punctual to the hour, he appeared in the street, driving through cheering crowds in an open car, whilst a band struck up the "Soldier's Song." Looking worn and haggard, but resolute as ever, he mounted the platform and surveyed the square that had been the scene of his own and of O'Connell's triumphs. Raising his hand for silence he began to speak, first in Irish, then in English. On the outskirts of the crowd an armoured car and a file of soldiers could be seen approaching. Scuffles began to take place, but above the commotion de Valera's voice was heard:

"I have come to tell you that I have never stood for destruction. I have never stood for brother's hand being raised against brother. I have always preached one gospel, the one and only gospel, that if we stand together and are united, we can achieve complete independence . . ."

A rifle-volley crashed into the middle of his next sentence. The soldiers were firing over the heads of the crowd, but so wildly that several people fell wounded. Another volley followed, and still another. A wild stampede took place, and when some of those on the platform started to rush for safety, de Valera, who had vainly shouted to the soldiers to stop firing, was thrown to the ground.

When he was seen to rise to his feet uninjured there was a renewed outburst of cheering. The soldiers appeared to be making ready to fire again when he advanced towards them and stopped them with a gesture. He was arrested immediately, bundled into a car and hurried under heavy guard to Dublin, where he was placed in solitary confinement in Arbour Hill Prison.

The Free State Government had, as an English newspaper put it, "elected itself at the point of the bayonet." But one constituency, at least, registered its opinion of what was being done in unmistakable terms. When the results were announced de Valera was still the Man for Clare. He had polled over 17,000 votes, more than twice the number given to his formidable opponent, Professor Eoin MacNeill.

(III)

When a man is in solitary confinement he has plenty of time to think. Michael Davitt planned the Land League whilst a convict in the stone quarries of Portland and emerged from prison with a clear-cut policy that was destined to shape the course of events in Ireland for the next twenty years. De Valera's thinking was equally fruitful.

The position he had to face was, despite the confusion of the time, clear enough in its essentials. The Republican cause had, for the time being, been heavily defeated. The Free State, however insecure its foundations, had been established. The country needed a long rest from war and turmoil. A majority of the people had accepted the new Government, and Republicans, though they could not co-operate with that Government, would have to recognise the fact of its existence. A resumption of the war was unthinkable.

It was evident, then, that a fresh beginning would have to be made. Neither of the two great objectives of the age-long Nationalist movement—independence and unity—had been attained. Partition was in force and Ireland was still part of the British Empire. Not only that, but already Free State Ministers appeared to be glorying in the fact. During the Treaty debates one of them, General Mulcahy, had declared: "None of us wants this Treaty. None of us wants the Crown. None of us wants the representative of the Crown. None of us wants our harbours occupied. None of us wants Partition." If he had accepted all those unwanted things it was, he said, because the alternative was the bitter one of hopeless war. But now that the Treaty had been fought for and the State which emerged from it established, there was a growing tendency on the part of its supporters to hold it up to the Irish people, not as the next best thing, but as the ultimate good, the fount from which all blessings flowed. "We walked into the Empire with our heads up!" declared Kevin O'Higgins. ("With your hands up!" retorted the Republicans). Loyalty to the Imperial institutions in Ireland began to be preached, however cautiously at first, as if it were loyalty to Ireland.

De Valera took account of all this. The Cosgrave Government was indebted to Britain for its success in the Civil War and the debt lay like a dead weight around its neck, making any further advance on its part in the direction of the National ideal almost impossible. The Treaty that had been claimed to be a stepping-stone had proved to be a millstone. So long as the issue continued to be one of Treaty *versus* Republic, the Government which took its stand upon the Treaty was bound to be anti-Republican. But the people were not anti-Republican; they were merely war-weary. Therein lay the hope for the future and the foundation on which a new policy could be built.

The cells at Arbour Hill are about sixteen feet by eight. A prisoner can take five paces each way. High up there is a small barred window through which a small glimpse of the sky can be seen and—if the cell is fortunately placed—the branch of a tree overtopping the lofty boundary wall of the exercise yard. Day after day de Valera paced up and down his cell, pausing once in a while to look up at the little window, through which no sunlight ever shone. (How many miles he covered during the eleven months of his imprisonment would be a simple calculation for his mathematical mind). His gaolers found him a satisfactory prisoner: one who accepted the deadly daily routine with philosophical serenity and who looked for no favours or privileges. Beyond the high boundary wall were the graves of his old comrades, the men who had been executed in Easter Week, Pearse, MacDonagh, Clarke, and the rest. He thought of them during the long night watches, of the high adventure on which they and he had set out, of the tragic interruption which had come to delay the achievement of the ideals for which they had laid down their lives. The words of the Easter Week Proclamation came back to him: " In the name of God and of the dead generations from which she receives her old tradition of nationhood, Ireland summons her children to her flag and strikes for freedom . . . We proclaim the Irish Republic as a Sovereign Independent State, and we pledge our lives to the cause of its freedom, of its welfare, and of its exaltation among the nations."

The idealism that informed these words had, he knew, been crushed. The violence of emotion had produced a natural reaction. The poetry and philosophy of the revolutionary era were experiencing a set-back. Even amongst thoughtful and unselfish people—people whose fundamental sympathies were never in doubt—there was a craving for a long interval that would be free from the hardships and anxieties of the period that had just ended. The natural temper of men in such circumstances was towards the enjoyment of what had been gained—and undoubtedly something had been gained—by the limited measure of independence that had been achieved. They wanted to go about their business, to cultivate material prosperity, to breathe freely, to have rest from revolution.

Recognising that the triumph of the principles of the revolutionary era, though postponed, was inevitable, de Valera set about formulating a policy that would have an appeal in the altered circumstances of the time. To heal the wounds of the civil war, to educate the people, to keep the Republican ideal constantly before their minds, to offer them a programme of self-reliance and self-sufficiency in national affairs, to press for a broad scheme of social reform—these were the fundamentals of the policy which he worked out during the eleven months that he spent in gaol.

(IV)

In July, 1924, he was released. In the previous October a mass hunger-strike of untried Republican prisoners had taken place in gaols and internment camps throughout the country, and at one time, after more than thirty days during which they had refused food, thousands of men were in danger of death through starvation. De Valera took no part in the strike, which caused three deaths and which failed pitiably to achieve its purpose. When it was over the prisoners were released in batches, the rank and file first, the leaders later.

Free State Ministers, now firmly entrenched, were inclined to be contemptuous of their opponents. De Valera, they believed, was utterly discredited. The man who, as one of them asserted, had "cost the country a civil war and seventeen million pounds," was not likely to stage a come-back. They proclaimed "a long farewell to rainbow-chasing," declared that they were determined "to get on with the nation's work," and offered the people, as a first instalment, an ambitious scheme under which the Shannon would be harnessed to supply the entire country with electricity for light and power.

But before the year was out a crisis sprang up which gravely damaged their prestige and which helped to turn the tide, however slowly, in de Valera's favour. Two Articles of the Treaty—Articles Five and Twelve—still remained to be implemented. Article Five provided for the setting up of a Commission to deal with the financial relations between Britain and the Free State. Article Twelve provided for a Boundary Commission "to determine, in accordance with the wishes of the inhabitants, the boundaries between Northern Ireland and the rest of Ireland."

During the Treaty debates Article Twelve had been used with deadly effect against de Valera and his supporters. Out of the Boundary Commission, Griffith had declared, unity would almost certainly emerge. It would, Collins had promised, add "immense anti-Partition areas" to the territory of the Free State. The harassed victims of Six-County rule in the counties of Tyrone and Fermanagh, in South Down and South Armagh, in Derry city and Newry town, in all of which places there were Catholic and Nationalist majorities, believed that it would reunite them with their fellow-countrymen across the Border. But, in the event, the Boundary Commission proved the worst of fiascos.

Sir James Craig from the beginning refused to have anything to do with it. The Six-County Government declined to appoint a representative, and Craig, deaf to all appeals, and safe in the knowledge that—despite the plain wording of the Treaty—he had the backing of the all-powerful British Conservative Party, contented himself with a parrot-like reiteration of the old Carsonite slogan, "Not an inch!" The Boundary dispute dragged on for the best part of two years. The British appointed Mr. J. R. Fisher to act for the Six Counties, and nominated Mr. Justice Feetham, a judge of the South African Supreme Court, as Chairman of the Commission. The Free State representative was Professor Eoin MacNeill. As soon as the Commission started its sittings, and while the matter to be decided was still *sub judice*, a campaign was launched in Britain to influence its findings. Lord Birkenhead, one of the signatories of the Treaty, declared that the purpose of Article Twelve was to preserve to Sir James Craig's Government jurisdiction over the whole Six Counties. Lloyd George, to whose ingenuity the Boundary Commission was primarily due, agreed with Birkenhead; the whole thing was, in his view, "a sectarian quarrel in a corner of Ireland"; his agreement with Collins and Griffith concerned nothing more than "an exchange of parishes." Sir Laming Worthington Evans, another signatory of the Treaty, stated that it was never intended that there should be "large transfers"; any British Government which attempted to enforce such an interpretation of Article Twelve would, he asserted, be guilty of "supreme folly." Lord Selborne, a Unionist leader in the House of Lords, published a secret pledge given by the British Government to the Six-County leaders at the time of the 1920 Partition Act, to the effect that the Border would remain unchanged "for good and all."

Collins and Griffith were in their graves and could not give the lie to the British signatories of the Treaty. They could not tell Lloyd George that, if he had not given them repeated assurances that the Boundary Commission would rectify the Border "in accordance with the wishes of the inhabitants," they would never have signed the Treaty or recommended it to their countrymen. It was left to de Valera to speak for them, which he did by publishing the letter written to him by Griffith during the negotiations, in which Griffith quoted Lloyd George's promise to the effect that, if the

R

Six-County Government refused to accept the Boundary Commission "he would fight, summon Parliament, dissolve, or pass an Act establishing an All-Ireland Parliament."

Well, the Six-County Government had refused, and they were backed up in their refusal by the very man who had given that pledge. What now? all Ireland was asking. What action would the Free State Government, who had proclaimed time and again that they were trustees for the policy of Collins and Griffith, take? The answer to that question, when it came at the end of 1925, was one that shocked the country.

No attempt was made by the Commission to hold a plebiscite, as demanded by the Nationalists in the Six Counties. Not that one was really necessary, for both the census returns and the results of numerous elections gave the Commission practically all the data it required. But it would have been a natural proceeding. MacNeill resigned from the Commission in November and disclosed that a Majority Report was being prepared which was in flagrant opposition to the provisions of Article Twelve. Judge Feetham, yielding to the pressure brought to bear upon him by British politicians and the British Unionist Press, was permitting political considerations to over-ride the wishes of the inhabitants. His view was that "the Act of 1920 and the time which had elapsed had created a *status quo*." He was contemplating nothing save minor adjustments of the Border.

Fierce anger blazed up in Ireland. Nationalists of all shades of opinion called upon the Cosgrave Government to act quickly and firmly. "Every device that cunning and chicanery could suggest," declared the *Irish Independent*—then, as now, a bitter critic of de Valera—" has been employed, openly and furtively, to prejudice the Commission," and it went on to say that if Article Twelve had been assumed capable of bearing the interpretation placed on it by Judge Feetham the Treaty " would never have received five minutes' consideration in this country." In face of the storm that had arisen, Free State Ministers hurried to London. There, it was hoped, they would present a united front to the British on the question of Partition and, if rebuffed, return home, rally the nation and renew the struggle. De Valera, however, was not hopeful. There had been so many surrenders that another was not unlikely. He gave it as his opinion that " the people of South Down, South Armagh, as well as Tyrone and Fermanagh are to be sacrificed," and he added that " if there are any people left who still believe in the Treaty policy they will be disillusioned."

His prophecy was fulfilled to the letter. In the settlement which emerged from the London conference both the Boundary Commission and the Financial Commission were thrown overboard. Partition—the Partition of the 1920 Act—was swallowed, hook, line and sinker. The Six Counties were handed over to Craig intact and the provision for a possible Council of Ireland, included both in the 1920 Act and the Treaty—the last shadowy safeguard of Ireland's geographical and political unity—was abolished.

The financial settlement was equally calamitous. Article Five, like Article Twelve, was capable of being given either an "Irish" or an "English" interpretation. "The Irish Free State," it read, "shall assume liability for the service of the Public Debt of the United Kingdom . . . in such proportion as may be fair and equitable, having regard to any just claims on the part of Ireland by way of set-off or counter-claim." Sums of great magnitude were involved. The British claimed from Ireland a sum amounting to roughly £160,000,000. Ireland's counter-claim was even more enormous. Taking their stand on the findings of two British Commissions, the Childers Commission of 1896 and the Primrose Commission of 1912, both of which found that Ireland had been grossly overtaxed ever since the Act of Union, Nationalists had assessed the sum owing from Britain as not less than £300,000,000. The second clause of the London Agreement cancelled the Free State's liability, but failed entirely to take into account the credit balance on Ireland's side.

Such was the agreement that the Free State Ministers brought home from London and which, in a public statement, they "confidently recommended to the Irish people." The people of the Free State, President Cosgrave asserted, had secured "a damned good bargain." "We have sown the seeds of peace. The settlement closes all financial questions which were left open by the Treaty of 1921." Neither statement, as time was to prove, bore any justification. In the eighteen years that have since elapsed Partition has remained a running sore that has brought untold misery to more than one-third of the population of the Six Counties, that has left a dismembered Ireland weakened economically and industrially, and that has poisoned the stream of friendship that might have begun to flow naturally between the peoples of Britain and Ireland. Nor was the financial settlement in any better case. Apart entirely from its inherent injustice, it was not, in spite of Cosgrave's assertion, final. The British, as we shall see, were to make a further claim, and that claim would not be disputed by Free State Ministers.

"An unmitigated betrayal," was the verdict of the Irish Labour Party on the Agreement. But Sir James Craig, who had taken part in the London conference, returned to Belfast "with feelings of rejoicing and relief."

(v)

De Valera and his followers, prevented by the Oath of Allegiance to the British King from entering the Dail, could only look on helplessly at what was happening. The protest that they made, registering their "abhorrence of the proposed dismemberment of their country," went unheeded. Nevertheless, the tide was turning. In by-elections that occurred about this time Republicans won four seats and de Valera's Party now numbered forty-eight. Cosgrave's numbered sixty-three. Slowly but surely the gap was being bridged.

In the October of 1924, whilst the Boundary crisis was maturing, there had been a general election in Britain and the Six Counties. De Valera travelled north to address a meeting in favour of the Republican candidate for County Down, but was arrested at Newry—which is in the partitioned area —by members of the Royal Ulster Constabulary, and escorted back across the Border. Refusing to obey an order which denied him the right of free travel in his own country, he made his way through Sligo and Donegal, eluding the guards who had been placed at all Border posts, to Derry City, where he was again arrested. When brought to trial before a Six-County Magistrate he refused to plead, holding, as he declared, that " this Court is the creature of a foreign power and therefore has not the sanction of the Irish people." He was sentenced to two months' imprisonment and lodged in Belfast Gaol. Of all his prison experiences it is the one of which he retains the most unhappy memories. The treatment he received was bad in the extreme and his health was temporarily impaired as a result. But he found a little solace in making an acquaintance with the poems of Francis Thompson, of which he managed to secure a copy. The ascetic temper and mystical prepossessions of the English Catholic poet suited his mood of depression.

It was probably the Boundary surrender that first shook his faith in the wisdom of the abstention policy. With every day that passed the Imperial shackles were being more firmly riveted on the country. Free State Ministers were attending levees at Buckingham Palace in Court dress; the Viceregal Lodge was a symbol of Imperialism; the Senate was a highly reactionary body; the whole stream of social life in Ireland was being insidiously diverted in the direction of anti-Republicanism. " Republicanism—*voila l'ennemi!* was the official motto of the time, even if it was regarded as a little premature to shout it openly in the Press or at the hustings. Repression continued to be the order of the day. A Treasonable Offences Act was passed through the Dail containing provisions so drastic that even Government supporters protested. Raids, searches, beatings and arrests continued unceasingly.

Republicans were not the only section of the Irish people to cry out against what was happening. The Army became restive, and a group of senior officers, headed by Major-Generals Tobin and Cullen, two of the men who had been intimately associated with Collins, mutinied. They had, they declared in a public statement, accepted the Treaty in the same spirit and for the same purpose as Michael Collins had—"as an advantageous position on the battlefield from which full independence could be won." They accused the Government of retreating from the ideals of independence and unity and called for a complete reversal of policy. The Government took alarm, temporised, and then struck swiftly and with force. The mutineers were silenced, but they were supported in their protest by one member of the Cosgrave Government, Joseph McGrath, Minister for Trade and Commerce, who resigned, along with eight other Deputies.

With only the small Labour Party to speak for them in the Dail, Republicans were, to all intents and purposes, disenfranchised, and, as a result, penalised. A political test was rigidly enforced and persons who refused to make a declaration of allegiance to the Free State Constitution were debarred from employment in the public services. Big business interests, which were almost all anti-Republican, discriminated in the same way, with the consequence that large numbers of Republicans found themselves unable to make a living in their own country. "There will be no Wild Geese this time," de Valera had declared, referring to the historic exodus which filled the armies of Europe with Irishmen after the fall of Limerick in 1691, but poverty and despair accomplished what the Black-and-Tans had not been able to do. By 1925 young Republicans were emigrating in thousands.

How to canalise all the dissatisfied and disillusioned elements of the nation into a stream that would sweep away the barriers that were being erected against the nation's further advance was the problem that de Valera now had to face. It was a problem full of complexities. So long as Republican Deputies remained outside the Dail the Party could do little more than meet in isolation, pass resolutions, and register protests. De Valera himself made it clear that he would enter the Dail and make use of the parliamentary machine if the test Oath were abolished, but many of his followers held that such a step would involve recognition of the Free State and did not hesitate to brand it as "treason" to the Republic. A large section of the Sinn Fein organisation and many of the I.R.A. leaders held that view. Were the Republicans, then, to be condemned to remain in the political wilderness for another generation? Was the long barren aftermath of the Parnell Split to be repeated? Those were questions that de Valera was turning over and over in his mind.

CHAPTER TWELVE

Victory

> " The people know that they need in their representative much more than talent, namely, the power to make his talent trusted."
>
> —EMERSON.

(I)

AT the end of 1925 the I.R.A. withdrew its support from de Valera and in the spring of 1926 a majority of the Executive of Sinn Fein followed suit. The Republican Left-Wingers in both organisations declared that they were prepared to spend the rest of their lives in the wilderness (which de Valera, if he could see an honourable way out, had no intention of doing) rather than recognise the Free State by making use of its established position. But the Republican leader had made up his mind. In April he launched a new organisation, to which he gave the name Fianna Fail.

It was to be a forward movement on strictly constitutional lines, designed, as its founder said, "to get the nation out of the paralysing Treaty dilemma." Its primary objects were threefold: (i) to unite the nation in a policy of cutting the bonds of British control one by one until the full internal sovereignty of the Twenty-six Counties was established; (ii) to rebuild the nation's structure on the basis of Irish culture and good economics; (iii) with a free and united Twenty-six Counties in existence to undertake the task of reuniting the people of the Partitioned area with the rest of Ireland. The vigorous economic policy that was foreshadowed included a revival of native industries under the shelter of protective tariffs and a revolution in agricultural methods under which the old ranching system would be replaced by tillage.

When he founded Fianna Fail de Valera was forty-four, and there were many, even amongst those sympathetic towards his aims, who believed that he would be an old man before he gained any of his chief objectives. The Treaty position had, so far as surface appearances went, been firmly consolidated. All executive authority in the Free State was vested in the British Crown. The King's Representative sat in the Viceregal Lodge like an English Viceroy of old. This Representative had the right to veto legislation and to appoint Ministers and judges. The Courts were subject to the decisions of the British Privy Council. Irish ports were in the hands of British naval forces and the Free State was bound to give Britain any facilities asked for in time of war. Every member of the Dail was required to take an oath of allegiance to the British King.

That was the position, humiliating to all who believed in Ireland's nationhood and perilous in the light of the international situation, which Fianna Fail set out to abolish. De Valera did not underestimate the difficulties which confronted him. From Free State Ministers he could expect no support. Tied by the provisions of the Treaty, they would strenuously oppose the fulfilment of ideals which once were theirs as well as his. From the extreme Left, the believers in physical force, he would receive no assistance. Banking interests and firms that had trade connections with Britain were also hostile. Even amongst the plain people there were many who, fearful lest the challenge of Fianna Fail should provoke fresh trouble with Britain, were slow to follow the new banner. They were only too painfully aware, since the Black-and-Tan War, of what trouble with Britain might mean.

Yet from the moment of its inception Fianna Fail began to make rapid headway. The " small men " of the country—the small working farmers, the small shopkeepers, the rural labourers, the artisans and clerks of the towns and cities, the University students, the younger section of the intelligentsia—had never been greatly in love with the bourgeois Government of which Mr. Cosgrave was the head and of which Mr. Kevin O'Higgins was the strong man. It was not merely that this Government had donned the Imperialist robe and was governing by methods of repression; that it appeared to be delimiting the national ideal to a share in an equality of nations within the British Empire; that it drew its party funds in the main from big business and from men of wealth who had always been enemies of the national cause; that its civil service was largely controlled by officials who scarcely appeared to be aware that they were no longer bound to report to Whitehall; or that the Senate was filled with relics of the decayed Anglo-Irish ascendancy class, whose spiritual home was London, not Dublin. An even greater cause of resentment was the fact that no attempt was being made to heal the wounds of the civil war or to pave the way for a position in which even moderate Republicans could take part in political life on constitutional lines. People saw de Valera being attacked week in and week out in language that was inexcusably brutal (and they also observed that, through all the campaign of scurrility, its victim, with an amazing power of self-command, kept a decent tongue in his head). They resented the fact that very little attempt was being made to put Arthur Griffith's policy of industrial self-sufficiency into operation, that social legislation fell woefully short of the needs of the community, that, in effect, the Cosgrave regime was as conservative in its policy and outlook as any Tory government in Britain. More and more they became attracted by a programme which promised to unite the nation, to assuage bitterness, to make Ireland economically self-contained, to speed up land division, to multiply tillage farms, to provide better houses for the workers, and, generally, to lay the foundations of a new Christian social system.

(II)

All through 1926 the campaign for the abolition of the Oath went ahead unceasingly and it brought many recruits to the ranks of Fianna Fail. Free State Ministers, however, were inclined to be contemptuous about the whole business. Why bother about the Oath? Was it not, when all was said and done, an "empty formality"? Let the country get on with its work. They, the Ministers, were busy attending Imperial Conferences in London, where they were succeeding in enlarging the scope of Dominion independence and establishing, as they claimed, a position under which the Free State was becoming master of its own destinies. At home they were busy reorganising agriculture, improving the quality of exported Irish produce, and making tentative beginnings for an industrial revival. Above all, they were establishing law and order. What more did the country want?

As it happened, the country wanted a good deal. If the Free State's "Dominion" status was all that Ministers claimed it to be, why not use it to abolish the Oath and give the second largest political party in the State an opportunity of entering the Dail? Intelligent citizens were well aware that there could be no stability in national affairs so long as a Government, committed to a repressive policy and with no Opposition save the small Labour Party, remained in power. Many of them began to suspect that Ministers were less concerned with the sanctity of the Constitution than with keeping de Valera and his followers in the wilderness.

Their suspicions were soon confirmed. Article 47 of the Constitution made special provision for the initiation of Bills by a Plebiscite and Article 48 provided for a Referendum. De Valera set about obtaining the number of signatures required—75,000—with the purpose of having an Abolition of the Oath Bill referred to the people. About the same time Dan Breen, noted guerilla chieftain in the War of Independence and uncompromising Republican, took the Oath—"just to show what he thought of it"—entered the Dail and introduced a similar Bill. Cosgrave refused it even a first reading, on the ground that it conflicted with the Treaty and the Constitution. Immediately afterwards, he rushed legislation through the Dail by which he abolished Articles 47 and 48, thus rendering a Referendum impossible.

There was an immediate outcry in the country. Was every avenue by which Republicans could enter political life on constitutional lines to be barred? Was the Constitution to be regarded as sacrosanct whenever the Government wished to invoke it and mutilated whenever it provided a loophole for Republicans? Labour, which had become more and more critical of Governmental methods, protested vehemently, and declared that, in the circumstances, the abolition of the right of Referendum was "monstrous."

In June, 1927, there was a General Election and the people were given their first opportunity of voting on the Fianna Fail policy. De Valera was still hampered by the lack of a newspaper in which to expound his programme. The Dublin dailies and most of the provincial press remained hostile. But he won 44 seats as against Cosgrave's 46. The Independents numbered 22, Labour 22, the Farmers 11, and Captain Redmond's National League Party, 8. The Farmers' Party, the Independents, and the National League Party continued to support Cosgrave, but Labour, in the main, was sympathetic. Fianna Fail was making progress.

(III)

A month later an event took place which was destined to affect the fortunes of both Cosgrave's party and de Valera's. Kevin O'Higgins, Minister for Justice and strong man of the Government, was assassinated. Those responsible were never apprehended, but Republicans had no hand in the crime. O'Higgins had been using a strong hand with the Army and the Police Force, in both of which discipline had become lax, and in the process he had incurred a good deal of enmity. Therein, it may be, lay the explanation of the murder. It was at once denounced by de Valera, who called upon the country to stand up against such outrages, declaring that the shooting of O'Higgins struck at the roots of all representative government.

The Free State Government's reaction to the crime was to introduce a drastic Public Safety Act which gave the authorities the widest powers of search and arrest. That, in itself, was understandable. But it was followed by another Act aimed, illogically and irrelevantly, at Fianna Fail, under which every candidate at parliamentary elections was obliged before nomination to declare that he would take the obnoxious Oath of Allegiance. This Act was in no way concerned with the public safety; it was political in its purpose. The Oath had prevented Republicans from entering the Dail; now it was to be used to prevent them from even taking part in elections.

De Valera was in a dilemma. If he accepted the new position not only was his movement doomed to remain in the wilderness for an indefinite period, but he was denied even the opportunity of giving the electorate an opportunity of pronouncing upon his policy. On the other hand, if he took the Oath he would be acting in defiance of the spirit of some of his most passionate pronouncements. He would be attacked both by the Right and the Left. The

Cosgrave party would find in his action another "twist" and the diehards of Sinn Fein and the I.R.A. would brand him as traitor.

To cut the knot, take the Oath and enter the Dail—as de Valera, after a period of painful heart-searching, decided to do—required an immense amount of moral courage. It was, everything considered, one of the bravest things he has ever done, as it was one of the most distasteful.

Later on—in 1932 when he was introducing the Act which abolished the Oath—de Valera defended his action at some length. He said:

> "I asked myself what my duty was and anything that was not wrong I was prepared to do. I would not have felt justified in committing perjury, or doing anything equivalent to perjury. The Party opposite [the Cosgravites] told the people that this was not an oath at all. I believe that the words 'I swear' mean an oath, but Deputies opposite thought differently and said that it was a formality, that anybody could take it. I asked myself whether in a crisis like that I would be justified in staying outside when this was a mere formality. There was only one way to find out. . . .
>
> "We [the Republicans] said that at least we were entitled to find out. What did I find? Instead of taking this oath openly, where the people could see what was done, as in other Parliaments, they hid it away in a dark room out of sight, so that the public would not know what it was. . . .
>
> "When I came to take this so-called oath I presented to the officer in charge that document [the Republican declaration that they did not regard the Oath of Allegiance as a binding oath] and told him that was our attitude, that we were not prepared to take an oath, and I have

here written document in pencil in Irish—the statement made to the officer who was supposed to administer that oath. I said: 'I am not prepared to take the oath—I am not going to take it. I am prepared to put my name down here in this book in order to get permission to get into the Dail, and it has no other significance. There was a Testament on the table and—in order that there might be no misunderstanding—I went over, took the Testament, put it away, and said, 'You must remember that I am not taking any oath.'"

There was hardly any need for such an elaborate defence, for the average Irish citizen had no sensitive feelings about an oath-taking business which was the result of duress and thoroughly approved of de Valera's decision. Politics is the art of the possible, and political methods are subject, like everything else, to time's mutations. It would have been sufficient if de Valera had said, with Emerson, to those who charged him with inconsistency, that consistency is the hobgoblin of little minds, or if he had replied, with George Moore, to those who called him a "trimmer," that a trimmer is not the statesman who changes his policy or his methods when the welfare of the country demands it, but the statesman who does so to reap personal gain. At any rate, it was an eminently practical step, and one of which nobody has ever doubted the wisdom.

Apart from Labour and the small "National League" group led by Captain Redmond, both of whom blessed the new departure, there was no welcome in the national assembly for de Valera and his forty-three followers. Only four years had elapsed since the termination of the civil war and

s

the old bitterness was still very much alive. Cosgrave's followers and those of de Valera glared at one another across the floor of the House as fiercely as many of them had done when they had guns in their hands in 1922.

Almost immediately a crisis sprang up. On August 16th, four days after Fianna Fail's entry into the Dail, Thomas Johnson, leader of the Labour Party, moved a vote of "No Confidence" in the Government. It was supported by the Republicans and by Captain Redmond's National League Party and it looked as if the Government would be defeated. But at the last moment one of Captain Redmond's followers, Alderman Jinks, of Sligo, allowed himself to be spirited away and the vote resulted in a tie—71 against 71. The Speaker's casting vote saved the Government.

Such a victory was, of course, tantamount to a defeat, and Cosgrave showed his appreciation of the fact by suddenly dissolving the Dail. At the General Election which followed—the second within three months—each of the two chief parties gained strength at the expense of the two smaller groups. The figures were: Cosgrave, 61; de Valera, 57; Labour, 13; Independents, 12; Farmers, 6; National Party, 2; Independent Labour, 1. Assured of the support of the Independents and the Farmers, the Cosgrave Party was given a further lease of life. But Fianna Fail was not far behind.

(IV)

The opening sessions of the new Dail were devoted to a *post mortem* on the Treaty and its tragic aftermath. It was a melancholy exhibition of party politics at their worst, with the rattling of dead men's bones as a macabre accompaniment. For de Valera, as was to be expected, the Cosgravites reserved their bitterest taunts and their most scathing denunciations, descending at times to unpardonable depths. Some of his supporters retorted in kind and the debate degenerated into a competition in invective as wearisome and unedifying as has ever disgraced a legislative assembly.

But through it all de Valera succeeded, miraculously, in maintaining the philosophic calm of an Alexander Hamilton. With thunders playing around his head he kept his temper and his dignity. Like Grattan, he knew how to be "severe and parliamentary at the same time." There was no lack of vigour or forthrightness in his defence of the policy he had pursued, but for the baser charges brought against him he showed his contempt by silence. The sufferings and anxieties and disillusionments of the dark years had schooled him in stoicism and taught him a patience that was not easily shaken. He was a party leader now, not leader of a nation, and he had already learnt something of the trials and the snares of party politics. The party machine is a lumbering cart that can easily throw an inexperienced or unskilful driver into the ditch. It needs a keen eye for the straight road, and the road that de Valera had marked out for himself, however straight it might be, was full of pitfalls. But as time went on and experience came, he proved himself a superb Parliamentarian, the ablest, probably, that Ireland has known since Parnell. From the first he was determined that he would never play party politics as a "game." There was nationally important work to be done—so important that until it was accomplished the country's very nationhood would be endangered—and he intended to use the position that his entry into the Dail had given him to carry it out. Always he kept his eyes on ideals that transcended party and which would some day, he hoped, reunite the nation. The Treaty episode and the Civil War were over and the sooner the evil memories born of them were buried the better.

That is not to say that he put party tactics aside or that he underestimated their importance in strengthening his position. Under the party system, unavoidable in a democracy, Oppositions have always indulged in tactical moves as a matter of course, and the Fianna Fail Opposition could be no exception. Early in the life of the new Dail the grievances of the Irish ex-servicemen—men who had fought in the British Army during 1914-1918—came under discussion. These men, belonging to the Irish branch of the British Legion, held that they had been denied a proportionate share of the grants-in-aid provided by the British Government for war veterans, and the Cosgrave Ministry had conducted negotiations on their behalf with Whitehall, but without any success. Captain Redmond, a Vice-President of the Legion, thereupon introduced a motion in the Dail calling for a commission of enquiry to investigate the claims of the ex-servicemen. The motion was resisted by Cosgrave, but supported by Labour and the Republicans, and when the vote was taken it was found that the Government had been defeated by a majority of two. There were not wanting cynics who declared that de Valera's action on this occasion was a dishonest party manœuvre. What sincerity could there be, they asked, in Republicans upholding the claims of men many of whom had enlisted in the Free State Army and fought against the Republic? The answer was, of course, that there was nothing dishonest, or even illogical, in any Irish political party supporting a body of Irishmen who believed that they had a legitimate claim. Parnell, in other years, had used the votes of the Irish Party in the British House of Commons in a similar manner, partly as a matter of tactics, partly because the opportunity arose of supporting some measure or motion towards which he was sympathetic. It was the votes of his party, for instance, that finally carried through a Bill for the abolition of flogging in the British Navy, a reform that was no direct concern of his, but one about which he had strong feelings. De Valera intended to use his position in the same way. So far as the policy of the Government went there was scarcely a single aspect of it—national, economic, industrial or agricultural—which he did not feel bound to oppose, and if he could secure the help of Labour or any other of the smaller groups in the Dail in his efforts to defeat the Ministry he had no intention of refusing it.

(v)

Before the end of 1927 a much bigger issue than the claims of the ex-servicemen was being raised in the Dail. Under the financial settlement of December, 1925, Ireland's liabilities to Britain had, the Free State Government announced at the time, been completely liquidated. "I have got from the

British the figure I wanted," Cosgrave had declared—" a huge 0." But less than a year later—in November, 1926—a British White Paper was published which disclosed the fact that, within three months of the London settlement, a secret agreement had been signed between Winston Churchill and Ernest Blythe, the Free State Minister for Finance, in which the Free State undertook to pay Britain the full amount of the Land Purchase Annuities. Under the Wyndham Act of 1903, which provided for expropriating the Irish landlords, the British Government had advanced the money enabling the tenant farmers to buy their land by floating guaranteed Irish Land Stock, and was to recover its advances by collecting from the farmers annuities payable half-yearly over sixty years. Everybody—except the Ministers of the two Governments involved in the transaction—had taken for granted that these payments to Britain had been wiped out by the London Agreement, as they had been wiped out, so far as the Six Counties were concerned, by the Act of 1920, and that they were being remitted to the Free State Exchequer. If all such liabilities had not been cancelled by the Agreement—the " damned good bargain " of which Cosgrave had spoken—what *quid pro quo* had the Free State Government received for handing over Nationalist territories, such as Tyrone and Fermanagh, to Sir James Craig? Was Ireland to be the loser in every arrangement made with Britain? Why was the whole affair kept hidden from the legislature and the people? Such were the questions asked in the Dail and throughout the country after the publication of the Churchill-Blythe

Agreement, and the answers forthcoming were not calculated to add to the prestige of the Cosgrave Ministry. "We have sold our nationals in Ulster and we have not got the price," declared Professor Magennis. "We have been burgled and we have bribed the burglar," commented Senator Colonel Maurice Moore.

Fianna Fail organised a strong campaign throughout the country, insisting that the Free State should retain its Land Annuities, as the Six-County Government had been allowed to retain theirs, and claiming that a secret agreement, unratified by the Dail, had no binding force. Legal opinion was taken and seven distinguished lawyers gave it as their opinion that the Free State should not be debited with the annuities.

Another factor which contributed to the growing strength of Fianna Fail was the question of public expenditure, which was made a constant target for attack. The Governor-General, for instance, was being paid a salary of £10,000, and the entire cost of his establishment was something in the neighbourhood of £40,000 a year. When de Valera asked if a country as poor as Ireland could afford to spend so much money on an office that could easily be abolished, he found plenty of willing listeners. Other official salaries were also brought under review and an all-round reduction was called for. Ministers sneered at what they called de Valera's "hair-shirt economics," but their sneers were lost on the small farmers and the workers. There was little prosperity in the country. The world slump had hit the export trade on which Irish farming mainly depended, unemployment was increasing, and discontent was rife. Some time previously, when the question of unemployment was raised in the Dail, the Minister for Industry in the Cosgrave Government had said acidly: " It is not any business of this Dail to provide work, and the sooner that is realised the better. The Government should not be held responsible for the provision of work in the country; it is not its business." All this, obviously, was playing into the hands of Fianna Fail. If that was the best a " realist " Government could do or say, perhaps, thought the workers, the country might be better served by the " visionaries." If unemployment was not the Government's affair, then, in God's name, whose affair was it? More and more they turned to Fianna Fail, with its promise that the country could be made self-supporting enough to feed and clothe its own people and to lighten the unemployment problem through the medium of new industries.

(VI)

The political pendulum continued to swing steadily back during the years 1928-1931. Fianna Fail won one bye-election after another, and it was becoming increasingly obvious that the country was no longer impressed by any talk of the Republicans as " wild men." Parliamentary government had become an established affair and Fianna Fail, vigilant and vigorous, was giving a remarkably good account of itself in Opposition.

These were strenuous years for de Valera. Conscious that the flowing tide was with him, he threw every ounce of energy he possessed into the struggle. Always an early riser, he worked from ten to twelve hours a day. Almost every morning the ramshackle old Ford car in which he drove to Dublin from his home in Greystones could be seen arriving at the headquarters of Fianna Fail in Mount Street. Other activities included visits to America, one in connection with a law-suit concerning the disposal of the Republican bonds, others to collect funds for the movement and, more particularly, for the purpose of starting a daily newspaper. His tall figure grew more and more lanky, his face more thin and gaunt. Some of his friends, fearful lest he would break down under the strain, remonstrated with him. But his only reply was a shrug or a smile. Victory, he felt, was not far off, and until it came he would not spare himself.

In the summer of 1931, when the life of the Sixth Dail was nearing its end, the Cosgrave Government proceeded to drive the final nail in its own coffin. The I.R.A., which all along had refused to acknowledge the Free State, had become increasingly active. Police barracks had been attacked and raided for arms, drilling was taking place, and Ministers went about heavily guarded. Many Republicans were in gaol. Claiming that the jury system had broken down owing to intimidation, Cosgrave introduced a new Public Safety Act of unexampled severity, and announced that he intended making it a permanent addition to the Constitution. Under the provisions of the Act Military Tribunals were to be set up and given almost absolute power. They could inflict the death penalty for the possession of arms; they could proclaim any organisation as illegal; anybody who was even suspected of being associated with such an organisation could be arrested and detained; those who were arrested must prove their innocence; premises could be searched at any hour of the day or night on mere suspicion; to crown it all, there was virtually no appeal from the decisions of the Tribunals.

Thousands of citizens who had hitherto supported the Cosgrave Ministry were shocked by the terms of this Draconian measure. After nearly ten years of iron rule things appeared to be getting worse instead of better. People who were old enough to remember the coercion regime of Arthur James Balfour recalled how that statesman had boasted he could solve the Irish problem by " twenty years of resolute government " and how completely he had failed. They had watched a native government employing the same weapon of coercion with the same lack of success for ten years. Naturally enough, they asked themselves whether the time had not come for a change of men and methods.

The Bill was fought at every step in the Dail by Fianna Fail and Labour, but it was rushed through by ' guillotine ' methods and rubber-stamped by a Senate which from the beginning had never shown the least sign of either independence or initiative.

In September of the same year de Valera's project for a new national newspaper materialised when the *Irish Press* came into existence. Under the brilliant editorship of Frank Gallagher, who had been associated with Erskine Childers in publicity work during the Black-and-Tan period and the Civil War, the new organ quickly established itself as a leading daily and became a pillar of strength to the Fianna Fail movement. The old Redmondite newspaper, the *Freeman's Journal*, was dead. Of the other two dailies with a nation-wide circulation, one, the *Irish Times*, still thought and spoke in terms of Unionism, whilst the other, the *Irish Independent,* was a strong supporter of the Commonwealth connection. Both were violently anti-de Valera. The *Irish Press* brought an entirely new note into Irish journalism. Until it appeared there was no daily paper in which Irish interests were made predominant. Now, at last, the people had a newspaper which stood for the full national claim—for independence, for unity, and for Irish culture—and which could be quoted abroad as expressing the distinctive outlook of the Irish nation on international affairs.

Five months after the founding of the *Irish Press*—in February, 1932—a General Election took place. De Valera threw himself into the struggle with all the dynamic energy and crusading ardour of a Gladstone conducting a Midlothian campaign. He journeyed north, south, east and west, addressing as many as three meetings a day, sometimes entering a town at midnight with bands blaring out wild music and torchlight processions leading the way. People were stirred to enthusiasm as they had not been since the great Sinn Fein election of 1918. What de Valera had prophesied when he gave the "Cease Fire" order in 1923 was coming true. "If the people have turned aside it is because they are weary and need a rest: a little time and you will see them recover and rally again to the standard."

The rally was evident when the figures were announced. Fianna Fail had won 72 seats and was easily the largest party in the State. The Cosgravites had been reduced from 61 to 57 and

Labour from 10 to 7. There were 17 Independents. Of the Independents nearly all were supporters of Cosgrave, and the small Labour Party therefore held the balance of power. There was little doubt as to which side it would give its support, and at the first meeting of the Seventh Dail de Valera was elected President and proceeded to nominate his Cabinet. Fianna Fail had arrived.

CHAPTER THIRTEEN

World Figure

" It was as if the Fates had laid a wager that they would daunt him; and in the end they had lost their bet."

—LYTTON STRACHEY on CARDINAL MANNING.

(1)

WHEN in March, 1932, de Valera's Party took over the reins of government there were underground rumblings of which the public were completely unaware at the time and of which even to-day there is no general knowledge. After the Civil War Free State Ministers had declared that they would drive " that man " out of political life for ever, and there was still a group in existence who were determined to attempt it, by fair means or foul. Preparations were made as soon as the results of the General Election were announced for a *coup d'état* with the object of suppressing parliamentary government and of setting up a military dictatorship. De Valera was to be got rid of at any price. The conspirators included two former members of the Cosgrave Ministry and a group of Army and Police officers. The *putsch* was to be carried out by means of a secret army organisation.

It was a desperate plot, and one which, if put into operation, could not have failed to plunge the country once more into civil war. But it miscarried.

Mr. Cosgrave refused to have anything to do with it, and a high ecclesiastical dignitary, to whom a rumour of what was on foot had come, let it be known that the Church would give it no countenance whatever. As a result the conspiracy was called off and the change of government was effected under conditions of peace.

There were few surprises when de Valera announced the composition of his Cabinet. All the new Ministers were men who had made their mark in Opposition and who had not wavered in their allegiance to the Republic. Sean T. O'Kelly, who had been associated with Arthur Griffith in the earliest days of Sinn Fein, became Vice-President of the Executive Council and was given the office of Minister for Local Government; Sean MacEntee became Minister for Finance; Sean Lemass, Minister for Industry and Commerce; Dr. James Ryan, himself a practical farmer, Minister for Agriculture; Tom Derrig, an Irish speaker who had had experience of teaching, Minister for Education. The pivotal office of Minister for Defence was given to Frank Aiken, who had been Republican Chief of Staff during the final stages of the Civil War. Significantly, de Valera reserved to himself the Ministry for External Affairs.

Time was to show that he had picked his team well. After twelve years all the Ministers mentioned are still members of the Government. At the outset there were some doubts and not a little uneasiness amongst even those who were sympathetic towards the new regime. What sort of relations, people asked, were likely to develop between the Army and the new Minister for Defence? The Higher

Command was composed almost entirely of men who had fought against the forces of which he had been Chief of Staff in the Civil War. Would these men give him the same loyalty that they had given his predecessor? These were natural questions, but they were soon answered. In his administration of Army affairs, big bluff Frank Aiken achieved a striking personal triumph within a remarkably short space of time. De Valera had made it clear on coming into office that he had no intention whatever of adopting a "spoils system," and even if in the Civil Service and the Army there were men in key positions who were his personal enemies, no official action would be taken against them so long as they served the State loyally. He believed, with Edmund Burke, that "magnanimity in politics is not seldom the truest wisdom." So the civil servants and the Army officers retained their posts and the governmental machine began to function smoothly. Frank Aiken became an immensely popular Minister for Defence and all danger of a military coup disappeared. From now onwards the Army was to be the Army of the State, not of a Party.

(II)

On St. Patrick's Day—a week after he had come into office—de Valera broadcast a message to the United States, in which he summarised the aims of the new Government by a quotation from the writings of Fintan Lalor, the ablest Irish political thinker of the nineteenth century:

> "Ireland her own and all therein, from the sod to the sky; the soil of Ireland for the people of Ireland to have and to hold from God alone

who gave it; to have and to hold for them and their heirs forever, without suit or service, rent or render, faith or fealty, to any power under heaven."

There was no mistaking the purport of those words. They bore a challenge and a warning. The wrong that had been done ten years before was going to be undone. De Valera was addressing the citizens of the Great Republic of the West, but his message was equally directed towards his own people and the people of England. He laid emphasis on his desire for a real and lasting friendship between the peoples of the two neighbouring islands, but he made it clear at the same time that no foundation for such friendship could be secured unless the principles of justice and fair dealing between nations were permitted to operate. "The will of our own people," he said, "must prevail in all matters concerning their sovereign rights, and as our people do not desire in any way to impose burdens or tests on the people of Great Britain they justly feel that no burdens or tests should be imposed on them."

That there would be any sympathetic response from Britain to his overtures at that particular moment was, he knew, in the highest degree unlikely. The British Press as a whole had interpreted his return to power as a sort of mad political interlude, a typical piece of tomfoolery indulged in occasionally by an incalculable people. Very soon, they asserted, the Irish electorate would get tired of de Valera's dangerous antics and throw themselves back into the safe arms of Mr. Cosgrave. A Labour Government was in office in England, but not in power; from Mr. Ramsay MacDonald's administration, dependent for its life on the good-will of politicians who persisted in looking upon Ireland in the old traditional way, there was nothing to be expected. British Labour, new to office and timid to a degree, would not depart by the smallest fraction from the policy of its predecessors.

But de Valera had no intention of waiting. Whatever British Ministers might do or say, he was about to launch the programme of Fianna Fail. Within a week from the date of the St. Patrick's Day broadcast Mr. J. W. Dulanty, the Irish Free State High Commissioner in London, handed to Mr. J. H. Thomas, the British Dominions Secretary, what the latter described to a startled House of Commons as "a very important and serious document." The document stated, on behalf of the Government of which Mr. de Valera was the head, that the Oath of Allegiance to the British King laid down by the Treaty of 1921 was being abolished; that it was regarded by the Irish people as "an intolerable burden, a relic of mediævalism, a test imposed from without under the threat of immediate and terrible war." Such a test, the statement added, was one which had "no parallel in treaty relationships between States"; it was "an imposition on the conscience of the people completely out of place in a political agreement between two countries."

Mr. Thomas at once accused de Valera of breaking the Treaty, to which de Valera replied, taking him on his own ground, that if Ireland was, as the British Government asserted, a Dominion of the British Empire, it had, like the other Dominions, the right of determining its own internal affairs. Had Mr. Thomas never heard of the Imperial Conference of 1926 or of the Statute of Westminster of 1931? The correspondence which followed showed that the Irish leader had nothing to learn from an English Labour politician with regard to political finesse. When the argument was put forward that an Irish Government which openly proclaimed its intention of seceding from the Empire had no right to claim the privileges of a Dominion, and that Mr. de Valera was trying to have it both ways, a ready reply was forthcoming. Ireland was having it only one way—the way which the English had left open to him. De Valera was keeping his election promise that he would work within the Constitution, and he was doing no more than taking advantage of the position which had been established at Imperial Conferences.

So, despite the heavy protests of Mr. Thomas, the hateful Oath of Allegiance was abolished. There was anger in Britain, but at home de Valera's stock rose tremendously. Here, at last, was a leader who had the courage of his convictions and who was not wanting in the art of diplomacy; the first, since Parnell, who refused, when dealing with British Ministers, to go hat in hand begging for favours.

(III)

Speedily, and without fuss, de Valera had carried out his first and most important election pledge. The Oath had gone. On the heels of its disappearance arose the question of the Land Annuities, which, the British Government was informed, were being retained in the Irish treasury. But on this occasion de Valera did not, as he had done in the case of the Oath, present Britain with a *fait accompli.* With regard to the Oath there had been no room for negotiation; it was a matter for Ireland and for Ireland only. The Annuities were a matter of a different sort. The Irish Government held, and they had the backing of high legal opinion, that they were entitled to withhold them, and withhold them they would. But, at the same time, to remove any doubts about the legality or morality of their action, they intimated their willingness to submit the question to a court of arbitration. In the meantime the Annuities would be collected from the farmers and banked in a reserve fund.

Mr. Ramsay MacDonald's Government was worried and not a little bewildered. This man de Valera was becoming a nuisance. He had not, it would appear, been indulging in heroics for vote-catching purposes when he had given the Irish people certain pledges. He had meant what he said and now he was translating his promises into action.

Mr. J. H. Thomas, the British Dominions Secretary, decided that he had better have a heart-to-heart talk with this strange Irishman, and in May he appeared in Dublin, accompanied by Lord Hailsham. The mountain had come to Mahomet. All Ireland was vastly intrigued. The reaction of British opinion to the event was expressed by Mr. Lloyd George when he told the House of Commons that "he was a little startled when he heard that two leading Cabinet Ministers were going to Ireland to negotiate."

The Dublin Conference, however, proved fruitless,

as might have been expected. It was not merely that the Irish leader and the British Dominion Secretary failed to discover any common ground on which to negotiate; they did not, so to speak, talk the same language. Poor Mr. Thomas had been an efficient General Secretary of the National Union of Railwaymen in his time, but he was sadly miscast on the diplomatic stage. His hail-fellow-well-met manner and his now-do-let-us-be-reasonable attitude were wasted on a man who would only give way if his case were to be proved legally or morally unsound. De Valera was courteous, but unshakeable. If the Irish claim was as untenable as Mr. Thomas asserted, why not submit it to arbitration? Mr. Thomas liked the idea: it provided a way out of the impasse. But Empire arbitrators, of course? Mr. de Valera shook his head. Memories of Empire arbitration in the case of the Boundary were too recent and too sad to permit of a similar fiasco happening again. The dispute was one between two nations, and if it went to arbitration it would have to be judged by an international tribunal of whose impartiality there could be no doubt.

Mr. Thomas gave up Mr. de Valera as a bad job and returned to London, where he told the House of Commons, in effect, that the British Government could not have any further agreements with an Irish Government which treated existing agreements as if they were non-existent. But it was Mr. Lloyd George, rather than Mr. Thomas, to whom the House listened most attentively on that particular occasion. The ex-Prime Minister, chief negotiator of the Treaty from which the matters in dispute had originated, had a good deal to say about Mr.

de Valera. "I have had some experience of Mr. de Valera and, frankly, I have never seen anything like him. Mr. de Valera is perfectly unique, and this poor distracted world has a good right to be profoundly thankful that he is unique." There was laughter in the House of Commons at the sally. In Ireland there was amusement. There the older people remembered that Gladstone had said very much the same sort of thing about Parnell. For an Englishman—or even a Welshman—to fail to understand an Irishman was nothing new. "What," continued Mr. Lloyd George, "is Mr. de Valera's demand in substance? Anyone who wants to know what he is driving at ought to read first all the correspondence that took place between the Government of which I was the head and Mr. de Valera before we had our first conference. He made it clear what his attitude was, and if you look at the correspondence between the Dominions Secretary and Mr. de Valera you will find that there is really no change in his attitude.

"His demand was, not that Ireland should be a part of the British Commonwealth of Nations with such rights as each Dominion has, whether by the Statute of Westminster or by any other Statute, but that Ireland should be a Sovereign State and should have the same relation to Britain and the Empire as Belgium and Holland have to Germany and Portugal to Spain. He has not changed one iota of that position, and let us not treat that as if it were a mere trumpery question of an oath."

The House of Commons cheered that statement and the cheers were re-echoed in Ireland, though for a different reason. Lloyd George had described de Valera's policy with his usual clarity, and it was a policy that was gaining new adherents amongst the Irish people with every day that passed. Courage is an infectious quality in a leader, and even those who had hitherto differed from de Valera found themselves beginning to admire the rock-like front that he was maintaining in his struggle with British Ministers.

"I am glad," concluded Lloyd George, amid loud and prolonged cheering, "that the Government have put their foot down. Do not let us be under any delusion that this is merely a trumpery and trivial discussion as to a form of an oath or as to your method of declaring allegiance to the British Empire. It is a clear demand from which Mr. de Valera has never swerved for one day. He is that type; he will never change right to the end."

It was profoundly true. On the fundamental issues that were bound up with his country's claim to sovereignty, de Valera had not changed, and would not change. He harboured no hatred towards England; a hundred times he had made that clear. But if a real lasting friendship were to be established it could only come when the right of the smaller nation to work out its own destiny had been secured.

Any hatred that existed at that moment was to be found on the Tory benches at Westminster which were filled with men who had learnt nothing and forgotten nothing. Like Lloyd George they demanded that Mr. Ramsay MacDonald's Government should "put its foot down," and they cheered frenziedly when Mr. Thomas announced that, as a reprisal for the retention of the Land Annuities, penal tariffs were to be imposed on imports from Ireland. That would teach Mr. de Valera! How long was his administration likely to survive in a country that depended for so much of its prosperity on its export cattle trade? Within a few months at the most, they calculated, the outraged and ruined farmers would turn and rend him. And that would be the end of another mad Irish interlude.

There was some excuse for the Tory politicians of Britain. They had never understood the Irish people. They had never tried to understand them. They still believed, those people who aired their views in the smoke-rooms of West End clubs or in the drawing-rooms of the great country houses, that, at heart, the Irish had neither the desire nor the capacity for self-government, and that if they were not bullied or misled by gunmen or visionaries, they would welcome the English back with open arms.

But there was not the same excuse for Mr. Cosgrave and his followers who, with a curious lack of prescience, appeared to share the Tory politicians' belief that the "Economic War" resulting from the Annuities dispute would speedily finish de Valera and his Government. Mr. Cosgrave denounced de Valera's action as "reckless folly" and called upon the farmers to repudiate him; the Land Annuities, he declared, were not being retained; as a result of the penal tariffs they were going over to Britain "on the horns of Irish cattle."

What the British and the Cosgravites both failed to realise was the extent to which the economic struggle was playing into de Valera's hands. His immediate retort to the penal tariffs was to impose similar tariffs on British imports. In season and out of season he had preached the revolutionary doctrine of a self-sufficing Ireland, an Ireland that would not be dependent for its economic life on its external trade. The new circumstances which had arisen rendered the moment an ideal one for putting his plans into operation. "We have said good-bye for ever," he declared at Ennis, "to the day in which this country was a grazing ranch for feeding other people, a dumping-ground for the manufactures of other people, and a country in which our own people were brought up for export like cattle." He appealed to those whose interests were most heavily involved in the struggle, the farmers, to support him. Let them turn from grazing to tillage; it would be better for the country and better for themselves in the long run. The transition period would be a hard one, but if they stood by the Government the Government would stand by them. The farmers, particularly the small working farmers, had borne the brunt of the Land War in the eighties and their courage and tenacity had given landlordism its death-blow. Victory would be theirs again if they stood firm. He appealed to them, the class from which he himself was sprung, over the heads of the British Government, over the heads of the Cosgravites, over the heads of the wealthy ranchers. As we shall see, his appeal was not made in vain.

(IV)

Towards the end of September, 1932, British Ministers were given a taste of the character and qualities of the man they were dealing with in a very different sphere. The scene was Geneva and the occasion the Thirteenth Meeting of the Assembly of the League of Nations. De Valera was presiding.

It was a day of gloomy skies and lashing rain. Dripping trees waved outside the tall glass panels of the Council Chamber, and across the lake the Swiss mountains looked ghostly in the mists. The President, the wits said, had brought Irish weather with him.

Within the great Hall, where men from almost every nation in the world had assembled, the atmosphere was as gloomy as without. After an existence of thirteen years the League of Nations had little on which to congratulate itself. In many lands poverty, hunger and oppression still existed. In wealthy countries like Britain and the United States unemployment had reached its peak figure. Everywhere there was unrest and the danger of war. The delegates who had come to Geneva had no reassuring stories to bring. Even in Switzerland itself, holiday-ground of the world, sensitive index to the state of Europe, the tale was one of deserted resorts and hard times.

De Valera, dressed in severe black, rose to address the Assembly. On his right hand sat Sir Eric Drummond, the Secretary-General, and Sir John Simon, the British Foreign Secretary. On his left sat M. Paul Boncour and Baron von Neurath. In the foreground were big Dr. Yen, the Chinese delegate, and little Mr. Nagoaya, the Japanese representative.

The President spoke for half-an-hour. There was no passion in his utterance; there was not even emphasis. Nobody applauded when he rose, and nobody applauded when he sat down. But the speech he delivered was the most forceful and the most striking that the Assembly had ever listened to.

Abandoning the customary practice of reviewing in detail the work of the League during the year, from material supplied by the Secretariat, de Valera went straight to the heart of things—things against which mere platitudes were of no avail. Both friends and enemies of the League, he declared prophetically, felt that the testing-time had come. They were watching to see if that test would reveal a weakness presaging ultimate dissolution or a strength that would be the assurance of a renewal of vigour and growth. There were on all sides complaint, criticism and suspicion. People were complaining that the League was devoting its activities to matters of secondary or minor importance, while vital international problems which touched the very existence of the peoples were being shelved, postponed or ignored; that equality of status did not apply in the things that mattered, and that the smaller States, whilst being given a voice, had little real influence in the final determination of League action.

"Out beyond these walls there is the public opinion of the world, and if the League is to prosper, or even survive, it must obtain the support and confidence of that public opinion. In the final analysis, the League has no sanctions but the force of world opinion."

There was dead silence in the assembly, but every eye was watching, every ear was strained. For the first time in years a cold blast of reality was sweeping through the Hall. Poles, Frenchmen, Germans,

Turks, Spaniards, Siamese, listened attentively. Newspaper men whispered excitedly to one another.

"There is a suspicion abroad," the level voice went on, "that little more than lip service is being paid to the fundamental principle on which the League was founded; there is a suspicion that the action of the League in the economic sphere would be paralysed by the pressure of powerful national interests, and that if the hand that was raised against the Covenant was sufficiently strong it could smite with impunity."

Big Dr. Yen, representative of a country of four hundred thousand square miles, whose territory had been forcibly occupied by the armies of another member of the League, beamed approval through his spectacles. Sir John Simon, who had given Japan's policy of imperial expansion a modified blessing, continued to gaze steadily at the papers in front of him.

"What," asked de Valera, "have we done to give a really effective answer to that criticism? The vast collection of surveys and reports and confidential records accumulated in our archives is not evidence that will disprove the charges brought against the League. The one effective way of silencing criticism and of bringing to the support of the League millions who at present stand aside in apathy or look upon its activities with undisguised cynicism is to say unmistakably that the Covenant of the League is a solemn pact, the obligations of which no State, great or small, will find it possible to ignore.

"On every side there is evidence of impending economic collapse. Twenty-five million unemployed are crying out for the recognition of the rights of themselves and their families to work and live. One hundred million people are faced with starvation, in the midst of a world of plenty, in a world in which mechanical development has reached a stage of production capable of meeting many times the people's needs.

"It is our duty to face this anomalous and desperate position frankly and honestly, not as the representatives of States or Parties or special interests, but as men who recognise that the primary duty of statesmen, national and international, is to plan for the well-being of their fellows, the plain, ordinary human beings of every country."

There followed a reference to Ireland. "Speaking of my own country," said the President, "I am confident that if we are left free to pursue our own policy we shall succeed not only in securing proper adjustment of our social and economic life, but shall be able to contribute more than our share to human progress throughout the world. I want you to believe that we in Ireland desire peace—peace at home and peace abroad. In spite of opinions you may have formed from misleading reports, I want you to know that our history is the history of a people who have consistently sought merely to be allowed to lead their own lives in their own way, at peace with their neighbours and the world."

The speech concluded with a sentence in the speaker's own Gaelic tongue. "Go dtugaidh Dia cabhair dúinn ins an obair mhóir atá romhainn agus nár leigidh Sé go dteipidh orainn. (May God assist us in our exalted task and may He not permit that we should fail)."

The "stony silence" with which, according to

Reuter, de Valera's pronouncement was received, probably reflected the uneasiness that it had created. "This speech," said the special correspondent of the *Manchester Guardian,* "was the best ever made by a President of the League Assembly. It was inspired by a true international spirit, and for the first time a President asked the members of the League to face the reality that the world has a less high opinion of them than they have of themselves. Perhaps it was for that reason that the speech was not applauded. The Assembly did not show Mr. de Valera the formal politeness customarily shown to any President of applauding him when he sat down. One would have expected the British delegation to lead the applause."

But if the delegates remained silent, the world was loud in its approval. Next day de Valera's speech was front-page news from Tokyo to Washington. "The best speech I have ever heard at the League Assembly," said the *Daily Herald* correspondent; "that is the opinion of almost every League journalist with whom I have spoken." "Geneva stunned by de Valera's onslaught," was the heading in the London *Daily Express,* which noted approvingly how "he had refused to repeat the customary rigmarole of pious platitudes drafted for him." The *New York Times* declared that the speech had made de Valera "*the* personality of the session and had revealed him as the League's strong man." "There is no doubt," said the *English Review,* "that in brushing aside the harmless text prepared for him and telling the League of Nations what he thought of it, the Fianna Fail leader voiced the views of millions of people all over the world."

Newspapers in almost every capital in Europe added their voices to the chorus of praise. From the *Neue Züricher Zeitung* came a vivid pen-picture as well as approval:

> "Eamon de Valera is probably the first President of the Council and Assembly of the League who has heard sentence of death passed upon him—which is perhaps still, as it was in Stendhal's time, the only proof that a man cannot be bought.
>
> "I heard this man eleven years ago speaking in the Dail, which was then still an Assembly of rebel conspirators, a good third of whom could share the tragic honour that an English court-martial had accorded him. De Valera has changed but slightly since then. His keen sea-hawk features have not become hardened by the terrible experience of the civil war, but only calmer and more decided. And now, as then, he speaks in a voice that has no seducingly melodious tones, but is matter-of-fact and earnest, with a much greater restraint in expression than might be expected of the adventurous leader, the conspirator and agitator who has waged war against the might of England, with such simplicity of feeling as has been shown by no other living man, not even Gandhi."

It was, everything considered, as complete a triumph as had ever been achieved by the leader of a small nation in an international assembly. No longer could a hostile English press hold up de Valera to the world as a mere agitator, an unpractical dreamer, a fanatic. In Geneva, at a moment of world crisis, he had revealed himself before impartial eyes as a statesman of unusual stature, as a man whose voice carried weight in the councils of the nations.

CHAPTER FOURTEEN

Achievement

"There are few tasks more difficult, and none more noble than the rebuilding of a nation."
—RICHARD LALOR SHEIL.

(I)

IN January, 1933, de Valera suddenly dissolved the Dail. During his ten months of office he had been dependent on the votes of the small Labour Party for his majority, and although on all major questions such as the abolition of the Oath and the retention of the Land Annuities, Labour had given him full support, he felt the position to be unsatisfactory. There was an immense amount of work to be done and he wanted a free hand. In a "straight" election there would be no doubt about the result, but under the system of Proportional Representation it would not be easy to secure an all-over majority. However, he was determined to try. After Geneva his prestige stood high, but the farmers were suffering severely from the effects of the Economic War with Britain, and the Opposition would not fail to make the fullest use of that.

The election, when it came, was fiercely contested. The Cosgravites told the farmers that the return of de Valera to power would mean their absolute ruin, that Fianna Fail's industrial revival policy was moonshine, and that tillage would never recompense them for the loss of a thriving cattle trade.

But the farmers, on whose votes the result of the election depended, were not impressed. At all times the backbone of the nationalist movement, they expressed their resentment at the penal tariffs, which they regarded as a typical example of the wielding of the big stick by Britain, by giving de Valera their united support. Only the big ranchers, who detested the change-over from grazing to tillage farming, clung to Cosgrave. The result was a de Valera triumph, the figures being: Fianna Fail, 77; Cosgrave, 48; Centre Party, 11; Independents, 9; Labour, 8. De Valera had gained an all-over majority and, possessed of a clear mandate from the country, was in a position to go ahead rapidly with his programme. English critics gave up Ireland as a bad job. Failing completely to understand de Valera's success or the tenacity of the nationalist tradition, they took refuge in silence. Irish news disappeared almost entirely from the columns of the English newspapers.

(II)

But before Fianna Fail could make a new start a fresh crisis developed at home. Out of the blue came the Blueshirts.

General Eoin O'Duffy, one of the most active members of the secret I.R.B. organisation and a close personal friend of Michael Collins, had taken a leading part on the anti-Republican side during the Treaty debates and the Civil War. During the siege of the Four Courts he had sought out the English Commander-in-Chief, General Macready, and taxed him with not bringing over supplies of guns and ammunition from England quickly enough. "O'Duffy," Macready records in his Memoirs, "did not fail to tell me that it was my fault, and said that he would telegraph to Mr. Churchill to say so, an Irishism for which I was quite prepared." After the Civil War he had been appointed Chief of Police by the Cosgrave Cabinet, and he still held that position when de Valera came into power.

It was a key position in the official life of the State. Other men in key positions had been bitter political opponents of de Valera, but his Government had not interfered with them. So long as they accepted the change-over and continued to serve the State loyally they would hold their jobs. There was to be no spoils system. Not only that, but de Valera's policy was, as the Americans put it, to "lean backwards," and he leant backwards deliberately. He could, by giving his political supporters positions, have evened things up a little and made them some material recompense for their days of outlawry. But he was determined to be fair to all sections and to accustom the country to the idea of continuity of government instead of violent revolutionary changes with every new administration.

General O'Duffy, however, lost the confidence of the Government and in February he was dismissed. His immediate retort was the founding of a "Shirt" movement, on Continental lines, with a "Corporative State" as the objective. The colour he chose was blue.

A League of Youth was established. The sons—and daughters—of the graziers were enrolled. The young women wore blue blouses and carried hat-pins in their berets, which they were recommended to make use of, if required, "in the most effective place." Incredibly, the whole of the Cosgrave Party and the Centre Party—the latter containing men of standing and ability like Frank MacDermot and James Dillon—went Blueshirt. A new Party was formed—called the United Ireland Party—and Mr. Cosgrave handed over the leadership to General O'Duffy.

Soon Ireland was threatened with a new convulsion. O'Duffy went on a raging, tearing campaign throughout the country, enlisting recruits, using Fascist symbols and the Fascist salute, announcing to the people that the object of his movement was to save the country from Communism. The Blueshirt flag, he declared, would soon be flying beside the Tricolour on Government Buildings. Outraged Republicans attempted to break up his meetings, clashes occurred, and there was general unrest. The big farmers refused to pay their rates and were supported by the Blueshirts, who cut telegraph wires, tore up railway lines, felled trees, trenched roads, and generally obstructed the officers of the law. For a few months the movement looked dangerous. Funds were provided by reactionary elements to whom the very name of de Valera had always been anathema. Heads of big business concerns asked their employees: "Why have you not your blue shirts on?" Strange recruits were attracted to the movement. Lord Muskerry told the young men of Ireland that by joining the Blueshirts they would be "following in the footsteps of St. Patrick." W. B. Yeats invited O'Duffy to his house and the entertaining spectacle was witnessed of the ageing poet discoursing on Hegel and Spengler to the bewildered General and promising him a marching song.

Soon, however, the Opposition leaders discovered that they had hitched their wagon, not to a star, but to a spluttering rocket. Whatever potentialities an Irish Fascist movement might have possessed under different leadership, it had little or none under General O'Duffy. He was completely miscast in the role of a Füehrer. His oratory was uninspiring, and not even a blue shirt, a blue beret and the Roman salute could succeed in making him look like Mussolini.

In March, 1934, de Valera, who had bided his time, struck. A Wearing of Uniforms (Restriction) Bill was passed through the Dail and the raising of private armies was made an offence against the law. De Valera's speech on this occasion was one of the greatest of his career. Declaring that the time had come to end "this tomfoolery of Blueshirting," he dealt faithfully with the pretence that it had been organised as a crusade to save the country from Communism. He was able to prove, from confidential reports supplied to the Government by General O'Duffy himself when Chief of Police, that Communism, or even Communistic activities, were virtually non-existent in Ireland.

"This country is not a natural breeding ground for Communism and everybody knows it. It is opposed to our religion; it is opposed to our individualistic tendencies; it is opposed to our whole scheme of life. If there is one country in the world which is unsuitable soil for Communism, it is this. . . . I have never stood for Communism in any form. I loathe and detest it as leading to the same sort of thing that I loathe and detest in the type of State that General O'Duffy would set up, because they are both destructive of human liberty."

He appealed to all Parties not to allow a condition of affairs to arise again similar to that which preceded the Civil War.

"When I was in the United States I travelled through the Southern States some sixty years after a civil war had been fought in that country. I was entertained at a banquet in a certain city. The chairman of the reception committee was a Federal judge, and although sixty years had passed there was the same bitterness in his heart against the 'Yankees,' as he called them, as there had been in the heart of his father. If that can be so in a country where people are separated territorially, how much more is it so in our country? Do we not know that there is a situation here far more dangerous than in Belgium, Holland or Switzerland? These countries have had no recent civil war. The leaders on opposite sides in these other countries are not relatively young men. We are relatively young. Every member on the opposite benches and on these benches could, if driven to it, be an active participant in a physical conflict to-day. I ask Deputies on the opposite benches not to do this thing."

In the Blueshirt campaign many of the doctrines of Continental Fascism had been rehashed and lauded from public platforms. Not only had anti-Semitism been openly preached, but some of the baser tongues, in an endeavour to give some semblance of reality to their anti-Communist crusade, went so far as to suggest that de Valera himself was of Jewish extraction.

There was passion in his voice as he dealt with this particular form of scurrility.

"In this House on one occasion I have had to speak on a personal matter. I did it, not because I cared a snap of my fingers regarding what anybody says about me personally, but because I am jealous, as long as I occupy this particular position, that my antecedents and my character shall not be attacked. Before, they went and soiled the steps of God's Altar; the same campaign is going on now in another guise, and I know that in order to get some basis for their Communistic attack on us they are suggesting that I am of Jewish origin."

There were loud cries of "No, no, not at all!" from all parts of the House. De Valera paused and then said:

"Go and read the *Cork Examiner*. The proprietor and editor sent me a letter apologising privately and saying that a certain thing was let through without his knowledge, showing what is happening at some of these meetings where this question of Communism is being discussed. There is not, so far as I know, a single drop of Jewish blood in my veins. I am not one of those who attack the Jews or want to make any use of the popular dislike of them. But as there has been, even from that bench over there, this dirty innuendo and suggestion carried, as I have said formally to God's Altar, I say that on both sides I come from Catholic stock. My father and mother were married in a Catholic church on September 19th, 1881. I was born in

October, 1882. I was baptised in a Catholic church. I was brought up here in a Catholic home. I have lived amongst the Irish people and loved them, and loved every blade of grass that grew in this land. I do not care who says or who tries to pretend that I am not Irish. I say I have been known to be Irish and that I have given everything in me to the Irish nation."

He finished with a warning that no section of the people, Right or Left, Blueshirt or I.R.A., would be allowed to raise a private army or prepare the way for a dictatorship in a country whose institutions and traditions were democratic, and with a moving appeal that all unauthorised arms in the country should be handed in "as the foundation of a monument to the Prince of Peace, as a pledge that Irishmen will never again fight one another."

(III)

The Blueshirts disappeared. General O'Duffy retired. Mr. Cosgrave resumed the leadership of the Opposition. Still another attempt to defeat de Valera and drive him out of public life by unconstitutional means had failed ignominiously.

Now, so far as Fianna Fail's social and economic programme was concerned, it was full steam ahead. The four years that elapsed between the General Election of 1933 and that of 1937 were extraordinarily productive. The country settled down to an era of peace and steady progress. De Valera's position had become almost impregnable and he was making full use of it to redeem the pledges which he had given the country before he came into office. The visionary was proving himself the practical man. The path-finder was becoming the road-builder.

What he set out to do was to translate the old Sinn Fein doctrine of self-sufficiency into solid achievement; to uproot the heresy that the test of a nation's prosperity is the volume of its external trade; to enable the country to feed and clothe itself and establish its own industries; and to put an end once and for all to Ireland's economic dependence on England.

Land division was speeded up, and on fertile plains where the herdsman and his dog had remained in undisputed possession from the days of the clearances and evictions, snug tillage farms began to appear. Gradually, the whole face of the countryside was changed. The ruined cabins of the Land War were swept away, and with the aid of Government grants new compact dwellings were erected. Wheat, beet, oats and barley took the place of grass. The area under wheat alone increased in five years from 20,000 acres to 220,000 acres. Three additional sugar factories were erected—one at Mallow, one at Thurles, one at Tuam—and the farmers were given a guaranteed market and a guaranteed price for their beet crop. Within two years the acreage under sugar beet increased from 15,000 to 57,000, almost sufficient to supply three-fourths of the needs of the whole population.

The change-over from pasture to crops was not effected without considerable opposition. The old legend, repeated in all the school-books in the days when Irish education was controlled from England, which pictured Ireland as "the fruitful mother of flocks and herds," did not die easily. The tradition of wheat-growing had been lost, and many farmers still believed the old story that both soil and climate were unsuitable. One Opposition Front Bencher declared that "he would not insult his land by attempting to grow wheat or beet."

There were other difficulties as well. There was a general slump in world prices for agricultural products which was felt in Ireland as much as elsewhere. The Opposition did not fail to make capital out of the fact, and the farmers were told that the depression was mainly due to the ruinous Economic War. Actually, the downward movement in prices had been in progress for some years before the Cosgrave Government fell and little had been done to lighten the blow to the country's agricultural economy. Tillage had remained at a standstill, and not only the bulk of the nation's wheat supply, but millions of pounds' worth of agricultural produce was being imported into a country which had at its disposal all the means of producing its own food.

What Fianna Fail aimed at was nothing less than a complete agricultural revolution, and de Valera's Government were determined that neither the world depression nor the Economic War would stand in the way. Both of these, in fact, had created circumstances in which the only salvation for the working farmers lay in a policy of self-sufficiency and exploitation of the home market. The farmer was "the man in the gap," and it was essential that he should be given help in the difficult period of transition. In addition to halving the Annuities, the Agricultural Grant was doubled, bacon and butter imports were stopped, dairy prices were stabilised, a system of bounties and subsidies was introduced, and legislation was passed providing that every miller must buy home-grown wheat up to a fixed amount. De Valera told the people that they would have to tighten their belts and go without certain things, but he promised them that the sacrifices they had to make would not go unrewarded. There were many who declared that he was making life too difficult, but those in the forefront of the fight—the working farmers—gave him loyal support. Tightening their belts a little was nothing new for a class who had never known luxury and whose powers of resistance had been strengthened throughout the years by the rigours of famine, rack-renting and evictions.

The industrial revival kept pace with the change-over in agriculture. Thirty years before, Arthur Griffith had pointed out that the economic life of the country could never be balanced without developing native industries. The swing-over from grazing to tillage was not enough. Ireland, to be economically independent, must not only feed herself, but supply herself with all the necessaries of life that could be produced at home; with such things as clothes and boots and machinery and building materials, and furniture and soap and cutlery. The Cosgrave Government had made tentative efforts to put Griffith's policy into operation by introducing a limited number of protective tariffs, but the pressure of British business interests had proved too much for them and the resultant advance in the direction of industrial self-sufficiency was ludicrously small.

The policy of de Valera, on the other hand, was

intensive and far-reaching. Making full use of the fiscal powers which it possessed, the Government established one industry after another, taking care not to make it a localised affair, but to spread the new factories as widely as possible throughout the country. This was not merely to avoid the evils that had followed in other countries from the over-centralisation of industry. It was part of a plan by which de Valera sought to provide work for farmers' sons and daughters near their own homes, to make industry conform to the general well-being of a country predominantly agricultural. Thus in the establishment of the new industries the location was regarded as of primary importance, and so it came about that Cork, Sligo, Limerick, Drogheda, Carlow, Waterford, Arklow, Ballyshannon, Portarlington, Tralee, Wexford, Nenagh, Galway, Thurles—a score of towns and cities shared in the industrial revival by having planted in their midst a factory or several factories which offered work to those who otherwise would have gone straight from the farm to the emigrant ship. In 1934 a Turf Development Board was set up and a Commission was sent to Russia and Germany to investigate the most up-to-date systems of turf-cutting and drying. A large area of bogland was taken over at Clonsast in Leix and an immense scheme for draining and cutting was begun. Other areas were taken over later, factories for the making of turf briquettes were erected, and the beginnings of a plan to make the country largely independent of imported coal were firmly laid.

The net value of industrial products increased from £18,218,000 in 1931 to £28,223,000 in 1940. The salaries and wages paid during the same period to workers engaged in the production of those goods increased from £8,009,000 to £13,701,000. 80,000 additional workers were put into employment. To illustrate the tremendous change that took place the figures relating to a single industry may be quoted. The year before de Valera came into office 5,158,000 pairs of boots and shoes had been imported; seven years later, as a result of home production, the figure had fallen to 266,000.

In addition to the tillage and industrial drives there was a rapid expansion of the social services. Between 1932 and 1938 some 120,000 houses were built or reconstructed, representing 90,000 more than in the previous decade. The amount paid in old age pensions was increased by approximately £1,000,000; a scheme of pensions for widows and orphans was put into operation; a Conditions of Employment Act was passed establishing a 48-hour week for adults and a 40-hour week for workers under 18, with an annual holiday with pay of at least six days, exclusive of statutory holidays. The same Act placed restrictions on the employment of women and children, and laid down special regulations with regard to night work and overtime. An Unemployment Assistance Act brought benefits to workers in non-insurable jobs—such as rural labourers—who had hitherto been excluded. Eleven and a half millions have been spent on Relief of Unemployment schemes by successive Fianna Fail Governments as compared with one million and a half under the Cosgrave regime. Grants for free milk for necessitous children were initiated and the yearly expenditure on school meals was doubled.

To-day the total amount expended on social services is something like twelve and a half millions annually, one of the highest, in proportion to revenue, in the world.

(IV)

In the constitutional sphere de Valera, true to his habit of never taking up a position which he could not hold, made his changes gradually and carefully. The abolition of the Senate was an exception. That body, which had given full, uncritical support to all the repressive measures of the Cosgrave regime, attempted, as soon as de Valera came into office, to establish itself as a barrier across the people's path. It held up the Abolition of the Oath Bill and the Blueshirt Bill, and was determined, apparently, to make the whole business of legislative reform a slow and cumbersome process. That decayed citadel of Irish landlordism, the Kildare Street Club—Dublin's counterpart of the London Carlton—from which Arthur Griffith, in an excess of generosity, had recruited so many of the Free State's original Senators, had never in all its history been distinguished for anything more admirable than a singularly myopic form of diehardism. It was the Kildare Street Club mind which still dominated the Senate when de Valera took office and which prevented it from seeing the writing on the wall. No statesman in de Valera's position could tolerate having a legislative programme approved by the people hampered at every turn by a thoroughly unrepresentative body and he acted swiftly and with determination. The Senate was abolished.

With regard to the Governor-Generalship he

adopted other methods. That it was almost universally unpopular there could be no doubt. Both as a symbol of the Free State's inferior status and as a very expensive ornament, it was irksome to the masses of the people. But to abolish it immediately would mean another Anglo-Irish crisis, and recurring crises were the last thing that de Valera wanted at a time when the immediate needs were peace and economic and social reform. Tim Healy, the first Governor-General, had enough sense of humour to grasp some of the anomalies of the position he occupied, and he was able to joke about it privately. "I'm Keeper of the King's Irish Cabbage Plot," he said to some English visitors whom he was entertaining at the Viceregal Lodge, "and you must admit"—pointing to the kitchen garden—"that they're good cabbages!" James MacNeill, a retired Indian Civil Service official who succeeded him, had brought home some memories of Durbar splendours and attempted to give the Viceregal building something of its old status. But he felt that there was no place for him under the democratisation of the Fianna Fail regime and soon handed in his resignation. Thereupon de Valera appointed in his place Donal Ua Buachalla (Donald Buckley), a Maynooth business man, and one of the few Volunteer leaders who had succeeded in bringing his men from the country to Dublin in Easter Week. Under him the office of Governor-General was shorn of all dignity and prestige. He attended no public functions and did not even occupy the official residence. In his place de Valera himself received envoys from foreign countries. The office was degraded, as it was intended that it should be degraded, and when the new Constitution came in 1937 it passed out of existence.

On the day following the abdication of Edward VIII de Valera introduced an External Relations Act in which, making use of the opportunity provided by that event, he further anticipated the Constitution and furnished a formula for international relations. The Act made it clear that, whilst the State might continue to make use of any instrument (e.g. the British Monarch) employed by any group or league of nations with which the State was associated for the purpose of international co-operation in matters of common concern, its relations with Britain or with any Dominion of the British Commonwealth were in future to be international relations in the fullest sense of the word. So far as the Twenty-six Counties were concerned, the definite status of inferiority imposed upon Ireland by the Treaty of 1921 was being steadily removed. With the coming of the new Constitution in 1937 it disappeared entirely.

(v)

In the Name of the Most Holy Trinity, from Whom is all authority, and to Whom, as our final end, all actions both of men and States must be referred,

We, the people of Eire,

Humbly acknowledging all our obligations to the Divine Lord, Jesus Christ, Who sustained our fathers through centuries of trial,

Gratefully remembering their heroic and unremitting struggle to regain the rightful independence of our Nation,

And seeking to promote the common good, with due observance of Prudence, Justice and

Charity, so that the dignity and freedom of the individual may be assured, true social order attained, the unity of our country restored, and concord established with other nations,

Do hereby adopt, enact and give to ourselves this Constitution.

Such was the Preamble to the historic document in which is embodied de Valera's greatest act of statesmanship, the new Irish Constitution of 1937.

The form and language of that Preamble could hardly come from any other country in the twentieth century world. It has the directness and simplicity of a prayer; it is the expression of a Catholic philosophy that has remained unchanged in a changing world; it is the dedication of a nation to the service of Christian and democratic principles.

Deliberately, the Constitution was drafted, not for twenty-six counties, but for the whole of the historic Irish nation. The framework which it was given is an anticipation of the day of unity.

There is no aspect of national or individual life which the Constitution does not cover. Equality of all citizens before the law, their personal rights, and their civil liberties are guaranteed by Article 40; the rights of the family by Article 41; freedom of education and the rights of the parent by Article 42; the right to private property by Article 43; freedom of conscience and of religion by Article 44. Article 45, clearly founded on the teachings of the great Encyclicals, and intended for the guidance of the legislative body, covers the whole domain of social justice. It lays down that the aim of the State is to ensure a distribution and control of ownership of the nation's material resources as will not only serve the common good, but give every citizen the means of livelihood. Free competition, which elsewhere has placed in the hands of financiers and monopolists so much power for evil, is to be watched and controlled. As many families as possible are to be placed on the land in economic security. "The State pledges itself to safeguard with especial care the economic interests of the weaker sections of the community, and where necessary to contribute to the support of the infirm, the widow, the orphan, and the aged."

Drawn up at a moment when new and conflicting ideologies were approaching their final clash in Europe, and when totalitarian doctrines were finding favour amongst powerful reactionary elements in Britain, the Constitution placed beyond all doubt the democratic basis of Ireland's governmental institutions. Article 5 lays down that "Ireland is a sovereign, independent, democratic State," and Article 6 that "all powers of government, legislative, executive and judicial, derive, under God, from the people, whose right it is to designate the rulers of the State, and, in final appeal, to decide all questions of national policy, according to the requirements of the common good." There was to be no truck with either Communism or Fascism.

Article 12 established the office of President of Ireland and set out the conditions and method of his election. A candidate must be nominated either by twenty members of the Oireachtas (Dail and Senate) or by not less than four County Councils, and the voting is by Proportional Representation. When elected the President takes an oath in the presence of both Houses, of the judges of the

Supreme Court and of other dignitaries, to dedicate himself to the service of the nation. He is in supreme command, like the President of the United States, of the country's armed forces, but his exercise of that command is subject to the control of the Dail. He cannot leave the country without permission of the Government, and can be impeached on a charge preferred by not less than thirty members of the Oireachtas. The Taoiseach, or Prime Minister, is appointed by the President on the nomination of the Dail.

Dr. Douglas Hyde became, after the enactment of the new Constitution, the first President of Ireland. Poet, playwright, folklorist, he had founded the Gaelic League forty-five years before, and in so doing had moulded the thought and outlook of the country to an extent not equalled by any thinker of his time. Like Wolfe Tone, Emmet, Davis and Mitchel, he is a product of Trinity College, Dublin, and like them he is a Protestant. It is a matter of no little significance that a Protestant should have been chosen to be the first President of a predominantly Catholic State. He has a Council of State, which is outside party politics, to advise him whenever a constitutional crisis arises.

The Senate was restored and re-fashioned under the Constitution. It consists of sixty members, eleven nominated by the Taoiseach, six elected by the Universities, and the remainder elected from panels representing such various interests as commerce, agriculture, public administration, and so on. The end in view was the creation of a Senate that would be vocational in character, but, in practice, the method of election has proved unsatisfactory and it is likely that some new plan will have to be devised. The Senate is, in its essence, an advisory body. It can hold up legislation for three months, it can initiate legislation, it can suggest amendments to the Dail, and it can refer matters in dispute to the President.

Article 29 deals with international relations and undoes the wrong that was done in the Treaty of 1921 and the dictated Constitution of 1922. The executive authority which those two documents vested in the British King is restored to its rightful place and vested in the people of Ireland, and Ireland is thereby given the status of a sovereign State in international affairs. Britain, to be sure, has not yet formally recognised or accepted the new Constitution or the new status, and by pretending to ignore what has happened, strives to keep alive the fiction that Ireland is still part of the British Commonwealth of Nations, but, as de Valera has remarked, " If they wish to keep on saying that we are in the Empire we cannot stop them."

Such, in brief, is the Constitution of 1937. It is a landmark in Ireland's struggle for independence and gives the citizens of Ireland a charter that is likely to endure. One would have thought that it would have been accepted, in broad outline, at any rate, by all political parties and debated at a high level of non-partisanship and constructive criticism. But that, some of de Valera's political opponents thought, would be giving its chief architect too much credit. The Constitution aimed directly, in some of its provisions, at wiping out the blunders of 1921 and 1922, and the

Cosgravites were still unwilling to admit that they had blundered. Ignoring both the logic of events and the remorseless march of history, they attacked the new document with venom and ferocity. The new Constitution, they alleged, would make de Valera a dictator (how, they never succeeded in explaining); they sneered at it as a "paper" Constitution (being a written Constitution it could not very well be anything else); they declared that it imperilled the liberty of the individual (though if there was one thing more rigidly safeguarded than another it was that). They declared that de Valera had established the office of Presidency for himself to fill. They strove to interpret the clause in Article 41 in which the State pledged itself "to endeavour to ensure that mothers shall not be obliged by economic necessity to engage in labour to the neglect of their duties in the home" as an attempt to interfere with the right of women to earn a living. The period that has elapsed since the Constitution was given the approval of the people has made nonsense of all such allegations. De Valera, who could probably have made himself a dictator without very much difficulty at any time during the past nine or ten years, remains the resolute democrat that he always was; the liberty of the individual remains unimpaired; the freedom of the Press and the radio and the right of free speech exist as before—save for the inevitable restrictions imposed by the war emergency; and no woman has had cause to complain that the Constitution has debarred her from making a livelihood.

As de Valera, whose hand and mind are to be

traced in almost every clause of the document, said in a broadcast in December, 1937: "The chief significance of the new Constitution coming at the present time is that it is in complete accord with national conviction and tradition in these matters, and that it bears upon its face, from the first words of its preamble to the dedication at its close, the character of the public law of a great Christian democracy." To-day that is generally accepted by the Irish people.

(VI)

On three important occasions between his first appearance at Geneva in 1932 and the coming of the second Great War de Valera intervened purposefully at the Assembly of the League of Nations. His 1932 warning had gone unheeded, and as year after year passed without any attempt being made to translate the principles of the Covenant of the League into concerted action that would bring peace to a distracted world, his belief in the sincerity of the bigger Powers was strained almost to breaking point. Yet he did not despair. If the League failed, he knew, there was little hope for the future. But that it should be allowed to fail, that the one powerful barrier standing between civilisation and barbarism should be pulled down by the hands of the very nations that had erected it, seemed to him a calamity of the first magnitude. He was determined to support the League to the end, but equally determined to frustrate every attempt on the part of the big Powers to degrade it into an instrument for achieving their own selfish ends.

In 1934 there arose the question of admitting

Russia to membership. De Valera favoured admittance, but disliked the methods that were being employed. There was little hope for unanimity, as there were members of the League who would resent the presence at Geneva of the representatives of a State, however powerful, that was committed to a philosophy which they regarded as destructive of Christian civilisation. Whatever decision might be reached, de Valera held, should be reached openly and not as the result of secret intrigues.

"The procedure to be adopted," he said, "should not be made a matter for consideration in hotel rooms where the voice of those delegates who might oppose Russia's entry would not be heard. The question should be openly and frankly faced. It is obvious that anyone who has the interests of the League at heart must desire to see in it a nation of such importance as Russia. I represent a country which, if you consider its political and religious ideals, is as far apart as the poles from Soviet Russia. But I would be willing to take the responsibility of saying openly and frankly here that I would support and vote for the entry of Russia into the League on account of the considerations I have mentioned."

He emphasised that he still believed in the League, but asked the Assembly to countenance nothing that would excite suspicion or give an impression of intrigue. M. Motta, the Swiss delegate, had suggested that, before being admitted, Russia should be asked to give certain guarantees. De Valera appealed to the Soviet representative. "It is not merely enough to concern oneself with politics. We must not exclude the purpose of human life. The only way that the human conscience can be eased is by an assurance given freely and by the action of the Russian Government itself. The things that count most in human life are being attacked in Russia. Hundreds of millions of Christians believe that to deprive a man of his religion is to deprive life of its meaning. Christians believe that the one hope of securing peace is by obedience to the primary Commandment of Our Saviour, 'Love one another.' Speaking as one who has hopes in the future of the League, and as the representative of a people that has no quarrel with the Russian Government, I urge the Russian Government to proclaim that the guarantee of liberty of conscience and freedom of worship, which they have guaranteed to American citizens in their agreement with America, shall be universalised and extended, not only to other citizens in Soviet Russia, but also to the inhabitants of that land."

A year later the League was confronted with the threat of aggressive action by Italy against Abyssinia. As in the case of the Sino-Japanese conflict, the big Powers shirked their obligations and no effective action was taken. De Valera's position was not an easy one, for the friendship that existed between Italy and Ireland was older and deeper than any based on merely political considerations. Yet there was no hesitation in his choice of a decision and no mincing of words when he came to criticise the League's display of impotence.

"Over fifty nations pledged themselves to one another in the most solemn manner, each to respect the independence and to preserve the integrity of the territories of the others. One of these nations turned its back on its pledges freely given and was adjudged almost unanimously by the remainder to have been an aggressor, and now, one by one, we have come to confess that we can do nothing about it. It is a sad confession as well as a bitter one."

The behaviour of the League in that crisis would, he declared, determine whether it was worthy to survive. If on any pretext it permitted the sovereignty of even the weakest of its members to be unjustly taken away, the whole foundation of the League would crumble into dust. Statesmen, not soldiers, should deal with Europe's problems. He warned the small nations not to become the tools of the great Powers and to resist to the utmost every attempt to force them into war against their will.

"The peace of Europe depends, as everybody knows, on the will of the great Powers. If the great Powers of Europe would only meet now in that peace conference which will have to be held after Europe has once again been drenched in blood, if they would be prepared to make now in advance only a tithe of the sacrifices each of them will have to make should war begin, the terrible menace that threatens us all to-day could be warded off."

When de Valera made his first speech at Geneva he was greeted with silence. On this occasion there was loud applause when he sat down. He had won the ear of the Assembly. "The speech of an idealist," said one delegate, "and of a prophet," added another. "He certainly hit a few boundaries," said an Australian. At home the Opposition attempted to make some capital out of his stand in the Abyssinian crisis, but he had little difficulty in justifying an attitude of which the vast majority of the Irish people approved. To critics of the Left, who seemed to find something to cavil at in the spectacle of Ireland and Britain travelling the same road on the Sanctions question, he replied with dry humour that if he should by chance find himself on the road to heaven in bad company he would be very foolish for that reason to go to the other place. And to Mr. Cosgrave, who spoke about bargaining, he retorted sharply that one did not barter about the right thing; in a question of right or wrong you either did the right thing or you did not do it.

The civil war which broke out a year later in Spain—the land of his father's fathers—was not only a source of deep personal distress to de Valera, but it placed him in a position of even greater delicacy than the Italo-Abyssinian conflict had done. The Church and almost the entire Catholic press were strongly, not to say violently, pro-Franco, and popular feeling in Ireland was greatly stirred. General O'Duffy organised and led a contingent to Spain to fight against the Reds. A Christian Front movement was started to assist Franco with money and medical supplies. But de Valera refused to be stampeded by any wave of popular emotion. He refused to recognise Franco, and gave his support to the League's policy of non-intervention. Whatever temporary unpopularity he incurred, his attitude gained in the long run the approval of the people who had kept their heads. O'Duffy's expedition proved a sorry fiasco, and the Christian Front movement, for which the Church had shown no great enthusiasm, was withered by a phrase.

Senator Frank MacDermot spoke of it as "cashing in on Christianity."

From the beginning de Valera held that the war in Spain was Spain's affair, but he was under no illusion that the non-intervention policy of the League was anything more than an elaborate pretence. Russia, Italy and Germany were deeply involved, and neither France nor Britain could boast of having clean hands in the affair. The usual intrigues were afoot at Geneva, and a draft resolution, instigated by a Power which was heavily embroiled in the conflict, was proposed, suggesting that the League should consider ending the policy of non-intervention unless foreign troops were withdrawn from Spain. De Valera at once opposed the resolution. Non-intervention—polite fiction though it was—had been adopted for the purpose of preventing the war overflowing the Spanish frontiers, and it had, whatever unreality lay behind it, so far succeeded in doing that. He demanded freedom of decision for each Government, and when the resolution came before the Assembly his lead was followed by several other States and the resolution defeated.

The League died, as de Valera prophesied that it would die, and the catastrophe that he had feared overtook Europe. But one small nation, at least, had no reason to be ashamed of the part that her representative had played in the deliberations at Geneva. In an Assembly where plain speech was not welcomed and where the art of enshrouding formidable meanings in a veil of amiable words had been brought to perfection, he had spoken his mind. No decoding was ever necessary in the case of de Valera's speeches. He had the courage, in a place where cynicism and insincerity were rife, to voice the instincts of his religious faith and to express the mind and the heart of common humanity.

(VII)

In April, 1938, the Economic War came to an end. De Valera went to London and there he and the son of the man who had killed Home Rule in the eighties reached a settlement which was greatly to the credit of both parties. Once again the truth was emphasised of the saying that it is only from the Tory Party in Britain that Ireland can ever hope to gain anything. The Tory Party alone has the power, and it was with a Tory Prime Minister, Neville Chamberlain, that de Valera negotiated across a table in Downing Street.

The London Agreement was more comprehensive and far-reaching than even the most optimistic could have hoped for. Britain relinquished her claim to the Land Annuities and accepted a lump sum of £10,000,000 in full and final settlement of all financial claims. The penal tariffs were removed and a revision of Customs duties was made for the purpose of facilitating trade and commerce between the two countries. More important and more dramatic was the abrogation of the defence provisions of the Treaty of 1921 and the handing back of the three naval ports, Cobh, Berehaven, and Lough Swilly. The British Care and Maintenance Parties were withdrawn and the ports and defences were transferred, unconditionally, to Ireland. England could no longer claim the right of entering or fortifying an Irish harbour in time of war and virtual recognition was at last given to Irish sovereignty over the Twenty-six Counties. With regard to Partition alone there was failure. De Valera strove with all his might to have the territorial unity of Ireland made part of the settlement, and no doubt indicated that the people and Government of the Twenty-six Counties were willing to make sacrifices to achieve that unity, but all to no purpose. Even Neville Chamberlain, who displayed both imagination and generosity, did not feel his position strong enough to give the settlement the finality that only the abolition of Partition could bring about. The Unionist diehards, traditional enemies of the Irish cause, and the British War Office, loath to surrender a last bridgehead in Ireland, blocked the way.

But even as it stood, the Agreement was a tremendous advance, as well as being a complete justification of the policy which, with patience and consummate skill, de Valera had pursued from the moment he returned to power. As such it was welcomed by the vast majority of the people of Ireland. The Cosgravites, to be sure, hardened in suspicion, tried to discover some grounds for criticism, and suggested that the settlement was too good to be true; underlying it and hidden out of sight, they hinted, there must be some compromising arrangement. There was none, of course, and when de Valera went to the country, as he did almost immediately, he was returned with what was, under the Proportional Representation system, an overwhelming majority. The figures were:

De Valera, 77; Cosgrave, 45; Labour, 9; Independents, 7.

De Valera's position was stronger than ever and he resolved to use it for the purpose of clearing away the last obstacle that stood in the way of a lasting friendship between Ireland and Britain. As a result of the Agreement Partition had become an isolated problem. He determined to bring all the forces of goodwill, not only in Britain and Ireland, but in the United States and the British Colonies, to bear upon it. He knew that he had a good case, and that if an all-Ireland plebiscite were taken on Partition there would be a majority of more than four to one against it. He recalled what Lloyd George himself, Partition's chief sponsor, had said to Craigavon in 1920: " Your proposal would stereotype a frontier based neither on national features nor broad geographical considerations, by giving it the character of an international boundary. Partition on these grounds the majority of the Irish people will never accept, neither could we conscientiously attempt to enforce it." But that was exactly what had been enforced, and de Valera planned, by means of an intensive educational campaign, to let the masses of the British people—always somewhat hazy about the realities of the Irish problem—know it.

But before his plans could be launched, the I.R.A. struck. Had Partition been ended by the London Agreement that secret organisation would have died an instant death, for there would no longer have been any justification for or any meaning in its existence. But the failure with regard to Partition gave it a new lease of life. Belfast, where there was one law for the Catholic and another for the Orangeman, where an armed constabulary, "Specials," and a Special Powers' Act kept one-third of the populace in subjection, and where the gaols were filled with political prisoners, was now its seeding-ground. Ignoring the success that had hitherto attended de Valera's step-by-step policy, the extremists of the I.R.A., with their eyes fixed on the pogroms and evictions in Belfast, began to hit out savagely and blindly. For the tactics of statesmanship they substituted bombs, and innocent people were killed in Britain in a campaign of terrorism similar to that of the Fenians in sixty-seven. But there was more excuse for the Fenians than for the 1938 terrorists. In 1867 the whole of Ireland lay under the iron heel and constitutional agitation was meeting with no success. Now, with a native Parliament in existence, with Ireland's voice heard frequently and forcefully at Geneva, and with all the machinery for a world-wide campaign against Partition at hand, the bombing methods of the I.R.A. were not only reckless, but criminal. De Valera denounced them with vehemence and adopted the strongest measures possible. But the harm had been done. After the London Agreement the relations between the peoples of the two islands had been more cordial than at probably any other moment for centuries, and the good feeling that had been engendered encouraged the hope that soon Partition would be added to the many injustices which had been swept away. The terrorist campaign threw the new movement back and spread a wave of anti-Irish feeling throughout Great Britain, a feeling which the British Press and certain members of the British judicial bench did nothing to allay. How de Valera would have coped with the new obstacle in his path, had world conditions remained normal, can now only remain a matter of speculation. Other forces, equally blind, had been let loose in the world and soon both Britain and Ireland were presented with problems infinitely greater than any arising from the terrorist methods of a small secret organisation.

(VIII)

When the second Great War broke out there was never any doubt as to the attitude Ireland would adopt. The whole of its history, ancient and modern, weighted the scales down crushingly on the side of neutrality. De Valera had paved the way that made neutrality possible; now he had merely to interpret the people's will. As far back as 1935, when the crisis was beginning to boil up in Europe, he had stated that the Irish nation had no intention of becoming embroiled in any world conflict. Now that the conflict had come he repeated that declaration with emphasis. That he was speaking for a united nation there was no question whatever. Not a single voice was raised in the Dail in favour of Ireland entering the war. Cosgravites, Labour and Independents were at one in declaring that neutrality was the only possible policy.

The four-and-a-half years that have since passed have tested de Valera's capacity for leadership more severely than any in the whole course of his political career. A multiplicity of problems, great and small, arising out of the war, have beset his Government. For a small nation, set in the midst of the war zone, with at the outset only the nucleus of a defence organisation, liable to be cut off from supplies of food, fuel, raw materials and petrol, with little or nothing in the way of shipping facilities, to adopt a policy of neutrality was one thing; to bring about a condition of affairs in which neutrality could survive was quite another. The tale of how it was successfully achieved will constitute, when it comes to be told, one of the romantic stories of Irish history. How an efficient and well-equipped army of a quarter-million men was brought into existence within a twelve-month, how the world was scoured for ships and a small fleet assembled in a time of shipping famine, how cargoes were brought from the ends of the world across perilous seas, how year after year the farmers of Ireland redoubled their efforts to ward off famine, how the Irish boglands were pressed into service to provide fuel for the people, how a tireless and most efficient Minister of Supplies succeeded in keeping the country's young industries vigorously alive, how thousands of makeshifts and experiments were put into operation, how employers kept employees on their pay-rolls for whom there was little work, how the workers shared out what employment there was so that as few as possible should lose their homes, how the State and the local authorities strove to lift the burdens off the shoulders of the poorest—the record of such achievements and the spirit of self-sacrifice which alone made them possible, have added a stirring chapter to Ireland's history.

Inspiring and dominating the whole united effort stands the figure of de Valera. To him, more than to any other single man, is due, under Heaven, that the Irish State stands outside the struggle that is devastating the world and that its people have so far escaped the worst horrors of war. At every moment of crisis it is for his voice they have waited; in every difficulty they have looked to him for guidance. When, in March, 1944, a demand that could not in the circumstances be regarded as otherwise than unjust and unreasonable was made to the Government of which he is the head by one belligerent nation and supported by another, the reply that he made to that demand—a reply that was characterised by dignity, firmness and tact—instantly rallied around him not only the people of Ireland but people of Irish blood in every country in the world.

There may have been moments when the stress and anxiety of the times have seemed to him an almost intolerable burden, but if so, he has shown no sign of it in public. Always, even on the occasions when he has had to issue grave warnings, his bearing has been one of quiet confidence. "If we stand united and are prepared to share in an equality of sacrifice, we shall come through," he has said. And the people have stood by him.

(IX)

In the General Election of June, 1943, Fianna Fail had secured only 67 seats out of 138. This in itself was, under the system of Proportional Representation, a considerable total, being more than twice that of the chief Opposition party and four times that of the other two Opposition groups, Labour and Clan na Talmhan, the latter a new party representing the small farmers of the West and

South-West. But it was less than a majority of the whole Dail and de Valera was dissatisfied. Declaring his policy on the first day's sitting of the new assembly, he pointed to the indecisive result of the election and said:

> "Is there any solution other than a solution by the people themselves? I do not see it. I feel satisfied that if there is to be good government in the country the people will again have to be appealed to. They know the results of their voting. . . . So far as we are concerned we are prepared to carry on, but we will not deviate by the slightest hair's-breadth from the path we should have pursued if we had an all-over majority."

Some eleven months later—on May 9, 1944—the Opposition parties combined to defeat the Government on a major measure—a Bill reorganising the whole transport system of the country and carrying a Government guarantee of interest on publicly-subscribed capital. Previously, there had been more speculative buying of railway stocks than usual, and the Opposition brought the charge that information about the guarantee, which should have been kept secret, had become known to individuals and demanded a public inquiry. De Valera at once agreed and set up an imposing tribunal of judges. But when the Transport Bill came up for Second Reading the Opposition made a further demand—that it should be postponed until the tribunal had reported. De Valera resisted the demand—in which two wholly unconnected things, the reorganisation of transport and certain Stock Exchange dealings, were linked up—and in the resultant division his Government was defeated by 64 votes to 63.

He at once appealed to the country, an action which took the Opposition parties, none of which desired an election, completely by surprise. They believed, apparently, that de Valera would not venture to face the electorate with charges of Stock Exchange gambling ringing in his ears. But they might have known that he has a deep, an almost mystical, belief in "the people" and that he would seek their judgment on the important issue that had arisen. The Cosgrave party had just lost its leader, who had retired into private life three months earlier, leaving the direction of the fortunes of Fine Gael in the hands of Richard Mulcahy, who as a political leader had yet to prove himself. The Labour Party had split into two over the question of Communist penetration; and the new party, Clan na Talmhan, had not fulfilled its early promise.

The results of the election thoroughly justified de Valera's faith in the good sense of the people. Despite a fierce campaign against the Government by the three Opposition parties and by all but one of the principal newspapers, he had the easiest of victories. The figures were: Fianna Fail, 76; Fine Gael, 30; Labour, 8; National Labour, 4; Clan na Talmhan, 9; Independents, 11. Such an impressive majority afforded ample proof that the electors still had the utmost confidence in a leadership which had steered the country safely through so many crises. As a London newspaper said, "The results of the election indicate that de Valera is to the people of Eire what Churchill is to the people of Britain."

 (D1238)

Photo [Irish Press

A section of the crowd at a de Valera meeting in College Green, Dublin,

CHAPTER FIFTEEN

"Dev."

> 'Tis a rugged road, more so than it seems, to follow a pace so rambling and uncertain as that of the soul: to penetrate the dark profundities of its intricate internal windings; to choose and lay hold of so many nimble motions.
>
> —MONTAIGNE.

(I)

IT is highly improbable that there will ever be a single, definitive estimate of, say, Pitt or Gladstone or O'Connell or Parnell, and it is equally certain that there will always be diverse opinions of the personal stature and historic achievement of de Valera. But of his significance in the modern history of the Irish nation there can never be any question. One can go even farther and say, with little fear of contradiction, that no Irishman at any time has so completely dominated the circumstances which gave him his opportunity.

The qualities that make for personal greatness are as rare as they are indefinable, but, when encountered, they are unmistakable. Abraham Lincoln was a man of rugged simplicity, who loved broad jokes, and who was often the despair of men whom he had gathered around him in a time of crisis. His greatness is not easily contained in any logic of historical causation, but nobody has ever doubted it who has read the words that he spoke at Gettysburg.

The same is true of de Valera, who resembles Lincoln in more than physical characteristics. To the English mind he is a puzzle, because both his character and his methods are different from anything that is to be found in their own gallery of great men. In the centuries from Elizabeth to Victoria, in all the period during which England was rising from the status of a small island nation to imperial greatness, the statesmen whom her people revered have been of quite another kind. The English tradition has been rationalist, pugnacious and materialist; it has accepted and thrived on a creed of progress through material welfare which has left no room for the mystical side of religion. It cannot understand a Gandhi, a Terence MacSwiney, a de Valera. When Gandhi enters upon a three weeks' fast in order to induce a sense of sin in those whom he regards as the oppressors of his country, they regard what he does as odd, freakish and impracticable. When MacSwiney dies in Brixton Gaol after a seventy-four days' fast with the purpose of focusing the eyes of the world upon the wrongs of his country, they greet his sacrifice with a puzzled, uneasy silence. When they encounter a man like de Valera, for whom material progress is only the least part of a nation's advance, and whose nationalism is emotional as well as intellectual, they regard him as an eccentric. Don Quixote was a Spaniard, not an Englishman, and de Valera has Spanish blood in his veins. If he is eager to go out and fight injustice and oppression and sometimes to tilt at windmills—and there is a good deal to be said for a man who occasionally tilts at windmills—by so much is he outside the tradition that a materialist world respects.

But his own people understand him. They, a people of whom Yeats has said that they "believe so much in the soul and so little in anything else that they are never entirely certain that the earth is solid under the footsole," have no cynical scorn for the knight-errant or the crusader. To them the lost cause often seems the only good cause. Their history is one of a people who, if "they went forth to battle and always fell," fell only to rise again. Always, for them, there was the prophecy of St. Malachi. Always there was a star in the darkness. And so it came about that a conquest which was always being completed never became final.

To most Englishmen—and, indeed, to many Irishmen—the finality of the conquest received its hallmark on December 6th, 1921. Thenceforth, they believed, there would be an end of a problem that had baffled the best brains in England for six centuries. Ireland, British statesmen hoped and believed, would accept with gratitude the undoubted material benefits that would spring from a limited measure of freedom and settle down thereafter to a place in the imperial sun. Their politicians and their newspapers hailed the Treaty as the end. But one man, whose mind crystallized Irish thought and tradition, knew that they were wrong. He knew that the spirit of nationhood could not thus easily be disposed of, that there were certain things with regard to which compromise is not merely cowardly, but morally indefensible. De Valera interposed his rock-like figure in the path of the stampede of a nation.

It is that, more than anything else, that gives him his stature in the eyes of the Irish people and that will give him an abiding place amongst the great names of Irish history.

(II)

At sixty-one Eamon de Valera is as straight and tall, though not nearly so thin or lanky, as when he led his men into Boland's Mills in 1916. He is now, as the Irish phrase has it, " a fine figure of a man," broad-shouldered, well-built and erect. His face is fuller and less gaunt than it was in the bitter years and his dark-brown hair has only the smallest touches of grey. Nobody would call him photogenic; cartoonists delight in him but he fills camera-men with despair. His eyes, which at one time threatened to fail entirely, are now, thanks to a successful operation by an Irish surgeon, quite strong again.

Sartorially, he is almost as undistinguished as Lincoln. He still affects black, clerical-looking attire, though in the summer of 1943 he surprised those who notice such things by appearing in a suit of pin-stripe blue. He wears a broad-brimmed black hat and a dark overcoat that is much too long to gain the approval of the editor of the *Tailor and Cutter*. When he goes on a long motor journey or for a tramp over the fields—he is a great walker—he exchanges the broad-brimmed hat for a close-fitting dark-blue beret.

His home is a modest detached villa in a Dublin suburb, which Mrs. de Valera, most capable of housekeepers, runs with the help of a single maid. Frugal comfort—a phrase that he has used many times in his speeches—is the keynote of his domestic life. He never smokes and hardly drinks at all, though on one occasion he created a mild sensation in temperance circles when he suggested that a light beer might prove a better national beverage than tea. But his tastes are simple rather than ascetic. Always he has been, comparatively, at any rate, a poor man; and he is a poor man still.

Of his five sons one, Brian, a popular and promising university student, was killed in a riding accident in the Phœnix Park in 1936, a tragedy which drew to him the sympathy of the whole nation. Of the others, Vivion, the eldest, is a Commandant in the Army; Eamon is a doctor; Rory, having completed his Army course, is studying archæology; Terry is a solicitor's apprentice. His daughter Emer is married; the other, Maureen, is a lecturer in botany at University College, Galway.

To everybody in Ireland, including his wife, Mr. de Valera is "Dev." The nickname is at once a tribute and a token of affection. Its universal use indicates a close bond of intimacy between the leader and the people. Parnell, who seldom lost his icy aloofness, was "The Chief"; Arthur Griffith was always Arthur Griffith and Mr. Cosgrave has remained Mr. Cosgrave; but de Valera, amongst his own, will be "Dev" to the end.

He is widely read and is fond of poetry, though some of the modern Irish poets, whose modernity is beyond him, allege that he is only interested in poetry because he believes that it is "good for the people": which, they declare, is absurd. To that one might reply that, at any rate, it is refreshing to find a twentieth-century statesman who thinks that people need poetry as well as bread; it is even refreshing to find a twentieth-century statesman who is interested in poetry at all. Admittedly, de Valera is nearer to the spirit of Davis than to that of Yeats, but even Yeats did not despise the poetry of Davis. He is not a regular theatre-goer, but is seen occasionally at a Shakespearian production, a Gaelic play, or a symphony concert. He is fond of the radio, but the films have passed him by.

He rises early and is usually in his office at Government Buildings by half-past nine. The office is a simply-furnished room with nothing in it to impress the visitor except the man himself. He puts in a long day, returning home for dinner and tea, and often working late into the night. He rarely takes a holiday and appears to thrive on hard work. Scrupulous in his attention to detail, but considerate towards those who work with him or under him, he inspires a deep affection in his colleagues. None of them has ever broken with him, and his Ministers are mostly the same men who started with him over twenty-five years ago.

The legend that he is a dour, morose man, with the temperament of a Carthusian monk, and no hobbies save quaternions, has long ago been killed. People have discovered that he can laugh heartily and that he enjoys a joke. During the stressful, anxious years the grave earnestness of his public pronouncements was seldom tempered by any light relief, but in recent times he has mixed humour with his arguments. In the 1943 Election the Opposition went to the country with a demand for a Coalition Government, for which there appeared to be no general enthusiasm. "This Coalition stunt," said de Valera, "reminds me of the story of the Chinaman who stood at a street corner day after day swinging a dead cat in his hand. People wondered why, and one day somebody asked him what he was doing with the dead cat. 'Oh,' said the Chinaman, 'it's for sale.' 'For sale! But surely nobody wants to buy a dead cat?' 'Maybe so,' said the Chinaman, 'but in case anybody does I have one here.'" When the election was over the Coalition was as dead as the cat.

His oratory is not at all in the Irish tradition. One searches his speeches in vain to discover any trace of the mighty eloquence of a Burke or a Grattan, the flashing wit of a Curran, the flamboyance and rollicking humour of an O'Connell, the Ciceronian periods of a Redmond, or the spell-bindery of a Jim Larkin. At his worst he is dull; at his best, he is direct, forceful, and extraordinarily effective. Nobody who listens to him when he is really roused, or on a big occasion, can fail to be impressed by a sense of his burning sincerity. Sometimes, when he broadcasts, one is given the inescapable impression of the old schoolmaster addressing a class: he becomes didactic, persuasive, patiently argumentative, or disarmingly simple. On St. Patrick's Day, 1943, he went to the microphone to give his annual talk, which contained the following remarkable passage:

> "The Ireland which we have dreamed of would be the home of a people who valued material wealth only as the basis of a right living, of a people who were satisfied with frugal comfort and devoted their leisure to the things of the spirit; a land whose countryside would be bright with cosy homesteads, whose

fields and villages would be joyous with the sounds of industry, with the romping of sturdy children, the contests of athletic youths, the laughter of comely maidens; whose firesides would be forums for the wisdom of old age. It would, in a word, be the home of a people living the life that God desires men should live."

It takes a big man to say a thing like that, to say it without insincerity or even self-consciousness, to say it in the year 1943 in the midst of a titanic war and an over-mechanised, over-sophisticated world. Some of his listeners murmured 'Utopia!' and the Dublin cynics cried, '1066 and all that!' But if it was an Arcadian picture that he drew, de Valera was speaking to a country whose civilisation is rural rather than urban, to a people whose standards of living have been moulded and simplified by centuries of persecution, spoliation and famine, to a people of whom he is one. An Englishman or a resident in a fashionable Dublin suburb might regard the sentiments expressed as hopelessly naïve, but the plain people of the Irish countryside listened with respect. They realised that the ideal put before them was the dream of a man who has seen so much of the horrors of war in his own country and in other countries that he has come to believe the world's salvation may lie in a return to a simpler and healthier way of living.

In the Dail his supremacy is unquestioned. He dominates the national assembly with, apparently, effortless ease. Amongst the rank and file of both the Government Party and the Opposition the debating standard is not high, and neither of the Front Benches is remarkable for its oratorical talent. Mr. Cosgrave is a facile and, on occasions, an eloquent speaker, but he lacks personality; Mr. Sean Lemass is lucidity itself, and his speeches often exhibit power and pugnacity; Mr. Sean MacEntee excels in the lightning thrust of rapier wit; Mr. James Dillon, readiest of phrasemakers, exhibits many of the qualities which gave Joseph Devlin the title of a 'duodecimo Demosthenes.' But de Valera stands head and shoulders above the rest. In any major debate everybody waits for the Taoiseach's pronouncement. Almost invariably he confines himself to big, broad issues and leaves the making of small debating points to others.

Once, when he was founding the newspaper of which he is still the controlling director, he interviewed a timid young man who had been appointed to the editorial staff. "Do you think you could write leading articles?" asked de Valera. "I'll try," said the young man, "but I'm not politically-minded." "Curiously enough, neither am I," said de Valera. Then the timid young man and the man who is one of the first statesmen in Europe both smiled. But, in a very real sense, what he said is true. For party politics as they are generally understood—for politics that are no more than a sort of "game"—de Valera has neither a liking nor an aptitude. He would, if it could conceivably be managed, conduct the affairs of the nation in an atmosphere as serene and elevated as that of the Institute of Higher Studies, which is his own creation and his very special pride.

Foreign visitors to Ireland who meet him seldom fail to be impressed by his personality. "One gets a definite impression of greatness from him," said

Professor C. E. M. Joad, who met him in the spring of 1943, " such as I, at least, derived from nobody else, certainly not from any other member of the Government or of the Opposition Party." "A striking figure, a most remarkable man," said Mr. Harold Nicolson, who met him about the same time. Mr. John Gunther, who was struck by his intellectual stature and by what he called his " terrific Irishness," was at a loss to reconcile his " obsessive hatred of Britain " with his emphatic declaration, made in 1935, that he would never allow Irish territory to be used by any foreign power as a base for attacking England. It was a bad slip on the part of Mr. Gunther, and all the more so because the book in which it appeared has had an enormous circulation on both sides of the Atlantic. At no time has de Valera cherished any hatred of England: his public pronouncements from 1917 to 1943 afford the clearest proof to the contrary. If he opposed the Treaty of 1921 it was because he was convinced that it would not bring peace between the two countries; and time has proved that he was right. What he has hated and what he has fought against all his life is the attempt on the part of a big nation to hold a smaller nation in complete or partial subjection—a very different thing.

(III)

" De Valera's Ireland " is a phrase that has been used more than once during recent years. It is a permissible phrase. The new Ireland bears the hallmark of his personality and achievements.

Under the Cosgrave regime the changes that took place did not strike very deeply into the roots of

Irish life. The strait-jacket of the Treaty made free movement difficult in the social as well as the political sphere. The acute discomfort it caused to those who had accepted it was evidenced by their strenuous efforts to loosen its bonds, efforts which met with a considerable measure of success during the period from 1926 to 1931. But their delimitation of the national ideal to the achievement of Dominion status within the British Empire inevitably prevented them from bringing about revolutionary changes in the fabric of Irish society. Britain was still the " predominant partner "; Dublin still looked to London. Provincialism was the keynote of the time, and the presence of an Irish Governor-General at the Viceregal Lodge emphasised rather than disproved that fact. Besides, the ten years from 1922 to 1932 were years of unrest, during which the Free State was being painfully born and during which its Ministers, through pressure of circumstances, were forced to ally themselves with the reactionary elements in the country. The changes that came about—soldiers dressed in green instead of khaki, the harp without the crown on the cap-badges of the police, green pillar boxes instead of red, new stamps and new coins—were superficial rather than fundamental. The way of thought had not changed greatly. Fashions and standards of life were much the same as before. The cynicism and disillusionment engendered by the Civil War told heavily against the creation of an Irish Ireland. The new bourgeoisie was hardly distinguishable from the old.

To-day the social revolution is almost complete. The Irish world which was the background of the novels of Joyce and George Birmingham and Somerville and Ross has vanished as utterly as the Irish world of the novels of Lover and Lever. The Big House has gone. Its former occupants are to be found neither in the countryside nor in the Senate nor on public boards. The few of the old gentry class who remain have completely isolated themselves. They take no part in the public life of the State and appear to have no interests save sport. The doom that one of their number, Standish O'Grady, prophesied for them fifty years ago has overtaken them. Here and there, in a decayed mansion in a remote rural back-water, a former landowner may be found living a lonely, almost solitary, existence, but the great majority have fled the country, preferring to end their days in the residential hotels of Torquay or Bournemouth.

De Valera did not will this. He had no desire to drive anybody away. When he abolished the Senate after he came into power it was not because it was largely composed of members of the old Ascendancy, but because it attempted to hold up the nation's advance to independence. If, as a consequence, the diehards went sulking to their tents, there was nothing that he could do about it.

On the other hand, the Protestants generally—Protestant was until recently almost synonymous with Unionist—have adapted themselves to the changing conditions. At the outset they had little love for the new regime, and in the prosperous residential suburbs of Dublin, in Trinity College, in the Protestant educational establishments, and in the Church of Ireland generally. Fianna Fail had few followers. To be sound on the question of de Valera was almost a necessary condition of political and social respectability. It took a long time before the Protestant doctors and lawyers and professors and business men could bring themselves to ponder on the case for the Revolution or to admit to themselves that the chief revolutionary was not the wild man they had imagined. But as time went on many of them were won over, and even those who still disagreed with him came to respect him. Geneva and the Blueshirt episode, of course, greatly increased his stature, but it was the character of the man that was mainly accountable for the change. His personal integrity, his unfailing courtesy, his broad tolerance, his avoidance of all that is cheap and petty in public controversy, his very simplicity of manner—all these combined to earn for him the good regard of people who were reared in a tradition and a creed diametrically opposed to his. De Valera is a fervent Catholic, and more than ninety per cent of the citizens of the Twenty-six Counties are Catholics, but under his Government no Protestant has ever suffered any loss on account of his religion. On scores of occasions, in fact, speakers at Protestant Synods have paid glowing tributes to the way in which the Protestant minority has been treated.

It is still true, however, that the real secret of de Valera's power is to be found in the support of the "small men." No doubt his economic and social policy favoured the class to which they belonged more than any other. Those who had been bred in an atmosphere of social inferiority began to come into their own. Class distinctions almost disappeared and British titles came to count for nothing. Power, for the first time in Ireland's history, was placed in the hands of a democracy. The nation, in fact, made a vigorous recovery after 1932, and initiative and self-reliance began to take the place of the old tradition of dependence upon Government grants and favours. De Valera's gospel of self-sufficiency has had spiritual as well as material results. The re-invigoration of the nation is no longer a matter for doubt. The farmers—to take only one example—have to work harder, but they take a natural pride in their wheatfields and their greatly improved farms. As an American ecclesiastic, revisiting the country in 1939, said: "In de Valera's Ireland the people's eyes are brighter and their backs straighter."

(IV)

Since the present war began many cultivated Englishmen have visited Ireland, to them—in a famous phrase—"a small country that we know nothing about." Many of them have come with the best possible intentions and the worst possible equipment: an education received at English public schools. All of them are anxious to discover why, in this crisis of civilisation, more than three-quarters of Ireland should, with an unparalleled demonstration of unity, have adopted a neutral position.

They look for Fascism and they fail to find it. They look for hostility to Britain and they discover very little. The one thing they do find, as Wendell Willkie found in Turkey, is that the people are almost aggressively neutral. Nobody in Eire—to employ the convenient but wrongly-used word—is, they soon come to realise, in the least anxious to plunge the country into war for 'a democratic civilisation,' for 'the defence of Christianity,' for 'the English way of living,' or, in fact, for any of those ideals which are the current coin of British propaganda. The people of Eire have little faith in British democracy; they prefer the Irish to the English way of living; they cannot, by any stretch of imagination, bring themselves to regard Britain as the sole champion of international good sportsmanship or as the saviour of small nations; and, so far from regarding the present European struggle as a holy crusade by Britain and her Allies against the Powers of Darkness, they suspect that it is, when probed to its full depth, the old recurring clash between two imperialisms, with finance, trade, colonies, power politics and international rivalries as its root causes. All of which is hurtful to the English visitor's pride and in direct conflict with what he has been taught to believe.

The week or two which he spends in Dublin will be all too short to clear his mind of prejudices and preconceived ideas or to give him the insight into Irish history and psychology which he failed to acquire at Rugby or Harrow. Yet he cannot be in Ireland long, if he is of an intelligent and exploratory turn of mind, before he realises that he is in a country which never forgets that it has experienced six centuries of oppression and only twenty years of restricted freedom; a country where men of forty retain vivid memories of the time when the heart of Cork City bore a striking resemblance to the Ypres of 1918; a country that still bears on its face many of the scars of the long years of persecution. Then, with a start, the honest Englishman may remember that it was *his* country, or, at any rate, *his* governing class, which was responsible for the invasions, plantations, and famines of the six tragic centuries; that it was British forces who burnt Cork and Balbriggan and Tuam twenty-two short years ago; that it was Britain who, after fifty thousand Irishmen had died fighting her battles in the last war, gave Ireland the Black-and-Tans and the Terror as a reward. When a British Cabinet Minister, visiting that part of Ireland which his country has forcibly severed from the rest, took occasion to lecture the Irish people on their attitude in the present war and to remind them of "the many battles for human freedom" they had fought during their long troubled history, de Valera was at no loss for a reply. He simply asked: "Against whom?"

If he probes a little further, however, the English visitor will discover that Ireland's attitude is not based merely upon memories that rankle or upon any innate anti-Britishism. It rests upon something deeper and more abiding; on the right that every free nation, great or small, has, or should have, to control its own destinies and to determine its own policy in international affairs. In fact, in declaring for neutrality, Ireland is doing no more than exercising the right which, Britain maintains, this war is being fought to safeguard. No nation, big or small, has entered the war of its own volition. Of the four great Powers on the Allied side in the conflict, two, Britain and France, entered it only when they believed their interests were endangered by the attack on Poland. Of the other two, Russia remained out of the war for nearly two years until it was attacked by Germany. The United States remained out of the war for over two years until it was attacked by Japan. In those two years "the battle for human freedom," of which Mr. Herbert Morrison spoke, was raging, and small nations—Poland, Denmark, Norway, Belgium, Holland, Greece, Yugo-Slavia—were invaded and occupied. But the two great Powers, Russia and the United States, did not enter the struggle until they were compelled to do so by an attack on their own territory. Ireland has no apology to make for taking the same stand. The Irish people feel that their country has had more than enough 'history': it badly needs a rest. It wants to live in peace, to stabilise its newly-founded institutions, to build up its young industries, to develop its native culture.

(v)

In all discussions about the war and neutrality, the English visitor finds that one name overshadows all the others: that of Eamon de Valera. In Ireland it is inescapable, as inescapable as that of Churchill in England, Hitler in Germany, Roosevelt in the United States, Salazar in Portugal. The war has made "Dev" much more than the leader of a party; it has made him what he was from 1917 to 1922—the leader of a nation. When he speaks on the major issue which is in everybody's mind, he speaks, not for a party or a section, but for the Irish people; and at least ninety-five per cent of the people are content that it should be so. This tall, rugged-featured man, who looks less than his sixty-one years, is to-day the very symbol of Ireland's separateness and nationhood. The visitor may learn something of his romantic career, his political honesty, his frugal manner of living, his unfailing personal charm. Somebody with a long memory may even recall how de Valera, when President of the Council of the League of Nations, warned the Assembly in an historic speech that all that has happened would happen if it did not put its house in order. " If the hand raised against the Covenant is sufficiently strong it can strike with impunity." Japan raised the strong hand against the Covenant in Manchukuo—and with impunity. But the voice that rang out in protest at Geneva was not that of the British delegate: it was that of Eamon de Valera; Sir John Simon was all for 'appeasement.' Abyssinia repeated the story. In spite of the centuries-old ties between Italy and Ireland, de Valera supported Sanctions: Sir Samuel Hoare helped Laval to sabotage them.

Englishmen have probably forgotten de Valera's part in those episodes, episodes which have had such disastrous consequences for the world. But Irishmen have not forgotten, and if they are told to-day that they should be fighting in a war for democracy, they must be pardoned if they look back to a time—little more than ten years ago—when 'democracy,' firmly planted in the saddle, showed scant respect for democratic principles at Geneva. The word democracy, in fact, has lost much of its old potency in Ireland. When they hear it used the people of the twenty-six Irish counties and a large section of the people of the remaining six are apt to concentrate their gaze upon the north-east corner of their island, where, in a territory smaller than Yorkshire, ruled from Whitehall, the investigations of the British Council of Civil Liberties found freedom and democratic rule almost non-existent.

And yet, the English visitor may find it comforting to learn, when the blitz struck Belfast, fire-engines and ambulances started out almost of their own accord from the Twenty-six Counties for the North, and the remarkable spectacle was witnessed of Dublin fire-fighters being cheered in the streets of the Orange stronghold. On that awful night, when the heart of Belfast was given over to death and destruction, de Valera was roused from sleep and told that an appeal had come for help. The decision he had to make was not an easy one; intervention, even in the cause of mercy, might possibly be regarded by a very powerful belligerent as a hostile act. Yet within less than five minutes he had made his decision—a decision, that, in the circumstances of the moment, had to be a personal one. "Go at once," he said to the Chief of the Dublin Fire Brigade, "and bring every available engine." "They are our people," he said afterwards, "and their sorrows are our sorrows; any help we give them is given whole-heartedly." What is the Englishman to assume from that? Let him beware of regarding it as an anti-German demonstration. There was, and is, a deep smouldering anger at the destruction of an Irish city, but there is also anger, no less deep, at the fact that it was Britain's partitioning policy that made such a disaster possible. Partition is the rock on which, to the great majority of Irishmen, Britain's claim to be fighting the battle of democracy breaks. Here, in a small island, with frontiers as clearly defined as any on earth, a corner of the national territory is torn away by the edict of the Legislature of another country, and an attempt is made on the principle of *divide et impera*, to make that wanton, arbitrary and immoral act permanent. That it cannot in the long run succeed does not render it any the less shocking to Irishmen whose democratic ideal is the establishment of the sovereignty of the people over every inch of their native soil. It is "an offence against the light of nations," the one outstanding obstacle in the way of a complete and lasting friendship between the two neighbouring islands.

30 years news

Nevertheless, things being what they are and geography being what it is, that is not the whole of the story. When the departing English visitor leans over the rail of the mail-boat and watches the blue mountains behind Dublin city fade away into the western mists, he cannot but be conscious that there are ties which bind as well as differences which sunder his people and the people he has left. The shores for which he is bound are only a couple of hours' run from the Irish coast. Britain is Ireland's nearest neighbour and the chief market for her surplus produce. English literature is the only literature known to the majority of Irish people. Ireland has given England not only navvies and dock-labourers and policemen, but statesmen, diplomats, generals, admirals, and men of eminence in every profession. The English visitor will have met nobody in Ireland who has not some friends or relatives across the Channel. turn to page 349

Irishmen, then, cannot view the present world war as if it were a struggle on Mars. Their unshakable attachment to neutrality does not mean, as de Valera has said, that their sympathies are not engaged. But they expect that if Britain is, as she claims to be, fighting the battle of democracy, she will continue to act in accordance with democratic principles and respect the right of her small neighbour to choose her own position at this cross-roads of history.

(v)

Ten years ago, on Abraham Lincoln's birthday, de Valera broadcast an address to the people of the United States. It ended with these words:

> "The veneration in which Lincoln is held by the American people is shared in no small measure by the people of Ireland. Having ourselves so long striven for freedom we honour him as the liberator of a race. Having had to suffer the partition of our territory, we revere him as the preserver of the unity of a nation. We esteem him for the love of truth which through all the vicissitudes of life inspired him, whether he was in the farm or in the store, in the court or in the capitol; for the charity which embraced even those who were ranged in battle against him; for the confidence in the ultimate triumph of right which upheld him in the darkest years of the Civil War."

If, in the years to come, somebody has occasion to broadcast an address in memory of Eamon de Valera, he can, if he chooses, borrow the concluding portion of that passage without the change of a comma.

EPILOGUE

SHORTLY after the second world war ended an American weekly published a striking cartoon in colour. It depicted Mr. Winston Churchill, a giant figure with legs apart, bestraddling, Colossus-like, the ruins of a smoking Europe. A huge cigar jutted from his mouth; there was the light of triumph in his eye; and his chin was thrust arrogantly forward. But in the east there was a red sunrise, through which could be clearly discerned the heavy features of Joseph Stalin. Stalin wore a mocking smile.

Its cruel comment apart, the cartoon was a faithful reflection of the mood—soon to be chastened by a sensational political landslide—which the victory of the Allied arms engendered in Mr. Churchill. That he should have felt proud and elated is no matter for wonder. He had done more than provide the people of Britain with an inspiring leadership in their darkest hour; he had made himself the living symbol of his country's war effort; without his courage and vision World War II might have ended very differently.

But Mr. Churchill's great qualities have never succeeded in blinding the world to the defects in his character. Always he has believed in the strong hand; always he has been on the side of the big battalions. The small nation, battling against great odds for its freedom, has never, save when an ally of Britain, engaged his sympathies. First and last, true to his ancestry and environment, he has been an imperialist. His concept of liberty has at all times been delimited by class and the lure of conquest.

In these pages has been recorded his amazing outburst when Erskine Childers was executed. A man of the highest integrity—a passionate friend of human liberty—had given his life for the cause he held dearest, and the Churchillian response was a whoop of joy. The days that immediately followed the Allied victory in 1945 witnessed a similar outburst. During the previous weeks the world had watched, not without cynicism, the spectacle of certain small European nations which had preserved their neutrality indulging in sudden "band-wagon" activities. Some who had openly favoured the Axis cause were now wooing the victor nations. But one small nation took no part in the *volte face*. At the beginning of the war Ireland, through its leader, and with the support of all political parties and of all sections of the people, had pledged itself to maintain a policy of neutrality to the end. Ireland honoured that pledge.

It was as the political head of a neutral nation that Mr. de Valera, when the news of Herr Hitler's death was reported, paid a visit to the German Legation in Dublin to convey a message of condolence. It was a conventional usage imposed by Ireland's neutral status and strictly in accordance with international practice. Had the position been reversed—had Mr. Churchill fallen whilst the German arms were crashing to triumph—Mr. de Valera would have acted in the same way. Had Herr Hitler gone to his death before the bombing of Pearl Harbour, there would have been a similar vote of condolence from President Roosevelt.

Mr. de Valera's action, which was understood and approved of by the vast majority of the Irish people, evoked a chorus of denunciation in the press of Britain and America. Neutrality and its obligations might, it would seem, be permitted to certain nations—including the United States before December 7th, 1941—but not to Ireland.

On Sunday, May 13th, 1945, Mr. Churchill broadcast his victory message to the world. Despite an occasional distinction of phrase, it did not rank with some of his earlier utterances. The hour of triumph evoked less from the British leader than the hour of adversity, and when he turned to Ireland he fell far beneath himself.

> "Owing to the action of Mr. de Valera," said Mr. Churchill, "so much at variance with the temper and instinct of Southern Irishmen, who hastened to the battle-front to prove their ancient valour, the approaches which the Southern Irish ports and airfields could so easily have guarded were closed by the hostile air-crafts and U-boats.
>
> This was indeed a deadly moment in our life, and if it had not been for the loyalty and friendship of Northern Ireland, we should have been forced to come to close quarters with Mr. de Valera, or perish forever from the earth.
>
> However, with a restraint and poise to which, I venture to say, history will find few parallels, His Majesty's Government never laid a violent hand upon them, though at times it would have been quite easy and quite natural, and we left the de Valera Government to frolic with the German and later with the Japanese representatives to their heart's content . . . . .
>
> I can only pray that, in years which I shall not see, the shame will be forgotten and the glories will endure, and that the peoples of the

British Isles and the British Commonwealth of Nations will walk together in mutual comprehension and forgiveness."

There was deep anger in Ireland. This was no knightly utterance, sprung from chivalry or magnanimity, but a piece of flamboyant trumpeting, compounded of deliberate falsehoods, mean innuendoes and petty sneers. During the war a leader-writer in the London *Times* had urged British statesmen to reach a better understanding of Ireland's position by "ceasing to regard their ancient neighbour as a unit in a stereotyped imperial system and looking upon her as a nation in a special and individual relation to their own." This advice was lost on Mr. Churchill. Familiar though he was with the events which in modern times had led to the restoration of independence over the greater part of Irish territory—in some of which he had been an active participator—his reference to Ireland in his victory broadcast displayed a vulgarity and a lack of understanding which only the cruder demands of the hustings could excuse.

When, three days later, Mr. de Valera went to Radio Eireann to reply, all Ireland listened-in. He began by recalling the circumstances which attended the adoption of Ireland's policy of neutrality—a policy, he emphasised, "supported by a unity rare to find amongst democratic peoples"—went on to thank the members of the Defence Forces for the sacrifices they had made in aid of the national effort, and issued a warning of trials still to come. Then came the words for which everybody had been waiting:

"Certain newspapers have been very persistent in looking for my answer to Mr. Churchill's recent broadcast. I know the kind of answer I am expected to make. I know the answer that first springs to the lips of every man of Irish blood who heard or read that speech, no matter in what circumstances or in what part of the world he found himself.

I know the reply I would have given a quarter of a century ago. But I have deliberately decided that that is not the reply I shall make to-night. I shall strive not to be guilty of adding any fuel to the flames of hatred and passion, which, if continued to be fed, promise to burn up whatever is left by the war of decent human feelings in Europe.

Allowances can be made for Mr. Churchill's statement, however unworthy, in the first flush of his victory. No such excuse could be found for me in this quieter atmosphere. There are, however, some things which it is my duty to say, some things which it is essential to say. I shall try to say them as dispassionately as I can.

Mr. Churchill makes it clear that, in certain circumstances, he would have violated our neutrality and that he would justify his action by Britain's necessity. It seems strange to me that Mr. Churchill does not see that this, if accepted, would mean that Britain's necessity would become a moral code and that when this necessity became sufficiently great, other people's rights were not to count.

It is quite true that other great Powers believe in this same code—in their own regard—and have behaved in accordance with it. That is precisely why we have the disastrous succession of wars—World War No. 1 and World War No. 2—and shall it be World War No. 3?

Surely Mr. Churchill must see that if his contention be admitted in our regard, a like justification can be framed for similar acts of aggression elsewhere and no small nation adjoining a great Power could ever hope to be permitted to go its own way in peace.

It is, indeed, fortunate that Britain's necessity did not reach the point when Mr. Churchill would have acted. All credit to him that he successfully resisted the temptation which, I have no doubt, many times assailed him in his difficulties and to which I freely admit many leaders might have easily succumbed. It is, indeed, hard for the strong to be just to the weak but acting justly always has its rewards.

By resisting his temptation in this instance, Mr. Churchill, instead of adding another horrid chapter to the already bloodstained record of the relations between England and this country, has advanced the cause of international morality an important step—one of the most important, indeed, that can be taken on the road to the establishment of any sure basis for peace.

As far as the people of these two islands are concerned, it may, perhaps, mark a fresh beginning towards the realisation of that mutual comprehension to which Mr. Churchill has referred and for which he has prayed and for which, I hope, he will not merely pray but work also, as did his predecessor who will yet, I believe, find the honoured place in British history which is due to him, as certainly he will find it in any fair record of the relations between Britain and ourselves.

That Mr. Churchill should be irritated when our neutrality stood in the way of what he thought he vitally needed, I understand, but that he or any thinking person in Britain or elsewhere should fail to see the reason for our neutrality I find it hard to conceive.

I would like to put a hypothetical question—it is a question I have put to many Englishmen since the last war. Suppose Germany had won the war, had invaded and occupied England,

and that after a long lapse of time and many bitter struggles she was finally brought to acquiesce in admitting England's right to freedom, and let England go, but not the whole of England, all but, let us say, the six southern counties.

These six southern counties, let us suppose, commanding the entrance to the narrow seas, Germany had singled out and insisted on holding herself with a view to weakening England as a whole, and maintaining the security of her own communications through the Straits of Dover.

Let us suppose, further, that after all this had happened, Germany was engaged in a great war in which she could show that she was on the side of the freedom of a number of small nations, would Mr. Churchill as an Englishman who believed that his own nation had as good a right to freedom as any other, not freedom for a part merely, but freedom for the whole—would he, whilst Germany still maintained the partition of his country and occupied six counties of it, would he lead this partitioned England to join with Germany in a crusade? I do not think Mr. Churchill would.

Would he think the people of partitioned England an object of shame if they stood neutral in such circumstances? I do not think Mr. Churchill would.

Mr. Churchill is proud of Britain's stand alone, after France had fallen and before America entered the war.

Could he not find in his heart the generosity to acknowledge that there is a small nation that stood alone not for one year or two, but for several hundred years against aggression; that endured spoliations, famines, massacres in endless succession; that was clubbed many times into insensibility, but that each time on returning consciousness took up the fight anew; a small nation that could never be got to accept defeat and has never surrendered her soul?

Mr. Churchill is justly proud of his nation's perseverance against heavy odds. But we in this island are still prouder of our people's perseverance for freedom through all the centuries. We of our time have played our part in that perseverance, and we have pledged ourselves to the dead generations who have preserved intact for us this glorious heritage, that we too will strive to be faithful to the end, and pass on this tradition unblemished.

Many a time in the past there appeared little hope except that hope to which Mr. Churchill referred, that by standing fast a time would come when, to quote his own words, 'the tyrant would make some ghastly mistake which would alter the whole balance of the struggle.'

I sincerely trust, however, that it is not thus our ultimate unity and freedom will be achieved, though as a younger man I confess I prayed even for that, and indeed at times saw no other.

In latter years, I have had a vision of a nobler and better ending, better for both our peoples and for the future of mankind. For that I have now been long working. I regret that it is not to this nobler purpose that Mr. Churchill is lending his hand rather than, by the abuse of a people who have done him no wrong, trying to find in a crisis like the present excuse for continuing the injustice of the mutilation of our country.

I sincerely hope that Mr. Churchill has not deliberately chosen the latter course but, if he has, however regretfully we may say it, we can only say, be it so.

Meanwhile, even as a partitioned small nation, we shall go on and strive to play our part in the world, continuing unswervingly to work for the cause of true freedom and for peace and understanding between all nations.

> As a community which has been mercifully spared from all the major sufferings as well as from the blinding hates and rancours engendered by the present war, we shall endeavour to render thanks to God by playing a Christian part in helping, so far as a small nation can, to bind up some of the gaping wounds of suffering humanity."

History has seldom recorded a more crushing retort from one statesman to another. Characterised by dignity and forbearance, and filled with merciless logic, de Valera's broadcast closed the issue with a finality that there was no mistaking.

His countrymen received it with delight. In restaurants, lounge bars and other public places where radio sets had been specially installed, the finish of the broadcast occasioned a scene of extraordinary enthusiasm. People rose to their feet clapping and cheering. There had been no histrionics, no flamboyance, no attempt to score debating points, and only the slightest betrayal of emotion. De Valera had refused to meet Mr. Churchill on his own level; he had refused to embitter the waters of Anglo-Irish controversy; he had refused to give the answer " that he might have given a quarter of a century ago." And the millions who listened to him, and the other millions who read his words, were doubly impressed as a result. Here, at least, was a statesman who scorned the petty ways of political debate and who displayed an unfailing sense of the balance of rights and the obligations of nations.

The passions and prejudices of the war are now fast fading away. What Mr. Winston Churchill thinks about Ireland has become a matter of supreme indifference to both Ireland and the world. Everybody, we know now, has lost the war. Victory has not brought happiness or prosperity to the victor nations. Everywhere there is political chaos, economic distress and social misery. Western civilisation has been shaken to its foundations and the cultural edifice built during the centuries by the best minds in Europe gapes with as many rents as Cologne Cathedral. The shadow of the atom bomb is over all, and we know that, unless the nations are able to reach a breadth of vision hitherto denied them, it will be used again and in even a more catastrophic form. If that happens it will make no basic difference who uses it on whom, for, as an American thinker has said: " In a profound sense the survivors will be deader than the corpses."

The Federation of the World is to-day as much a dream as it was when Tennyson coined the phrase. Power politics continue to dominate the international scene, and the United Nations' Organisation has not brought stable peace any nearer than the old League to which de Valera addressed his historic warning in 1932. Ireland, which might have brought at least a spiritual contribution to it, has been banned from its counsels by the veto of one Great Power. But U.N.O.'s loss is greater than Ireland's.

Index

Index

Index